HARDPRESS.NET
HOME OF HARD-TO-FIND BOOKS

The Beauties of the British Poets, With a Few
Introductory Observations
by George Croly

Address:
HardPress
8345 NW 66TH ST #2561
MIAMI FL 33166-2626
USA
Email: info@hardpress.net

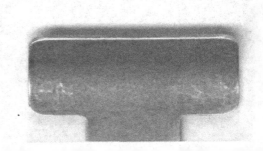

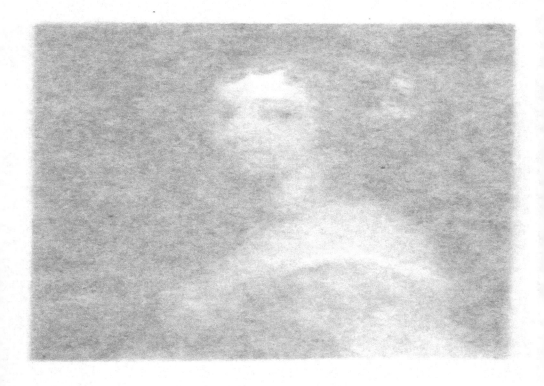

THE

BEAUTIES

OF THE

BRITISH POETS,

WITH A FEW

INTRODUCTORY OBSERVATIONS

By the Reb. George Croly.

BOSTON:
PHILLIPS, SAMPSON, AND COMPANY.
1857.

201830

INTRODUCTORY OBSERVATIONS.

ENGLISH POETRY constitutes one of the most brilliant portions of the intellectual history of Modern Europe. The era of English Poetry commences with the Norman Invasion. Anglo-Saxon Poems had existed; but their topics, their rudeness, or the decay of the language, extinguished them in the presence of a superior dialect and a more fortunate time. The few that remain, are merely memorials of some barbarian event, or harsh attempts to throw some superstitious fable into metre. The violence of the Norman Conquest, that shook the laws and institutions of England, also shook the language. But here the violence was more than compensated by the novelty, richness, and vigour of the results. The poetical soil was ploughed roughly; but, in the act, its native fertility was put in motion—

the old incumbrances were swept away, and a new and lovely vegetation was left free to spread and luxuriate. The transfer of the Norman Court to England, was the transfer of a warlike, romantic, and regal system, into a land of native generosity and courage, yet hitherto but little acquainted with the higher arts of nations. The Conqueror, and his descendants, brought with them many noble recollections, much spirit-stirring pomp, and much picturesque ceremonial. Italy was then the golden fount, from which the minor urns drew light: and the intercourse of the Norman princes, the universal conquerors, with the finest regions of Europe, had raised their court to a comparative height of civilization. The Minstrel followed the Monarch, and was essential, not more to his indulgence than to his fame. The wild traditions of the North; the French and Italian narratives of bold exploit, or idolatrous devotion to the Sex; and those oriental tales, whose high-coloured conceptions of supernatural agency, royal grandeur, and superb enjoyment, captivate us, even in our day of cold and chastised fancy, moved before the young mind of England like a new creation. If England had been left to the full exercise of her powers, thus awakened, probably no nation of Europe would have made a more rapid progress to the highest intellectual excellence. But war came across her, as the thunderbolt across the eagle's wing; and her natural vigour was bitterly expended in the struggles of rival usurpers, and in foreign wars, fruitless of all, but those apples of Sodom, the glories of the sword.

Yet Poetry is a part of human nature, and exists wherever man exists. A succession of poets rose in even this tumultuous period. But their efforts perished, either from defect of ability, or from the want of popular leisure, when life and possessions were in perpetual hazard. At length, Chaucer* appeared, and established a fame, that forced its way through the difficulties of his age. It is a fine remark of Bacon, that, ' while Art perfects things by parts, Nature perfects all together.' The triumphant periods of nations have this excellence of Nature—opulence, arms, and intellect flourish at the same time : the vegetation of the imperial tree is urged at once through all the extremities, and throws out its vigour alike in branch, leaf, and bloom. The reign of Edward III. had placed England in a high European rank, and with her rank came intellectual honours.

Chaucer's mind was cast in the mould of Poetry, and his genius was practised and enriched by the most

* Born in London, 1328, died 1400.
1*

singular diversity of knowledge and situation. He was a classical student, a lawyer, a soldier, a mathematician, and a theologian. His successive employments placed the whole round of life before his eyes. He began, by being a member of both universities; he then travelled on the Continent; returned to study law; became an officer of the palace; went to Italy as an envoy; was a comptroller of the customs; was an exile for the reformation; was a prisoner; and closed his various and agitated career, by retiring from the world, to correct those Poems by which he was to live when the multitude of his glittering and haughty compeers were forgotten.

Chaucer was the earliest successful cultivator of the harmony of the English language. His quaintnesses and occasional irregularities of thought and diction, belong to his time; but he has passages of copious and honeyed sweetness that belong to the finest poetic perception alone.

Spencer* arose in the most memorable period of English history, the reign of Elizabeth. And his career, though less diversified than that of his great predecessor, yet had much of similar interest and change. He was early introduced to the stately

* Born in London, 1553—Died 1599.

court of Elizabeth, and was led there by Sydney, the very genius of romance and heroism. He next visited the Continent, then vivid with arts and arms; and, as the envoy of Lord Leicester, visited it in a rank which gave him the most fortunate opportunities. In Ireland he next saw the contrast of a people naked of the arts and indulgences of life, but exhibiting singular boldness and love of country; a rude magnificence of thought and habit; a stately superstition; and a spirit of proud and melancholy romance, cherished by the circumstances, climate, and landscape of their soil. To those influences on the poet's mind may be attributed some of the characteristics of his poetry, for in Ireland, and in the midst of its most delicious scenery, he completed the "Fairy Queen."

The faults of this celebrated poem are obvious, and must be traced to Spencer's admiration of the Italian poets. The attempt to personify the passions, and the prominent characters of his time, involves the story in confusion. Continued allegory exhausts and defeats the imagination. But his excellence is in his language; and few can think of the story, in the incomparable sweetness and variegated beauty of his lines. To this hour Spencer is a spring of English inexhaustible, from which all the leading poets have drawn, and which is still fresh and sparkling as ever.

Panegyric sinks before the name of Shakespeare.* His dramatic fame has become proverbial, and is now beyond increase or diminution by posterity. If the conduct of his plays be sometimes dilatory, perplexed, and improbable ; no man ever redeemed those errors by such triumphant power over the difficulties character and poetry. His knowledge of the workings of the human breast in all the varieties of passion, gives us the idea that he had either felt and registered every emotion of our being, or had attained the knowledge by some faculty restricted to himself. He is, above all poets, the poet of passion ; not merely of the violent and gloomy distortion into which the greater trials of life may constrain the mind, but of the whole range of the simple, the lovely, and the sublime. His force and flow have the easy strength of the tide; and his lights and shadows are thrown with the rich negligence, yet with the intensity and grandeur of the colours of heaven on the ocean.

Shakespeare's fertility increases the surprise at this accumulation of poetic power. Within twenty-three years he produced thirty plays, indisputably genuine ; and contributed largely to five more, if he did not altogether write them. Of the thirty, twelve are

* Born at Stratford upon Avon, 1564—died, 1616

master-pieces, whose equals are not to be found in the whole compass of the living languages, nor perhaps of the dead. Yet, susceptible as he must have been of the poet's delight in praise, he seems to have utterly disregarded fame. He left his writings to the false and garbled copies of the theatre. It is not known that he even cared whether they ever passed to posterity. He retired from active life—from the pleasures of general society, which he must have been eminently capable of enjoying—and from authorship, a still severer sacrifice,—while he was yet in the prime of years, and gave himself up to the quiet obscurity of the country, without allowing us room for a suspicion that he ever regretted his abandonment of the world.

No man ever seems to have been so signally unconscious of what mighty things he was doing, or of the vast space that he must fill in the eyes of the future. And this unconsciousness, the rarest distinction and clearest evidence of great minds, crowns his supremacy; for it must have proceeded from either the creative facility that made all effort trivial, or the still nobler faculty, that sense of excellence, which makes all that genius can do feeble and dim, to the vivid and splendid form of perfection perpetually glowing before the mind

Milton's* genius was equal to his theme, and his theme comprehended the loftiest, loveliest, and most solemn subjects that touch the heart or elevate the understanding of man. We live at too remote a period to discover how far his powers may have been excited or trained by his time. But the characteristic of the poetic mind is, to be impressed by all influences, to be laying up its treasures from every event and vicissitude, to be gathering its materials of future brilliancy and power from the highest and lowest sources, from the visible and the invisible, till it coerces those vaporous and unformed things into shape, and lifts them up for the admiration of the world, with the buoyancy and radiance of a cloud painted by the sun. The stern superstitions of the republicans, the military array of the land, the vast prayer-meetings, and the fierce and gloomy assemblages, whether for war, council, or worship, are to be traced in Milton ; and the most unrivalled fragments of the ' Paradise Lost,' may be due to his having lived in the midst of an age of public confusion, of sorrow and of slaughter.

Milton was the most learned of poets. Learning oppresses the nerveless mind, but invigorates the powerful one. The celestial armour of the Greek hero,

* **Born in London, 1608, died 1674.**

which let in death to his feeble friend, only gave celestial speed and lightness to the limbs of the chosen champion. But the true wonder is, the faculty by which Milton assimilates his diversified knowledge, and makes the most remote subservient to his theme. His scholarship is gathered from all times and all languages; and he sits in the midst of this various and magnificent treasure from the thousand provinces of wisdom, with the majesty of a Persian king.

Dryden* revived poetry in England, after its anathema by the Puritans, and its corruption by the French taste of Charles II. and his court. He was the first who tried the powers of the language in satire to any striking extent: and his knowledge of life, and his masculine and masterly use of English, placed him at the summit of political poets, a rank which has never been lowered. No English poet wrote more voluminously, and none retained a more uncontested superiority during life. By a singular fortune, his vigour and fame increased to the verge of the grave.

A rapid succession of Poets followed, of whom Pope retains the pre-eminence. His animation and poignancy made him the favourite of the higher ranks; a favour which seldom embodies itself with the permanent

* Born, 1631, died 1700

feelings of a people. But the poetry of the ' Essay on Man,' however founded on an erroneous system, has the great preservative qualities that send down authorship to remote times. Its dignity, force, and grandeur fix it on the throne of didactic poetry. Pope's compliance with habits, then sanctioned by the first names of society, has humiliated his muse. But no man will desire to extinguish the good for the sake of the evil; and in the vast and various beauty, morality, and grace of Pope, we may wisely forget that he ever wrote an unworthy line.

It is not the purpose of this rapid sketch to more than allude to subsequent writers. Our own age has produced individuals, whose ability will be honoured to the latest period of the language. But the genuine praise of the Poet rests with posterity : and of those noble ornaments of our country, and it can possess none nobler, happily all survive, with the exception of Keats, Wolfe, and the mightier name of Byron.

Keats died at an early age, probably long before his powers were matured ; but not till he had given promise of excellence in his peculiar style. His versification was chiefly formed on the model of Spencer; and few as his poems are, they exhibit a rich and delicate conception of the beauty of our language

Wolfe's fame chiefly rests on a fine poem to the memory of Sir John Moore.

Lord Byron's merits and defects, as a poet, have been largely attributed to the personal temperament that accounts for, and palliates, his personal career. The constitutional irritability which embittered his days, probably gave birth to the pride, sternness, and misanthrophy of his style, its love of the darker passions, and its sullen and angry views of human life. But the error was often nobly redeemed by the outbreak of a noble mind, by touches of the finest feeling; flashes of sunshine through the gloom; vistas of the rosiest beauty, through a mental wilderness that seemed to have been bared and blackened in the very wrath of nature.

Like all men of rank, he had temptations to contend with, that severely try man. Fortune, flattering companionship, and foreign life, were his natural perils; and we can only lament that, when a few years more might have given him back to his country, with his fine faculties devoted to her service, and cheered by true views of human life, his career was closed. His moral system as a poet is founded on the double error, that great crimes imply great qualities; and, that virtue is a slavery. Both maxims palpably untrue; for crime is so much within human means, that the most stu

2

pendous crime may be committed by the most abject
of human beings. And common experience shows,
that to be superior to our habits and passions is the
only true freedom ; while the man of the wildest license
is only so much the more fettered and bowed down.
But on the grave of Byron there can be but one inscrip-
tion—that living long enough for fame, he died too
soon for his country. All hostility should be sacrificed
on the spot where the remains of the great poet sleep ;
and no man worthy to tread the ground, will approach
it but with homage for his genius, and sorrow that such
genius should have been sent to darkness, in the hour
when it might have begun to fulfil its course, and,
freed from the mists and obliquities of its rising, run its
high career among the enlighteners of mankind.

The object of this volume is to give such a selection
from our eminent writers, as may best exhibit their
styles of thought and language. All their beauties it
would be impossible to give. But the following pages
contain many of those passages on which their authors
would perhaps be most content to be tried at the

tribunal of popularity. There are other Authors from whom this volume would gladly have adduced extracts, but its size was previously restricted; and such is the opulence of English poetry, that to comprehend all, many volumes must have been formed, instead of one.

I feel the more privileged to speak favourably of the following Selection, from the limited part which I have borne in it; a considerable portion of the materials having been collected before the work came into my hands. The volume was commenced, and in a great measure carried on, by a literary friend, to whom the idea originally suggested itself as a personal amusement; and who persevered in it from the feeling, that the writings of the great poets of England cannot be put into the popular hand too often, in too pleasing a form, or under too accessible circumstances.

CONTENTS.

2*

CONTENTS.

CONTENTS.

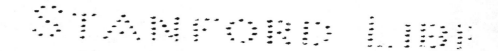
BEAUTIES OF THE POETS

CHAUCER.

FROM THE PROLOGUE TO THE CANTERBURY TALES

Befelle, that in that season on a day,
In Southwark at the Tabard as I lay,
Ready to wenden on my pilgrimage
To Canterbury, with devout courage,
At night was come into that hostelrie
Well nine and twenty in a companie
Of sundry folk, by aventure yfalle
In fellowship, and pilgrims were they all
That toward Canterbury wolden ride.
The chambers and the stables weren wide,
And well we weren eased at best.
And shortly, when the sun was gone to rest
So had I spoken with them every one,
That I was of their fellowship anon,
And made agreement early for to rise,

3

To take our way there as I you advise,
 But natheless, while I have the time and **space**
Before I further in the tale do pass,
It seemeth me accordant unto reason,
To tell unto you all the condition
Of each of them, so as it seemed me,
And who they weren, and of what degree;
And eke in what array they all were in,
And at a Knight then will I first begin.

 A KNIGHT there was, and that a worthy man
That from the time that he at first began
To riden out, he loved chivalrie,
Truthe and honour, freedom and courtesie.
Full worthy was he in his lord's war,
And thereto had he ridden, near and farre,
As well in Christendom as in Heatheness,
And ever honoured for his worthiness.
At Alisandr' he was when it was won,
Full oftentime he had the field outdone
Aboven all the nations warring in Prusse.
In Lettone had he travelled, and in Russe
 * * * * * * *
With many a noble army had he been.
Of mortal battles had he seen fifteen,
 * * * * * *
And evermore he had a sovereign praise,
And though that he was worthy he was wise.
And of his port as meek as is a maid,
He never yet no villany had saide
In all his life, unto no man or wight,
He was a very perfect noble Knight.

But for to tellen you of his array,
His horse was good, but yet he was not gay,
Of fustian he weared a gipon,
All besmutted with his habergeon,
For he was lately come from his voyage,
And wenten for to do his pilgrimage.

With him there was his son, a fresh young SQUIRE
A lover and a lusty bachelor,
With locks curled as they were laid in press ;
Of twenty years of age he was I guess.
Of his stature he was of equal length,
And wonderf'ly agile, and great of strength ;
And he had something seen of chivalrie,
In Flanders, in Artois, and Picardie,
And borne him well, as of so little space,
In hope to standen in his ladies grace.
Embroidered was he, as it were a meade
All full of fresh flowers, white and red,
Singing he was, or fluting all the day,
He was as fresh as is the month of May.
Short was his gown, with sleeves full long and **wide**
Well could he sit on horse, and fairly ride.
He could songs make, and well endite,
Juste, and eke dance, and well pourtray and write.
Courteous he was, lowly and serviceable,
And carved for his father at the table.

A YEOMAN had he, and servants no mo
At that time, for him pleased to ride so ;
And he was clad in coat and hood of green,
A sheafe of peacock arrows bright and keen

Under his belt he bare full thriftily ;
Well could he dress his tackel yeomanly .
His arrows drooped not with feathers low
And in his hand he bare a mighty bow.
    A round head had he, with a brown visage;
Of wood craft knew he well all the usage ;
Upon his arm he bare a gay bracer,
And by his side a sword and buckler,
And on that other side a gay dagger,
Harnessed well, and sharp as point of spear ;
A cristofre on his breast of silver shene ;
An horn he bare, the baudrick was of green.
A forester was he soothly I guess.

    There also was a NUN, a Prioress,
That in her smiling was full simple and coy ;
Her greatest oath was but by Saint Eloy ;
And she was cleped Madame Eglantine.
Full well she sang the service divine,
Entuned in her nose full sweetly ;
And French she spake full faire and fetisly,
After the school of Stratford at Bow,
For French of Paris was to her unknowe.
At meat was she well ytaught withall ;
She let no morsel from her lips fall,
Nor wet her fingers in her sauce deep ;
Well could she carry a morsel, and well keep,
That no drop neer fell upon her breast.
In courtesie was set full much her lest.
  *   *   *   *   *   *   *   *   *
And certainly she was of great disport,
And full pleasant, and amiable of port,

And took much pains to imitate the air
Of court, and hold a stately manner,
And to be thoughten high of reverence.
But for to speaken of her conscience,
She was so charitable and so piteous,
She would weep if that she saw a mouse
Caught in a trap, if it were dead or bled;
Two small hounds had she that she fed
With roasted flesh, and milk, and wasted bread,
But sore she wept if one of them were dead,
Or if men smote it with a staff smarte:
She was all conscience and tender heart.
  Full seemely her wimple pinched was;
Her nose was strait; her eyes were grey as glass
Her mouth full small, and thereto soft and red;
But certainly she had a fair forehead.
It was almost a span broad I trow,
For certainly she was not undergrowne.
  Full handsome was her cloak, as I was 'ware
Of small coral about her arm she bare
A pair of beads, gauded all with green;
And thereon hung a broach of gold full shene,
On which was first ywritten a crowned A,
And after, *Amor vincit omnia.*
  Another NUN also with her had she
That was her chaplain, and of PRIESTS three.

  A MONK there was, full skilful in the chace,
A bold-rider, no better in that place,
A manly man, to be an Abbot able,
Full many a daintie horse had he in stable,
And when he rode, men might his bridle hear
3*

Gingling in a whistling wind, as clear,
And eke as loud, as doth the chapel bell ;

    *   *   *   *   *   *   *

This jolly Monk he let old things pass,
And held after the new world the trace.
He gave not for the text a pulled hen,
That saith that hunters be not holy men ;
And that a Monk, when he is reckless,
Is like unto a fish that is waterless ;
That is to say, a Monk out of his cloister ;
This ilke text held he not worth an oyster ;
And I shall say that his opinion was good.
Why should he study, and make himself mad
Or upon a book in cloister alway pore,
Or toil with his hands, and labour,
As Austin bid ? how shall the world be served
Let Austin have his toil to him reserved.
Therefore he was a hard rider a right :
Greyhounds he had as swift as fowl of flight ;
Of pricking and of hunting for the hare
Was all his lust, for no cost would he spare.
    I saw his sleeves all gauded at the hand
With fur, and that the finest of the land.
And for to fasten his hood under his chin,
He had of gold a curiously wrought pin :
A love knot in the greater end there was.
His head was bald, and shone as any glass,
And eke his face, as it had been anoint.
He was a lord full fat and in good point,
His eyes were deep, and rolling in his head,
That steamed as a furnace of lead.

CHAUCER.

His boots souple, his horse in great estate,
Now certainly he was a fair prelate,
He was not pale as a tormented ghost ;
A fat swan loved he best of any roast :
His palfrey was as brown as is a berry.

A good man there was of religion,
That was a poor PARSONE of a town ;
But rich he was in holy thought and work,
He was also a learned man, a clerk,
That Christ's gospel truely would preach.
His parisheus devoutly would he teach,
Benigne he was and wondrous diligent,
And in adversity full patient :
And such he was yproved often times ;
Full loth were he to cursen for his tithes,
But rather would he given, out of doubt,
Unto his poor parishioners about,
Of his offering, and eke of his substance ;
He could in little thing have suffisance.
Wide was his parish, and houses far asunder,
But he nor felt nor thought of rain or thunder,
In sickness and in mischief to visit
The farthest in his parish, much and oft,
Upon his feet, and in his hand a staff.
This noble ensample to his sheep he gave,
That first he wrought, and afterward he taught,
Out of the gospel he the words caught,
And this figure he added yet thereto,
That if gold rust, what should iron do ?
And if a priest be foul, on whom we trust,
No wonder if a common man do rust;

CHAUCER

Well ought a priest ensample for to give,
By his cleanness, how his sheep should live.
He set not his benefice to hire,
Or left his sheep bewildered in the mire,
And ran unto London, unto Saint Paul's,
To seeken him a chanterie for souls,
Or with a brotherhood to be withold :
But dwelt at home, and kept well his fold,
So that the wolf ne made it not miscarry.
He was a shepherd and no mercenarie,
And though he holy were, and virtuous,
He was to sinful men not dispiteous,
Nor of his speech dangerous nor high,
But in his teaching discrete and benigne.
To draw his folk to heaven, with fairness,
By good ensample, was his business :
But if were any person obstinate,
Whether he were of high, or low estate,
Him would he reprove sharply for the nones,
A better priest I trow that nowhere is.
He waited after neither pomp ne reverence,
Nor maked him no spiced conscience,
But Christ's lore and his Apostles twelve
He taught, but first he followed it himselve.

CHAUCER.

DESCRIPTION OF THE KINGS OF THRACE AND INDIA.

There mightst thou see, coming with Palamon,
The great Lycurgus, sovrein king of Thrace :
Black was his beard, and manly was his face ;
The restless glancing of his eyen bright,
Shone with a glowing and a fearful light,
And like a griffon looked he about.
 * * * * * * * *
His limbs were great, his sinews hard and strong,
His shoulders broad, his arms were round and long
And, as the manner was in his countree,
Full high upon a car of gold stood he,
Drawen by four bulls of milk-white hue.
And in the place of any coat of mail,
He had a bear's skin, black as is a coal.
His hair was long, and braided down his back,
As any raven's feather shining black.
A coronet of gold, of greatest weight,
Upon his head sat, full of jewels bright,
Of rubies fine, and sparkling diamonds.
About his car there wenten snow-white hounds,
Twenty and more, as great as any steer,
To hunten at the lion or the deer ;
And followed him, with muzzle fast ybound.

With Arcite came Emetrius, king of Inde,
Upon a bay steed, trapped o'er with steel,
Covered with cloth of gold, embroidered well,
Riding like the dreadful war god, Mars.
His coat armour was of a cloth of Tarse,

Covered with pearls, white, round, and great
His saddle was of pure gold, newly beat;
A mantle upon his shoulders hanging,
Studded with rubies, like red fire sparkling;
His crisp hair into ringlets ran,
Yellow, and bright, and shining as the sun:
His nose was high, his eyen bright and keen.
His lippes round, his colour was sanguine,
And as a lion he his looks did fling;
His voice was like a trumpet thundering;
Upon his head he wore of laurel green
A garland, fresh and beauteous to be seen:
And on his hand he bare, for his delight,
An eagle tame, as any lily white;
About him ran and played their wilful game
Full many a lion and a leopard tame.

SPENCER

THE CAVE OF DESPAIR

Ere long they come, where that same wicked wight
His dwelling has, low in a hollow cave,
Far underneath a craggy cliff ypight,
Dark, doleful, dreary, like a greedy grave,
That still for carrion carcases doth crave :
On top whereof ay dwelt the ghastly owl,
Shrieking his baleful note, which ever drave
Far from that haunt all other cheerful fowl ;
And all about it wandering ghosts did wail and howl.

And all about old stocks and stubs of trees,
Whereon nor fruit nor leaf was ever seen,
Did hang upon the ragged, rocky knees ;
On which had many wretches hanged been,
Whose carcases were scattered on the green,
And thrown about the cliffs.   Arrived there,
That bare-head Knight, for dread and doleful teene,
Would fain have fled, ne durst approachen near ;
But the other forced him stay, and comforted in fear

That darksome cave they enter, where they find
That cursed man, low sitting on the ground,
Musing full sadly in his sullen mind ;
His grisly locks, long growen and unbound,
Disordered hung about his shoulders round,
And hid his face; through which his hollow eyne
Looked deadly dull, and stared as astound ;
His raw-bone cheeks, through penury and pine,
Were shrunk into his jaws, as he did never dine:

His garment, nought but many ragged clouts,
With thorns together pinned and patched was,
The which his naked sides he wrapped abouts :
And him beside there lay upon the grass
A dreary corse, whose life away did pass,
All wallowed in his own yet lukewarm blood,
That from his wound yet welled, fresh, alas !
In which a rusty knife fast fixed stood,
And made an open passage for the gushing flood.

Which piteous spectacle approving true
The wofull tale that Trevisan had told,
When as the gentle red-cross knight did view,
With fiery zeal he burnt in courage bold,
Him to avenge before his blood was cold ;
And to the villain said, " Thou damned wight,
The author of this fact we here behold,
What justice can but judge against thee right,
With thine own blood to price his blood, here shed
    sight ?"

" What frantic fit," quoth he, " hath thus distraught
Thee, foolish man, so rash a doom to give ?
What justice ever other judgment taught,
But he should die who merits not to live ?
None else to death this man despairing drove,
But his own guilty mind deserving death.
Is't then unjust to each his due to give ?
Or let him die that loatheth living breath ?
Or let him die at ease, that liveth here uneath ?

" Who travels by the weary wandering way,
To come unto his wished home in haste,
And meets a flood, that doth his passage stay,
Is't not great grace to help him over past,
Or free his feet, that in the mire stick fast ?
Most envious man, that grieves at neighbours' good,
And fond, that joyest in the wo thou hast ;
Why wilt not let him pass, that long hath stood
Upon the bank, yet wilt thyself not pass the flood ?

" He there does now enjoy eternal rest
And happy ease, which thou doest want and crave,
And further from it daily wanderest ;
What if some little pain the passage have,
That make frail flesh to fear the bitter wave ?
Is not short pain well borne, that brings long ease,
And lays the soul to sleep in quiet grave ?
Sleep after toil, port after stormy seas,
Ease after war, death after life, doth greatly please."
4

The knight much wondered at his sudden wit,
And said, " The term of life is limited,
Nor may a man prolong nor shorten it:
The soldier may not move from watchful sted,
Nor leave his stand until his captain bid."
" Who life did limit by almighty doom,
Quoth he, "knows best the term established ;
And he, that points the sentinel his room,
Doth license him depart at sound of morning drum

" Is not his deed, whatever thing is done
In heaven and earth ? did not he all create
To die again? all ends that are begun :
Their times in his eternal book of fate
Are written sure, and have their certain date.
Who then can strive with strong necessity,
That holds the world in his still changing state?
Or shun the death ordained by destiny ?
When hour of death is come, let none ask whence nor why

"The longer life, I wot the greater sin ;
The greater sin, the greater punishment :
All those great battles which thou boasts to win,
Through strife, and blood-shed, and avengement
Now praised, hereafter dear thou shalt repent :
For life must life, and blood must blood repay.
Is not enough thy evil life forespent ?
For he, that once h— ui missed the right way,
The further he do— go, the further he doth stray.

" Then do no further go, no further stray ;
But here lie down, and to thy rest betake,
Th' ill to prevent, that life ensewen may.
For what hath life, that may it loved make,
And gives not rather cause it to forsake ?
Fear, sickness, age, loss, labour, sorrow, strife,
Pain, hunger, cold, that makes the heart to quake ;
And ever fickle fortune rageth rife ;
I which, and thousands more, do make a loathsome life.

" Thou, wretched man, of death hath greatest need,
If in true balance thou wilt weigh thy state ;
For never knight, that dared warlike deed,
More luckless disadventures did await.
Witness the dungeon deep, wherein of late
Thy life shut up for death so oft did call ;
And though good luck prolonged hath thy date,
Yet death then would the like mishaps forestall,
Into the which, hereafter, thou maist happen fall.

" Why then dost thou, O man of sin, desire
To draw thy days forth to their last degree ?
Is not the measure of thy sinful hire
High heaped up with huge iniquity
Against the day of wrath, to burden thee ?
Is't not enough, that to this lady mild
Thou falsed hast thy faith with perjury,
And sold thyself to serve Duessa vile,
With whom in all abuse thou hast thyself defiled ?

" Is not he just that all this doth behold
From highest heaven, and bears an equal eye ?
Shall he thy sins up in his knowledge fold,
And guilty be of thine impiety ?
Is not his law, Let every sinner die,
Die shall all flesh ? what then must needs be done,
Is it not better to die willingly,
Than linger till the glass be all outrun ?
Death is the end of woes : die soon, O fairy's son."

The knight was much enmoved with this speech,
That as a sword's point through his heart did pierce;
And in his conscience made a secret breach,
Well knowing true all that he did rehearse,
And to his fresh remembrance did reverse
The ugly view of his deformed crimes ;
That all his manly powers it did disperse,
As he were charmed with enchanted rhymes,
That oftentimes he quaked, and fainted oftentimes.

In which amazement when the miscreant
Perceived him to waver weak and frail,
(Whiles trembling horror did his conscience daunt,
And hellish anguish did his soul assail,)
To drive him to despair, and quite to quail,
He showed him painted in a table plain,
The damned ghosts that do in torments wail,
And thousand fiends, that do them endless pain,
With fire and brimstone, which for ever shall remain

The sight thereof so thoroughly him dismayed,
That nought but death before his eyes he saw,
And ever-burning wrath before him laid,
By righteous sentence of the Almighty's law.
Then gan the villain him to over-craw,
And brought unto him swords, ropes, poison, fire,
And all that might him to perdition draw ;
And bade him choose what death he would desire :
For death was due to him, that had provoked God's ire.

But whenas none of them he saw him take,
He to him brought a dagger, sharp and keen,
And gave it him in hand : his hand did quake,
And tremble like a leaf of aspen green,
And troubled blood through his pale face was seen
To come and go with tidings from the heart,
As it a running messenger had been.
At last, resolved to work his final smart,
He lifted up his hand, that back again did start.

THE CAVE OF MAMMON.

That house's form within was rude and strong,
Like an huge cave hewn out of rocky clift,
From whose rough vault the ragged breaches hung,
Embossed with massy gold of glorious gift,
And with rich metal loaded every rift,
That heavy ruin they did seem to threat :
And over them Arachne high did lift
Her cunning web, and spread her subtle net,
Enwrapped in foul smoke, and clouds more black than jet

Both roof, and floor, and walls were all of gold,
But overgrown with dust and old decay,
And hid in darkness, that none could behold
The hue thereof: for view of cheerful day
Did never in that house itself display,
But a faint shadow of uncertain light ;
Such as a lamp whose life doth fade away ;
Or as the moon, clothed with cloudy night,
Does show to him that walks in fear and sad affright
    *   *   *   *   *   *   *

And over all sad Horror, with grim hue,
Did always soar, beating his iron wings;
And after him owls and night-ravens flew,
The hateful messengers of heavy things,
Of death and dolour telling sad tidings ;
Whiles sad Celleno, sitting on a clift,
A song of bale and bitter sorrow sings,
That heart of flint asunder could have rift ;
Which having ended, after him she flieth swift.

DESCRIPTION OF PRINCE ARTHUR.

At last she chanced by good hap to meet
A goodly knight, fair marching by the way,
Together with his squire, arrayed meet :
His glittering armour shined far away,
Like glancing light of Phœbus' brightest ray ;
From top to toe no place appeared bare,
That deadly dint of steel endanger may ;
Athwart his breast a baldrich brave he ware,   [rare :
That shined like twinkling stars, with stones most precious

And in the midst thereof one precious stone,
Of wondrous worth, and eke of wondrous might,
Shaped like a ladies head, exceeding shone,
Like Hesperus, amongst the lesser lights,
And strove for to amaze the weaker sights ;
Thereby his mortal blade full comely hung
In ivory sheath, ycarved with curious slights ;
Whose hilts were burnished gold, and handle strong,
Of mother-pearl, and buckled with a golden tongue.

His haughty helmet, horrid all with gold,
Both glorious brightness and great terror bred ;
For all the crest a dragon did enfold
With greedy paws, and over all did spread
His golden wings : his dreadful, hideous head.
Close couched on the beaver, seemed to throw
From flaming mouth bright sparkles, fiery red,
That sudden horror to faint hearts did show ;
And scaly tail was stretched down his back full low.

Upon the top of all his lofty crest,
A bunch of hairs, discoloured diversely,
With sprinkled pearl and gold full richly drest,
Did shake, and seemed to dance for jollity ;
Like to an almond tree, ymounted high
On top of green Selinis, all alone,
With blossoms brave bedecked daintily ;
Whose tender locks do tremble, every one,
At every little breath that under heaven is blown.

His warlike shield all closely covered was,
Ne might of mortal eye be ever seen;
Not made of steel, nor of enduring brass,
(Such earthly metals soon consumed beene,)
But all of diamond, perfect, pure, and clean
It framed was, one massy, entire mould,
Hewn out of adamant rocks with engine keen,
That point of spear it never piercen could,
No dint of direful sword divide the substance would.

The same to wight he never would disclose,
But whenas monsters huge he would dismay,
Or daunt unequal armies of his foes,
Or when the flying heavens he would affray :
For so exceeding shone its glistening ray,
That Phœbus' golden face it did attaint,
As when a cloud his beams doth overlay ;
And silver Cynthia waxed pale and faint,
As when her face is stained with magic arts constraint.

THE CAVE OF MERLIN.

Forthwith themselves disguising, both in strange
And base attire, that none might them bewray,
To Maridunum, that is now, by change
Of name, Cayr-Merdin called, they took their way :
There the wise Merlin, whylome wont (they say)
To make his wonne, low underneath the ground,
In a deep delve, far from the view of day ;
That of no living wight he mote be found,
Whenso he counseld, with his sprites encompast round

And if thou ever happen that same way
To travel, go to see that dreadful place :
It is an hideous hollow cave (they say)
Under a rock that lies a little space
From the swift Barry, tumbling down apace
Amongst the woody hills of Dynevowre :
But dare thou not, I charge, in any case,
To enter into that same baleful bower,
For fear the cruel fiends should thee un'wares devour

But standing high aloft, low lay thine ear,
And there such ghastly noise of iron chains,
And brazen cauldrons thou shalt rumbling hear,
Which thousand spirits, with long enduring pains,
Do toss, that will stun thy feeble brains ;
And oftentimes great groans and grievous stounds
When too huge toil and labour them constrains ;
And oftentimes loud strokes and ringing sounds
From under that deep rock most horribly rebounds.

The cause, some say, is this : a little while
Before that Merlin died, he did intend
A brazen wall in compass to compile
About Cairmardin, and did it commend,
Unto these sprites to bring to perfect end ;
During which work the Lady of the Lake,
Whom long he loved, for him in haste did send,
Who thereby forced his workmen to forsake,
Them bound till his return their labour not to slake.

In the meantime, through that false lady's train,
He was surprized and buried under bier,
Ne ever to his work returned again ;
Natheless those fiends may not their work forbear,
So greatly his commandement they fear,
But there do toil and travail day and night,
Until that brazen wall they up do rear ;
For Merlin had in magic more insight
Than ever him before or after living wight.

For he by words could call out of the sky
Both sun and moon, and make them him obey ;
The land to sea, and sea to mainland dry,
And darksome night he eke could turn to day.
Huge hosts of men he could alone dismay,
And hosts of men of meanest things could frame,
When so him list his enemies to fray ;
That to this day for terror of his fame,
The fiends do quake, when any him to them does name

SHAKESPEARE.

SOLITUDE.

          Are not these woods
More free from peril than the envious court?
Here feel we but the penalty of Adam,
The seasons' difference; as the icy fang,
And churlish chiding of the winter's wind;
Which when it bites and blows upon my body,
Even till I shrink with cold, I smile, and say,
This is no flattery: these are counsellors
That feelingly persuade me what I am.
Sweet are the uses of adversity;
Which like the toad, ugly and venomous,
Wears yet a precious jewel in his head;
And this our life, exempt from public haunt,
Finds tongues in trees, books in the running brooks,
Sermons in stones, and good in every thing.

MUSIC.

I am never merry when I hear sweet music.

The reason is, your spirits are attentive :
For do but note a wild and wanton herd,
Or race of youthful and unhandled colts,
Fetching mad bounds, bellowing, and neighing loud,
Which is the hot condition of their blood ;
If they but hear perchance a trumpet sound,
Or any air of music touch their ears,
You shall perceive them make a mutual stand,
Their savage eyes turn'd to a modest gaze,
By the sweet power of music : therefore the poet
Did feign that Orpheus drew trees, stones, and floods
Since nought so stockish, hard, and full of rage,
But music for the time doth change his nature.
The man that hath not music in himself,
Nor is not moved with concord of sweet sounds,
Is fit for treasons, stratagems, and spoils ;
The motions of his spirit are dull as night,
And his affections dark as Erebus :
Let no such man be trusted.

If music be the food of love, play on,
Give me excess of it ; that, surfeiting,
The appetite may sicken, and so die.
That strain again ;—it had a dying fall :
O! it came o'er my ear like the sweet south
That breathes upon a bank of violets,
Stealing and giving odour

STANTON

HUMAN LIFE.

Reason thus with life,——
If I do lose thee, I do lose a thing
That none but fools would keep: **a breath thou art,**
(Servile to all the skiey influences,)
That do this habitation, where thou keep'st,
Hourly afflict: merely, thou art Death's fool;
For him thou labour'st by thy flight to shun,
Yet run'st toward him still: thou art by no means valiant;
For thou dost fear the soft and tender fork
Of a poor worm; thy best of rest is sleep,
And that thou oft provok'st; yet grossly fear'st
Thy death, which is no more. Thou'rt not thyself;
For thou exist'st on many a thousand grains
That issue out of dust: happy thou art not;
For what thou hast not, still thou striv'st to get;
And what thou hast, forget'st; thou art not certain;
For thy complexion shifts to strange effects,
After the moon: if thou art rich, thou art poor;
For, like an ass, whose back with ingots bows,
Thou bear'st thy heavy riches but a journey,
And death unloads thee: friend hast thou none;
For thy own bowels, which do call thee sire,
The mere effusion of thy proper loins,
Do curse the gout, serpigo, and the rheum,
For ending thee no sooner: thou hast nor youth, nor age;
But, as it were, an after-dinner sleep,
Dreaming on both! for all thy blessed youth
Becomes as aged, and doth beg the alms
Of palsied eld; and when thou'rt old, and rich.
Thou hast neither heat, affection, limb, nor **beauty,**

5

To make thy riches pleasant.   What's yet in this
That bears the name of life?   Yet in this life
Lie hid more thousand deaths : yet death we fear,
That makes these odds all even.

    All the world's a stage,
And all the men and women merely players :
They have their exits and their entrances ;
And one man in his time plays many parts,
His acts being seven ages.   At first the infant,
Mewling and puking in the nurse's arms.
And then, the whining school-boy, with his satchel
And shining morning face, creeping like snail
Unwillingly to school.   And then, the lover,
Sighing like furnace, with a woful ballad
Made to his mistress' eyebrow.   Then, the soldier,
Full of strange oaths, and bearded like the pard ;
Jealous in honour, sudden and quick in quarrel,
Seeking the bubble reputation
Even in the cannon's mouth.   And then, the justice
In fair round belly, with good capon lined,
With eyes severe, and beard of formal cut,
Full of wise saws and modern instances ;
And so he plays his part.   The sixth age shifts
Into the lean and slippered pantaloon ;
With spectacles on nose, and pouch on side ;
His youthful hose well saved, a world too wide
For his shrunk shank ; and his big manly voice,
Turning again toward childish treble, pipes
Tnd whistles in his sound.   Last scene of all,
Ahat ends this strange eventful history,
Is second childishness, and mere oblivion ;
Sans teeth, sans eyes, sans taste, sans every thing

MERCY.

The quality of mercy is not strained ;
It droppeth as the gentle rain from heaven
Upon the place beneath : it is twice blessed ;
It blesseth him that gives, and him that takes :
'Tis mightiest in the mightiest ; it becomes
The throned monarch better than his crown :
His sceptre shows the force of temporal power,
The attribute to awe and majesty,
Wherein doth sit the dread and fear of kings ;
But mercy is above this sceptred sway,
It is enthroned in the hearts of kings,
It is an attribute to God himself ;
And earthly power doth then show likest God's,
When mercy seasons justice.

MOONLIGHT.

How sweet the moonlight sleeps upon this bank !
Here will we sit, and let the sounds of music
Creep in our ears ; soft stillness and the night,
Become the touches of sweet harmony.
Sit, Jessica : look, how the floor of heaven
Is thick inlaid with patines of bright gold :
There's not the smallest orb, which thou behold'st,
But in his motion like an angel sings,
Still quiring to the young-eyed cherubims :
Such harmony is in immortal souls ;
But, whilst this muddy vesture of decay
Doth grossly close it in, we cannot hear it.

HENRY IV AND RICHARD II.

YORK. Then, as I said, the duke, great Bolingbroke,
Mounted upon a hot and fiery steed,
Which his aspiring   rider seemed to know,
With slow, but stately pace, kept on his course,
While all tongues cried—God save thee, Bolingbroke !
You would have thought the very windows spake,
So many greedy looks of young and old
Through casements darted their desiring eyes
Upon his visage ; and that all the walls,
With painted imagery, had said at once—
Jesu preserve thee ! welcome, Bolingbroke !
Whilst he from one side to the other turning,
Bare-headed, lower than his proud steed's neck,
Bespake them thus—*I thank you, Countrymen :*
And thus still doing, thus he pass'd along.
　　DUCH. Alas ! poor Richard ! where rid he the while !
　　YORK. As in a theatre, the eyes of men,
After a well graced actor leaves the stage,
Are idly bent on him that enters next,
Thinking his prattle to be tedious :
Even so, or with much more contempt, men's eyes
Did scowl on Richard ; no man cried, God save him ;
No joyful tongue gave him his welcome home ;
But dust was thrown upon his sacred head ;
Which with such gentle sorrow he shook off,
His face still combating with tears and smiles,
The badges of his grief and patience,——
That had not God, for some strong purpose, steeled
The hearts of men, they must perforce have melted,
And barbarism itself have pitied him.

WOLSEY.

Nay then, farewell,
I have touched the highest point of all my greatness ;
And from that full meridian of my glory,
I haste now to my setting : I shall fall
Like a bright exhalation in the evening,
And no man see me more.
So farewell to the little good you bear me.
Farewell, a long farewell, to all my greatness !
This is the state of man ; to-day he puts forth
The tender leaves of hope, to-morrow blossoms,
And bears his blushing honours thick upon him :
The third day comes a frost, a killing frost ;
And, when he thinks, good easy man, full surely
His greatness was a ripening,—nips his root,
And then he falls, as I do.   I have ventured,
Like little wanton boys that swim on bladders,
These many summers in a sea of glory ;
But far beyond my depth : my high blown pride
At length broke under me ; and now has left me,
Weary and old with service, to the mercy
Of a rude stream, that must for ever hide me.

Vain pomp and glory of this world, I hate ye;
I feel my heart new opened : O, how wretched
Is that poor man that hangs on princes' favours.
There is, betwixt that smile we would aspire to,
The sweet aspect of princes, and our ruin,
More pangs and fears than war or women have ; -
5*

And when he falls, he falls like Lucifer,
Never to hope again.

  Cromwell, I did not think to shed a tear,
In all my miseries ; but thou hast forced me
Out of thy honest truth to play the woman.
Let's dry our eyes: and thus far hear me, Cromwell;
And, when I am forgotten, as I shall be,
And sleep in dull cold marble, where no mention
Of me must more be heard—say, I taught thee,—
Say, Wolsey, that once trod the ways of glory,
And sounded all the depths and shoals of honour,
Found thee a way, out of his wreck, to rise in ;
A sure and safe one, though thy master missed it.
Mark but my fall, and that which ruined me :
Cromwell, I charge thee, fling away ambition ;
By that sin fell the angels : how can man then,
The image of his Maker, hope to win by it ?
Love thyself last; cherish those hearts that hate thee ;
Corruption wins not more than honesty.
Still in thy right hand carry gentle peace,
To silence envious tongues.   Be just, and fear not :
Let all the ends thou aim'st at be thy country's,
Thy God's, and Truth's, then if thou fall'st, O Cromwell,
Thou fall'st a blessed martyr.   Serve the king ;
There take an inventory of all I have,
To the last penny : 'tis the king's ; my robe,
And my integrity to heaven, is all .
I dare now call my own.   O Cromwell, Cromwell.
Had I but served God with half the zeal
I served my king, he would not in mine age
Have left me to mine enemies.

DEATH.

To be, cr not to be, that is the question :
Whether 'tis nobler in the mind to suffer
The slings and arrows of outrageous fortune,
Or to take up arms against a sea of trouble
And, by opposing, end them ?—To die—to sleep—
No more ;—and by a sleep to say we end
The heart-ache, and the thousand natural shocks
That flesh is heir to :—'tis a consummation
Devoutly to be wished.   To die,—to sleep ;—
To sleep ! perchance to dream ; aye, there's the rub ;
For in that sleep of death what dreams may come,
When we have shuffled off this mortal coil,
Must give us pause :—there's the respect,
That makes calamity of so long life :
For who would bear the whips and scorns of time,
The oppressor's wrong, the proud man's contumely,
The pangs of despised love, the law's delay,
The insolence of office, and the spurns
That patient merit of the unworthy takes,
When he himself might his quietus make
With a bare bodkin ? who would fardels bear,
To groan and sweat under a weary life ;
But that the dread of something after death,—
The undiscovered country, from whose bourn
No traveller returns,—puzzles the will ;
And makes us rather bear the ills we have,
Than fly to others that we know not of!
This conscience does make cowards of us all ;

And thus the native hue of resolution
Is sicklied o'er with the pale cast of thought ;
And enterprises of great pith and moment,
With this regard, their currents turn awry,
And lose the name of action.

HUMAN LIFE.

To-morrow, and to-morrow, and to-morrow,
Creeps in this petty pace from day to day,
To the last syllable of recorded time ;
And all our yesterdays have lighted fools
The way to dusty death.   Out, Out, brief candle !
Life's but a walking shadow ; a poor player,
That struts and frets his hour upon the stage,
And then is heard no more : it is a tale
Told by an idiot, full of sound and fury,
Signifying nothing.

I have lived long enough : my way of life
Is fallen into the sere, the yellow leaf :
And that which should accompany old age,
As honour, love, obedience, troops of friends,
I must not look to have ; but in their stead,
Curses, not loud, but deep ; mouth-honour, breath,
Which the poor heart would fain deny, but dare not

MILTON.

FROM SAMPSON AGONISTES.

A LITTLE onward lend thy guiding hand
To these dark steps, a little further on;
For yonder bank hath choice of sun or shade:
There I am wont to sit, when any chance
Relieves me from my task of servile toil,
Daily in the common prison else enjoined me;
Where I, a prisoner chained, scarce freely draw
The air imprisoned also, close and damp,
Unwholesome draught: but here I feel amends,
The breath of heaven fresh blowing, pure and sweet,
With day-spring born; here leave me to respire.
This day a solemn feast the people hold
To Dagon their sea-idol, and forbid
Laborious works: unwillingly this rest
Their superstition yields me: hence with leave,
Retiring from the popular noise, I seek
This unfrequented place to find some ease;
Ease to the body some, none to the mind,
From restless thoughts, that like a deadly swarm
Of hornets armed, no sooner found alone,

But rush upon me thronging, and present
Times past, what once I was, and what am now.

O wherefore was my birth from heaven foretold
Twice by an Angel, who at last, in sight
Of both my parents, all in flames ascended
From off the altar, where an offering burned,
As in a fiery column charioting
His godlike presence,—
Why was my breeding ordered and prescribed
As of a person separate to God,
Destined for great exploits ; if I must die
Betrayed, captived, and both my eyes put out,
Made of mine enemies the scorn and gaze ;
To grind in brazen fetters under task
With this heaven-gifted strength ? O glorious strength
Put to the labour of a beast, debased
Lower than bond-slave !   Promise was, that I
Should Israel from Philistian yoke deliver :
Ask for this great deliverer now, and find him
Eyeless in Gaza, at the mill with slaves,
Himself in bonds under Philistian yoke.

                    But chief of all
O loss of sight, of thee I most complain !
Blind among enemies, O worse than chains,
Dungeon, or beggary, or decrepit age !
Light, the prime work of God, to me extinct,
And all her various objects of delight
Annulled, which might in part my grief have eased ;
Inferior to the vilest now become
Of man or worm : the vilest here excel me ;
They creep, yet see ; I, dark in light, exposed

To daily fraud, contempt, abuse, and wrong :
Within doors or without, still, as a fool,
In power of others, never in my own.
O dark, dark, dark, amid the blaze of noon,
Irrecoverably dark, total eclipse,
Without all hope of day!
O, first-created Beam, and thou, great Word,
' Let there be light,' and light was over all,
Why am I thus bereav'd thy prime decree?
The sun to me is dark
And silent as the moon,
When she deserts the night,
Hid in her vacant interlunar cave.
Since light so necessary is to life,
And almost life itself, if it be true
That light is in the soul,
She all in every part ; why was the light
To such a tender ball as th' eye confined,
So obvious and so easy to be quenched ?
And not as feeling through all parts diffused,
That she might look at will through every pore ?
Then had I not been thus exiled from light,
To live a life half dead, a living death,
And buried : but, O yet more miserable !
Myself my sepulchre, a moving grave ;
Buried, yet not exempt
By privilege of death and burial,
From worst of other evils, pains, and wrongs ;
But made hereby obnoxious more
To all the miseries of life,
Life in captivity
Among inhuman foes.

FROM THE SAME.

Many are the sayings of the wise,
In ancient and in modern books enrolled,
Extolling patience as the truest fortitude ;
And to the bearing well of all calamities,
All chances incident to man's frail life,
Consolatories writ
With studied argument, and much persuasion sought
Lenient of grief and anxious thought ;
But with the afflicted in his pangs their sound
Little prevails, or rather seems a tune
Harsh, and of dissonant mood from his complaint ;
Unless he feel within
Some source of consolation from above,
Secret refreshings that repair his strength,
And fainting spirits uphold.

FROM "PARADISE LOST." BOOK III.

Hail, holy light, offspring of heaven first born,
Or of the eternal, co-eternal beam !
May I express thee unblamed ? Since God is light.
And never but in unapproached light
Dwelt from eternity, dwelt then in thee,
Bright effluence of bright essence uncreate
Or hearest thou, rather, pure etherial stream,
Whose fountain who shall tell ? Before the Sun,
Before the Heavens thou wert ; and at the voice
Of God, as with a mantle, did invest

MILTON.

The rising world of waters, dark and deep,
Won from the void and formless infinite.
Thee I revisit now with bolder wing,
Escaped the Stygian pool, though long detained
In that obscure sojourn, while in my flight
Through utter and through middle darkness borne,
With other notes than to the Orphean lyre,
- sung of Chaos and eternal Night,
Taught by the heavenly muse to venture down
The dark descent, and up to reascend,
Though hard and rare : Thee I revisit safe,
And feel thy sovereign, vital lamp ; but thou
Revisitst not these eyes, that roll in vain
To find thy piercing ray, and find no dawn ;
So thick a drop serene hath quenched their orbs,
Or dim suffusion veiled. Yet not the more
Cease I to wander where the Muses haunt,
Clear spring, or shady grove, or sunny hill,
Smit with the love of sacred song ; but chief,
Thee, Zion, and the flowery brooks beneath,
That wash thy hallowed feet, and warbling flow,
Nightly I visit : nor sometimes forget
Those other two, equalled with me in fate.
So were I equalled with them in renown,
Blind Thamyris and blind Mœonides,
And Tiresias and Phineas, prophets old ;
There feed on thoughts that voluntary move
Harmonious numbers ; as the wakeful bird
Sings darkling, and, in shadiest covert hid,
Tunes her nocturnal note. Thus with the year
Seasons return ; but not to me return
Day. or the sweet approach of even or morn,

Or sight of vernal bloom, or summer's rose
Or flocks, or herds, or human face divine ;
But cloud instead, and ever-during dark
Surrounds me, from the cheerful ways of men
Cut off, and for the book of knowledge fair,
Presented with a universal blank
Of Nature's works, to me expunged and rased,
And wisdom, at one entrance, quite shut out.
So much the rather thou, celestial Light,
Shine inward, and the mind through all her powers
Irradiate ; there plant eyes ; all mist from thence
Purge and disperse ; that I may see and tell
Of things invisible to mortal sight.

FROM THE SAME. BOOK IV.

O thou that with surpassing glory crowned,
Lookst from thy sole dominion like the god
Of this new world ; at whose sight all the stars
Hide their diminished heads ; to thee I call,
But with no friendly voice, and add thy name
O Sun, to tell thee how I hate thy beams,
That bring to my remembrance from what state
I fell, how glorious once above thy sphere ;
Till pride and worse ambition threw me down,
Warring in Heaven against Heaven's matchless King ;
And wherefore ?   He deserved no such return
From me, whom he created what I was
In that bright eminence, and with his good
Upbraided none ; nor was his service hard.
What could be less than to afford him praise,

The easiest recompense, and pay him thanks,
How due! yet all his good proved ill in me,
And wrought but malice; lifted up so high,
I 'sdained subjection, and thought one step higher
Would set me highest, and in a moment quit
The debt immense of endless gratitude,
So burdensome, still paying, still to owe,
Forgetful what from him I still received,
And understood not that a grateful mind
By owing owes not, but still pays, at once
Indebted and discharged; what burden then?
O had his powerful destiny ordained
Me some inferior angel, I had stood
Then happy; no unbounded hope had raised
Ambition. Yet why not? some other power
As great might have aspired, and me though mean
Drawn to his part: but other powers as great
Fell not, but stood unshaken from within,
Or from without, to all temptations armed.
Hadst thou the same free will and power to stand?
Thou hadst; whom hast thou then, or what t'accuse,
But Heaven's free love dealt equally to all?
Be then his love accursed, since love or hate,
To me alike it deals eternal wo.
Nay, cursed be thou; since against his thy will
Chose freely what it now so justly rues.
Me miserable! which way shall I fly
Infinite wrath, and infinite despair?
Which way I fly is Hell; myself am Hell;
And in the lowest deep a lower deep
Still threatening to devour me, opens wide,
To which the Hell I suffer seems a Heaven,

O then at last relent; is there no place
Left for repentance, none for pardon left?
None left but by submission; and that word
Disdain forbids me, and my dread of shame
Among the spirits beneath, whom I seduced
With other promises and other vaunts
Than to submit, boasting I could subdue
The Omnipotent. Ah me, they little know
How dearly I abide that boast so vain,
Under what torments inwardly I groan,
While they adore me on the throne of hell,
With diadem and sceptre high advanced,
The lower still I fall, only supreme
In misery; such joy ambition finds.
But say I could repent, and could obtain
By act of grace my former state: how soon
Would height recall high thoughts, how soon unsay
What feigned submission swore? ease would recant
Vows made in pain, as violent and void.
For never can true reconcilement grow
Where wounds of deadly hate have pierced so deep;
Which would but lead me to a worse relapse
And heavier fall: so should I purchase dear
Short intermission bought with double smart.
This knows my punisher; therefore as far
From granting he, as I from begging peace:
All hope excluded thus, behold instead
Of us outcast, exiled, his new delight
Mankind created, and for him this world.
So farewell, hope, and with hope, farewell fear,
Farewell remorse: all good to me is lost;
Evil be thou my good: by thee at least

MILTON.

Divided empire with Heaven's King I hold,
By thee, and more than half perhaps will reign :
As man ere long, and this new world, shall know.

FROM THE SAME.

  O unexpected stroke, worse than of death !
Must I thus leave thee, Paradise ? thus leave
Thee, native soil ! these happy walks and shades,
Fit haunt of gods ? where I had hope to spend,
Quiet though sad, the respite of that day
That must be mortal to us both.   O Flowers,
That never will in other climate grow,
My early visitation and my last
At even, which I bred up with tender hand
From the first opening bud, and gave ye names !
Who now shall rear ye to the sun, or rank
Your tribes, and water from the ambrosial fount ?
Thee, lastly, nuptial bower ! by me adorned
With what to sight or smell was sweet ! from thee
How shall I part and whither wander down
Into a lower world ; to this obscure
And wild ?   How shall we breathe in other air
Less pure, accustomed to immortal fruits ?

FROM THE SAME.   BOOK XI.

  To whom thus Michael.   Death thou hast seen
In his first shape on man ; but many shapes
Hath Death, and many are the ways that lead
6*

To his grim cave all dismal ; yet to sense
More terrible at the entrance, than within.
Some, as thou sawest, by violent stroke shall die ;
By fire, flood, famine, by intemperance more
In meats and drinks, which on the earth shall bring
Diseases dire, of which a monstrous crew
Before thee shall appear ; that thou mayst know
What misery the inabstinence of Eve
Shall bring on men.
                              Immediately a place
Before his eyes appeared, sad, noisome, dark ;
A lazar-house it seemed ; wherein were laid
Numbers of all diseased ; all maladies
Of ghastly spasm, or racking torture, qualms
Of heart-sick agony ; all feverous kinds ;
Convulsions, epilepsies, fierce catarrhs,
Intestine stone and ulcer, colick pangs,
Demoniack frenzy, moping melancholy,
And moon-struck madness ; pining atrophy,
Marasmus, and wide-wasting pestilence ;
Dropsies, and asthmas, and joint-racking rheums.
Dire was the tossing, deep the groans.   Despair
Tended the sick, busiest from couch to couch ;
And over them triumphant Death his dart
Shook ; but delayed to strike, though oft invok'd
With vows, as their chief good, and final hope.
  Sight so deform what heart of rock could long
Dry-eyed behold ?   Adam could not, but wept,
Though not of woman born : compassion quelled
His best of man, and gave him up to tears
A space, till firmer thoughts restrained excess ;
And scarce recovering words, his plaint renewed.

L'ALLEGRO.

Hence, loathed melancholy,
Of Cerberus, and Blackest Midnight born,
  In Stygian cave forlorn,
'Mongst horrid shapes, and shrieks, and sights unholy
  Find out some uncouth cell,
Where brooding darkness spreads his jealous wings,
  And the night raven sings;
There under ebon shades and low browed rocks
  As ragged as thy locks,
In dark Cimmerian desert ever dwell.
  But come thou goddess fair and free,
In Heaven yclept Euphrosyne,
And by men, heart-easing Mirth,
Whom lovely Venus at a birth,
With two sister-graces more,
To ivy-crowned Bacchus bore,
Or whether (as some sages sing)
The frolic wind that breathes the spring,
Zephyr, with Aurora playing,
As he met her once a-maying,
There on beds of violets blue,
And fresh blown roses washed in dew,
Filled her with a daughter fair,
So buxom, blithe, and debonair.
Haste thee, Nymph, and bring with thee
Jest and youthful Jollity,
Quips and cranks, and wanton wiles,
Nods and becks and wreathed smiles,
Such as hang on Hebe's cheek,

MILTON.

And love to live in dimple sleek;
Sport that wrinkled Care derides,
And Laughter holding both his sides,
Come and trip it as you go;
On the light fantastic toe;
And in thy right hand lead with thee,
The mountain nymph sweet Liberty;
And if I give thee honour due,
Mirth, admit me of thy crew,
To live with her and live with thee
In unreproved pleasures free;
To hear the lark begin his flight
And singing startle the dull night,
From his watch-tower in the skies,
Till the dappled dawn doth rise;
Then to come in spite of sorrow,
And at my window bid good morrow,
Through the sweet briar or the vine,
Or the twisted eglantine:
While the cock with lively din,
Scatters the rear of darkness thin,
And to the stack or the barn-door
Stoutly struts his dames before;
Oft listening how the hounds and horn
Cheerly rouse the slumbering morn,
From the side of some hoar hill,
Through the high wood echoing shrill,
Sometime walking not unseen
By hedge row elms, on hillocks green,
Right against the eastern gate,
Where the great sun begins his state,
Robed in flames, and amber light,

MILTON.

The clouds in thousand liveries dight,
While the plowman near at hand
Whistles o'er the furrowed land,
And the milkmaid singeth blithe,
And the mower wets his scythe,
And every shepherd tells his tale
Under the hawthorn in the dale.
Straight mine eye hath caught new pleasures
Whilst the landscape round it measures:
Russet lawns, and fallows gray,
Where the nibbling flocks do stray,
Mountains on whose barren breast,
The labouring clouds do often rest;
Meadows trim with daisies pied,
Shallow brook and rivers wide.
Towers and battlements it sees
Bosomed high in tufted trees,
Where perhaps some beauty lies,
The Cynosure of neighbouring eyes.
Hard by a cottage chimney smokes,
From betwixt two aged oaks,
Where Corydon and Thyrsis met,
Are at their savoury dinner set,
Of herbs, and other country messes,
Which the neat handed Phyllis dresses:
And then in haste her bower she leaves,
With Thestylis to bind the sheaves;
Or if the earlier season lead
To the tanned haycock in the mead.
Sometimes with secure delight
The upland hamlets will invite,
When the merry bells ring round,

MILTON.

And the jocund rebecks sound,
To many a youth and many a maid,
Dancing in the chequered shade;
And young and old come forth to play
On a sunshine holiday;
Till the live-long daylight fail;
Then to the spicy nut-brown ale,
With stories told of many a feat,
How fairy Mab the junkets eat,
She was pinched and pulled, she said,
And he, by friars, lantern led;
Tells how the drudging goblin sweat,
To earn his cream bowl duly set,
When in one night ere glimpse of morn,
His shadowy flail had threshed the corn
That ten day labourers could not end;
Then lays him down the lubber fiend,
And stretched out all the chimney's length
Basks at the fire his hairy strength,
And crop-full out of doors he flings,
Ere the first cock his matin rings.
Thus done the tales, to bed they creep,
By whispering winds soon lulled asleep.
Towered cities please us then,
And the busy hum of men,
Where throngs of knights and barons bold,
In weeds of peace high triumphs hold;
With store of ladies, whose bright eyes
Rain influence, and adjudge the prize,
Of wit, or arms, while both contend
To win her grace whom all commend.
There let Hymen oft appear

In saffron robe, with taper clear,
And Pomp, and Feast, and Revelry,
With Mask, and antique Pageantry,
Such sights as youthful poets dream,
On summer eves by haunted stream.
Then to the well-trod stage anon,
If Johnson's learned sock be on,
Or sweetest Shakespeare, Fancy's child,
Warble his native wood-notes wild.
And ever against eating cares,
Lap me in soft Lydian airs,
Married to immortal verse,
Such as the meeting soul may pierce,
In notes of many a winding bout
Of linked sweetness long drawn out,
With wanton heed, and giddy cunning,
The melting voice through mazes running,
Untwisting all the chains that tie
The hidden soul of harmony;
That Orpheus self may heave his head
From golden slumber on a bed
Of heaped Elysian flowers, and hear
Such strains as would have won the ear
Of Pluto to have quite set free
His half-regained Eurydice.
These delights, if thou canst give,
Mirth, with thee I mean to live.

MILTON.

IL PENSEROSO.

Hence vain deluding Joys,
The brood of Folly, without father bred,
    How little you bested,
Or fill the fixed mind with all your toys?
    Dwell in some idle brain,
And fancies fond with gaudy shapes possess,
    As thick and numberless
As the gay motes that people the sunbeams;
    Or likest hovering dreams,
The fickle pensioners of Morpheus' train.
    But hail, thou Goddess sage and holy,
Hail, divinest Melancholy,
Whose saintly visage is too bright
To hit the sense of human sight,
And therefore to our weaker view,
O'erlaid with black, staid Wisdom's hue;
Black, but such as in esteem
Prince Memnon's sister might beseem;
Or that starred Ethiop queen that strove
To set her beauty's praise above
The sea-nymphs, and their powers offended
Yet thou art higher far descended,
Thee bright haired Vesta long of yore
To solitary Saturn bore;
His daughter she, (in Saturn's reign
Such mixture was not held a stain,)
Oft in glimmering bowers and glades
He met her, and in secret shades

Of woody Ida's inmost grove,
While yet there was no fear of Jove.
Come, pensive nun, devout and pure,
Sober, steadfast, and demure,
All in a robe of darkest grain,
Flowing with majestic train,
And sable stole of Cyprus lawn,
Over thy decent shoulders drawn.
Come, but keep thy wonted state,
With even step and musing gait ;
And looks commercing with the skies,
Thy rapt soul sitting in thine eyes ;
There held in holy passion, still,
Forget thyself to marble, till
With a sad leaden downward cast,
Thou fix them on the earth as fast :
And join with thee calm Peace and Quiet,
Spare Fast that oft with Gods doth diet,
And hears the Muses in a ring
Aye round about Jove's altar sing :
And add to these retired Leisure,
That in trim gardens takes his pleasure ;
But first and chiefest with thee bring,
Him that yon soars on golden wing,
Guiding the fiery-wheeled throne,
The cherub Contemplation ;
And the mute silence hist along,
'Less Philomel will deign a song.
In her sweetest, saddest plight,
Smoothing the rugged brow of night,
While Cynthia checks her dragon yoke,
Gently o'er the accustomed oak ;

7

MILTON

Sweet bird that shunn'st the noise of folly,
Most musical, most melancholy !
Thee, chauntress, oft the woods among,
I woo to hear thy evening song;
And missing thee, I walk unseen
On the dry smooth shaven green,
To behold the wandering moon
Riding near her highest noon,
Like one that had been led astray
Through the heaven's wide pathless way;
And oft, as if her head she bowed,
Stooping through a fleecy cloud.
Oft on a p.at of rising ground,
I hear the far off curfew sound,
Over some wide watered shore,
Swinging slow with sullen roar ;
Or if the air will not permit,
Some still removed place will fit,
Where glowing embers through the room
Teach light to counterfeit a gloom ;
Far from all resort of mirth,
Save the cricket on the hearth,
Or the bellman's drowsy charm,
To bless the doors from nightly harm.
Or let my lamp at midnight hour,
Be seen in some high lonely tower,
Where I may oft out-watch the Bear,
With thrice great Hermes, or unsphere
The spirit of Plato, to unfold
What worlds or what vast regions hold,
The immortal mind that hath forsook
Her mansion in this fleshly nook ;

MILTON.

And of those demons that are found
In fire, air, flood, or under ground,
Whose power hath a true consent
With planet, or with element.
Sometime let gorgeous Tragedy
In sceptred pall come sweeping by,
Presenting Thebes' or Pelops' line,
Or the tale of Troy divine,
Or what (though rare) of later age,
Ennobled hath the buskined stage.
But O, sad Virgin, that thy power
Might raise Musæus from his bower,
Or bid the soul of Orpheus sing
Such notes as warbled to the string,
Drew iron tears down Pluto's cheek,
And made Hell grant what Love did seek.
Or call up him that left half told
The story of Cambuscan bold,
Of Camball, and of Algarsife,
And who had Canace to wife,
That owned the virtuous ring and glass,
And of the wondrous horse of brass,
On which the Tartar king did ride;
And if aught else great bards beside
In sage and solemn tunes have sung,
Of tourneys and of trophies hung,
Of forests and enchantments drear,
Where more is meant than meets the ear.
Thus night oft see me in thy pale career,
Till silver-suited morn appear;
Not trickt and frounced as she was wont,
With the Attic boy to hunt,

MILTON

But kerchiefed in a comely cloud,
While rocking winds are piping loud,
Or ushered with a shower still,
When the gust hath blown his fill,
Ending on the rustling leaves,
With minute drops from off the eaves
And when the sun begins to fling
His flaring beams, me, Goddess bring
To arched walks of twilight groves,
And shadows brown that Sylvan loves,
Of pine or monumental oak,
Where the rude axe with heaved stroke,
Was never heard the nymphs to daunt,
Or fright them from their hallowed haunt.
There in close covert by some brook,
Where no profaner eye may look,
Hide me from Day's garish eye,
While the bee with honied thigh,
That at her flowery work doth sing,
And the waters murmuring,
With such concert as they keep,
Entice the dewy-feathered sleep :
And let some strange mysterious dream
Wave at his wings, in airy stream
Of lively portraiture displayed,
Softly on my eyelids laid.
And, as I wake, sweet music breathe
Above, about, or underneath,
Sent by some spirit to mortals good,
Or the unseen Genius of the wood.
But let my due feet never fail
To walk the studious cloister's pale,

MILTON.

And love the high embowed roof,
With antique pillars, massy proof;
And storied windows, richly dight,
Casting a dim religious light;
There let the pealing organ blow
To the full-voiced quire below,
In service high, and anthems clear,
As may with sweetness through mine ear
Dissolve me into ecstacies,
And bring all Heaven before mine eyes.
And may, at last, my weary age,
Find out the peaceful hermitage,
The hairy gown, and mossy cell,
Where I may sit, and rightly spell
Of every star that Heaven doth shew,
And every herb that sips the dew;
Till old Experience do attain
To something like prophetic strain.
These pleasures, Melancholy, give,
And I with thee will choose to live.

LYCIDAS.

Yet once more, O ye Laurels, and once more,
Ye Myrtles brown, with Ivy never sere,
I come to pluck your berries, harsh and crude,
And with forced fingers rude
Shatter your leaves before the mellowing year.
Bitter constraint, and sad occasion dear,
Compels me to disturb your season due ;
For Lycidas is dead, dead ere his prime ;
Young Lycidas, and hath not left his peer.
Who would not sing for Lycidas?   He knew
Himself to sing, and build the lofty rhyme.
He must not float upon his watry bier
Unwept, and welter to the parching wind,
Without the meed of some melodious tear.
Begin then, Sisters of the sacred well,
That from beneath the seat of Jove doth spring ;
Begin, and somewhat loudly sweep the string.
Hence with denial vain, and coy excuse,
So may some gentle Muse
With lucky words favour my destined urn ;
And, as she passes, turn,
And bid fair peace be to my sable shroud.
For we were nursed upon the self-same hill,
Fed the same flock, by fountain, shade, and rill.
Together both, ere the high lawns appeared
Under the opening eyelids of the morn,
We drove a-field, and both together heard
What time the gray fly winds her sultry horn,
Battening our flocks with the fresh dews of night,

Oft till the star that rose at evening bright
Toward heaven's descent had sloped his west'ring wheel.
Meanwhile the rural ditties were not mute,
Tempered to the oaten flute;
Rough Satyrs danced, and Fauns with cloven heel,
From the glad sound would not be absent long,
And old Damœtas loved to hear our song.
But, O the heavy change! now thou art gone,
Now thou art gone, and never must return!
Thee, Shepherd, thee the woods and desert caves,
With wild thime and the gadding vine o'ergrown,
And all their echoes, mourn.
The willows, and the hazel copses green,
Shall now no more be seen
Fanning their joyous leaves to thy soft lays.
As killing as the canker to the rose,
Or taint-worm to the weaning herds that graze;
Or frost to flowers, that their gay wardrobe wear,
When first the white-thorn blows;
Such Lycidas, thy loss to shepherd's ear.
Where were ye, Nymphs, when the remorseless deep
Closed o'er the head of your loved Lycidas?
For neither were ye playing on the steep,
Where your old bards, the famous Druids, lie,
Nor on the shaggy top of Mona high,
Nor yet where Deva spreads her wizard stream.
Ah me! I fondly dream!
Had ye been there—for what could that have done?
What could the Muse herself, that Orpheus bore,
The Muse herself, for her enchanting son,
Whom universal nature did lament,
When by the rout that made the hideous roar,

His gory visage down the stream was sent,
Down the swift Hebrus to the Lesbian shore ?
   Alas ! what boots it with incessant care
To tend the homely slighted shepherd's trade,
And strictly meditate the thankless Muse ?
Were it not better done, as others use,
To sport with Amaryllis in the shade,
  r with the tangles of Neæra's hair ?
Fame is the spur that the clear spirit doth raise
(That last infirmity of noble minds)
To scorn delights, and live laborious days ;
But the fair guerdon when we hope to find,
And think to burst out into sudden blaze,
 omes the blind Fury with th' abhorred shears,
And slits the thin-spun life.　'But not the praise,'
Phœbus replied, and touched my trembling ears ;
Fame is no plant that grows on mortal soil,
Nor in the glistering foil,
Set off to the world, nor in broad rumour lies ;
But lives and spreads aloft by those pure eyes,
And perfect witness of all-judging Jove ;
As he pronounces lastly on each deed,
Of so much fame in Heaven expect thy meed.
   O fountain Arethuse, and thou honoured flood,
Smooth-sliding Mincius, crowned with vocal reeds,
That strain I heard was of a higher mood :
But now my oat proceeds,
And listens to the herald of the sea
That came in Neptune's plea ;
He asked the waves, and asked the felon winds,
What hard mishap hath doomed this gentle swain ?
And questioned every gust of rugged winds,

That blows from off each beaked promontory :
They knew not of his story ;
And sage Hippotades their answer brings,
That not a blast was from his dungeon strayed,
The air was calm, and on the level brine
Sleek Panope with all her sisters played.
It was that fatal and perfidious bark,
Built in th' eclipse, and rigged with curses dark,
That sank so low that sacred head of thine.
   Next Camus, reverend sire, went footing slow,
His mantle hairy, and his bonnet sedge,
Inwrought with figures dim, and on the edge
Like to that sanguine flower inscribed with wo.
Ah ! who hath reft (quoth he) my dearest pledge ?
   Last came, and last did go,
The pilot of the Galilean lake ;
Two massy keys he bore of metals twain,
(The golden opes, the iron shuts amain)
He shook his mitred locks, and stern bespake :
How well could I have spar'd for thee, young swain,
Enow of such, as for their bellies' sake
Creep, and intrude, and climb into the fold ?
Of other care they little reckoning make,
Than how to scramble at the shearers' feast,
And shove away the worthy, bidden guest ;
Blind mouths ! that scarce themselves know how to hold
A sheep-hook, or have learned ought else the least,
That to the faithful herdman's art belongs ;
What recks it them ? What need they ? They are sped ;
And, when they list, their lean and flashy songs
Grate on their scrannel pipes of wretched straw :
The hungry sheep look up, and are not fed,

But, swoln with wind, and the rank mist they draw,
Rot inwardly, and foul contagion spread :
Besides what the grim wolf with privy paw,
Daily devours apace, and nothing said,
But that two-handed engine at the door
Stands ready to smite once, and smite no more.
    Return, Alpheus, the dread voice is past,
That shrunk thy streams ; return, Sicilian Muse,
And call the vales, and bid them hither cast
Their bells and flowerets of a thousand hues.
Ye valleys low, where the mild whispers use
Of shades, and wanton winds, and gushing brooks,
On whose fresh lap the swart-star sparely looks,
Throw hither all your quaint enamelled eyes,
That on the green-turf suck the honied showers,
And purple all the ground with vernal flowers.
Bring the rath primrose that forsaken dies,
The tufted crow-toe, and pale jessamine,
The white pink, and the pansy freaked with jet,
The glowing violet,
The musk-rose, and the well attired woodbine,
With cowslips wan, that hang the pensive head,
And every flower that sad embroidery wears :
Bid amaranthus all his beauty shed,
And daffodillies fill their cups with tears,
To strew the Laureat hearse where Lycid lies.
For, so to interpose a little ease,
Let our frail thoughts dally with false surmise.
Ah me ! Whilst thee the shores and sounding seas
Wash far away, where'er thy bones are hurled,
Whether beyond the stormy Hebrides,
Where thou perhaps, under 'he whelming tide

Visit'st the bottom of the monstrous world ;
Or whether thou, to our moist vows denied,
Sleep'st by the fable of Bellerus old,
Where the great vision of the guarded mount,
Looks toward Namancos and Bayona's hold ;
Look homeward, Angel, now, and melt with ruth ;
And, O ye dolphins, waft the hapless youth.
　　Weep no more, woful shepherds, weep no more,
For Lycidas, your sorrow, is not dead,
Sunk though he be beneath the watery floor ;
So sinks the day-star in the ocean bed,
And yet anon repairs his drooping head,
And tricks his beams, and with new-spangled ore
Flames in the forehead of the morning sky :
So Lycidas sunk low, but mounted high,
Through the dear might of Him that walked the waves
Where other groves and other streams along,
With nectar pure his oozy locks he laves,
And hears th' unexpressive nuptial song,
In the blest kingdoms meek of joy and love.
There entertain him all the saints above,
In solemn troops, and sweet societies,
That sing, and, singing in their glory move,
And wipe the tears for ever from his eyes.
Now, Lycidas, the shepherds weep no more ;
Henceforth thou art the Genius of the shore,
In thy large recompense, and shalt be good
To all that wander in that perilous flood

FROM COMUS.

LADY.   This way the noise was, if mine ear be true,
My best guide now; methought it was the sound
Of riot and ill-managed merriment,
Such as the jocund flute, or gamesome pipe,
Stirs up among the loose unlettered hinds,
When for their teeming flocks and granges full,
In wanton dance they praise the bounteous Pan,
And thank the Gods amiss.   I should be loth
To meet the rudeness and swilled insolence
Of such late wassailers; yet oh, where else
Shall I inform my unacquainted feet,
In the blind mazes of this tangled wood?
My brothers, when they saw me wearied out
With this long way, resolving here to lodge
Under the spreading favour of these pines,
Stept, as they said, to the next thicket side,
To bring me berries, or such cooling fruit
As the kind hospitable woods provide.
They left me then, when the gray-hooded even,
Like a sad votarist in Palmer's weed,
Rose from the hindmost wheels of Phœbus' wain.
But where they are, and why they came not back,
Is now the labour of my thoughts; 'tis likeliest
They had engaged their wandering steps too far,
And envious darkness, e'er they could return,
Had stole them from me; else, O thievish night,
Why shouldst thou, but for some felonious end,
In thy dark lantern thus close up the stars,
That nature hung in Heaven, and filled their lamps

With everlasting oil, to give due light
To the misled and lonely traveller?
This is the place, as well as I may guess,
Whence even now the tumult of loud mirth
Was rife and perfect in my listening ear;
Yet nought but single darkness do I find.
What might this be? A thousand fantasies
Begin to throng into my memory,
Of calling shapes, and beckoning shadows dire,
And airy tongues that syllable men's names
On sands, and shores, and desert wildernesses.
These thoughts may startle well, but not astound
The virtuous mind, that ever walks attended
By a strong siding champion, Conscience.
O welcome pure-eyed Faith, white-handed Hope,
Thou hovering angel, girt with golden wings;
And thou, unblemished form of Chastity,
I see ye visibly, and now believe
That he, the Supreme Good, t'whom all things ill
Are but as slavish officers of vengeance,
Would send a glist'ring guardian, if need were,
To keep my life and honour unassailed.
Was I deceived, or did a sable cloud
Turn forth her silver lining on the night?
I did not err, there does a sable cloud
Turn forth her silver lining on the night,
And cast a gleam over this tufted grove.
I cannot halloo to my brothers, but
Such noise as I can make to be heard farthest
I'll venture; for my new enlivened spirits
Prompt me; and they perhaps are not far off.

Lady sings

SONG

Sweet echo, sweetest nymph, that liv'st unseen
    Within thy airy shell,
    By slow Meander's margent green,
And in the violet embroidered vale,
    Where the love-lorn nighingale
Nightly to thee her sad song mourneth wel ;
Canst not tell me of a gentle pair
    That likest thy Narcissus are ?
      Oh if thou have
    Hid them in some flowery cave,
    Tell me but where,
  Sweet Queen of parly, daughter of the sphere,
  So may'st thou be translated to the skies,
And give resounding grace to all Heaven's harmonies.

Comus. Can any mortal mixture of earth's mould,
Breathe such divine, enchanting ravishment ;
Sure something holy lodges in that breast,
And with these raptures moves the vocal air
To testify his hidden residence :
How sweetly did they float upon the wings
Of silence, through the empty vaulted night,
At every fall, smoothing the raven down
Of darkness till it smiled ! I have oft heard
My mother Circe, with the Syrens three,
Amidst the flow'ry-kirtled Naiades,
Culling their potent herbs and baleful drugs,
Who as they sung, would take the prisoned soul
And lap it in Elysium ; Scylla wept.

And chid her barking waves into attention,
And fell Charybdis murmured soft applause.
Yet they in pleasing slumber lulled the sense,
And in sweet madness robbed it of itself;
But such a sacred and home-felt delight,
Such sober certainty of waking bliss,
I never heard till now.   I'll speak to her,
And she shall be my queen.

SONNETS.

ON HIS BLINDNESS

When I consider how my light is spent
    Ere half my days, in this dark world and wide,
    And that one talent which is death to hide,
    Lodged with me useless, though my soul more bent
To serve therewith my Maker, and present
    My true account, lest he, returning, chide :
    " Doth God exact day-labour, light denied ?"
    I fondly ask : but Patience to prevent
That murmur, soon replies, ' God doth not need
    Either man's work, or his own gifts ; who best
    Bear his mild yoke, they serve him best : his state
Is kingly ; thousands at his bidding speed,
    And pass o'er land and ocean without rest ;
    They also serve, who only stand and wait.'

MILTON

ON HIS DECEASED WIFE.

Methought I saw my late espoused saint
   Brought to me like Alcestis from the grave,
   Whom Jove's great son to her glad husband gave,
   Rescued from death by force, though pale and faint.
Mine, as whom washed from spot of childbed taint
   Purification in the old law did save ;
   And such as yet once more I trust to have
   Full sight of her in Heaven without restraint,
Came vested all in white, pure as her mind :
   Her face was veiled, yet to my fancied sight,
   Love, sweetness, goodness, in her person shined
So clear, as in her face with more delight ;
   But O, as to embrace me she inclined,
   I waked, she fled, and day brought back my night.

ON THE MASSACRE IN PIEDMONT

Avenge, O Lord, thy slaughtered saints, whose bones
   Lie scattered on the Alpine mountains cold ;
   Even them who kept thy truth so pure of old,
   When all our fathers worshipped stocks and stones,
Forget not : in thy book record their groans
   Who were thy sheep, and in their ancient fold
   Slain by the bloody Piedmontese, that rolled
   Mother with infant down the rocks. The moans
The vales redoubled to the hills, and they
   To heaven. Their martyred blood and ashes sow
   O'er all the Italian fields, where still doth sway
The triple tyrant ; that from these may grow
   A hundred fold, who, having learned thy way,
   Early may fly the Babylonian wo.

TO MR. LAWRENCE.

Lawrence, of virtuous father, virtuous son,
  Now that the fields are dank, and ways are mire,
  Where shall we sometimes meet, and by the fire
  Help waste a sullen day, what may be won
From the hard season gaining? Time will run
  On smoother till Favonius re-inspire
  The frozen earth, and clothe in fresh attire
  The lily and rose that neither sowed nor spun.
What neat repast shall feast us, light and choice
  Of Attic taste, with wine, whence we may rise
  To hear the lute well touched, or artful voice
Warble immortal notes and Tuscan air;
  He who of these delights can judge, and spare
  To interpose them oft, is not unwise.

TO CYRIAC SKINNER.

Cyriac, whose grandsire, on the royal bench
  Of British Themis, with no mean applause
  Pronounced, and in his volumes taught, our laws,
  Which others at their bar so often wrench:
To-day deep thoughts resolve with me to drench
  In mirth that, after, no repenting draws;
  Let Euclid rest, and Archimedes pause,
  And what the Swede intends, and what the French:
To measure life learn thou betimes, and know
  Toward solid good what leads the nearest way;
  For other things mild Heaven a time ordains,
And disapproves that care, though wise in show,
  That when superfluous burden loads the day,
  And, when God sends a cheerful hour, refrains.

8*

TO THE SAME.

Cyriac, this three-years-day, these eyes, though clear,
  To outward view, of blemish or of spot,
  Bereft of light, their seeing have forgot ;
  Nor to their idle orbs doth sight appear
Of sun, or moon, or star, throughout the year,
  Or man, or woman.　Yet I argue not
  Against Heaven's hand or will, nor bate a jot
  Of heart or hope ; but still bear up and steer
Right onward.　What supports me, dost thou ask ?
  The conscience, Friend, to have lost them overplied
  In liberty's defence, my noble task,
Of which all Europe rings from side to side.
  This thought might lead me thro' the world's vain mask
  Content, though blind, had I no better guide.

WHEN THE ASSAULT WAS INTENDED TO THE CITY.

Captain, or Colonel, or Knight in arms,
  Whose chance on these defenceless doors may seize,
  If deed of honour did thee ever please,
  Guard them, and him within protect from harms
He can requite thee ; for he knows the charms
  That call Fame on such gentle acts as these,
  And he can spread thy name o'er lands and seas,
  Whatever clime the sun's bright circle warms.
Lift not thy spear against the Muses' bower :
  The great Emathian conqueror bid spare
  The house of Pindarus, when temple and tower
Went to the ground ; and the repeated air
  Of sad Electra's poet had the power
  To save th' Athenian walls from ruin bare.

DRYDEN.

VENI CREATOR

CREATOR Spirit by whose aid
The world's foundations first were laid,
Come visit every pious mind ;
Come pour thy joys on human kind ;
From sin and sorrow set us free,
And make thy temples worthy thee.

O, source of uncreated light,
The Father's promised Paraclete!
Thrice holy fount, thrice holy fire,
Our hearts with heavenly love inspire
Come, and thy sacred unction bring
To sanctify us while we sing.

Plenteous of grace, descend from high,
Rich in thy sevenfold energy!
Thou strength of his Almighty hand,
Whose power does heaven and earth command.
Proceeding Spirit, our defence,
Who dost the gift of tongues dispense
And crownst thy gift with eloquence '

Refine and purge our earthly parts:
But, oh, inflame and fire our hearts!
Our frailties help, our vice control,
Submit the senses to the soul;
And when rebellious they are grown,
Then lay thy hand, and hold them down.

Chase from our minds th' infernal foe,
And peace, the fruit of love, bestow;
And, lest our feet should step astray,
Protect and guide us in the way.

Make us eternal truths receive,
And practice all that we believe:
Give us thyself, that we may see
The Father, and the Son, by thee.

Immortal honour, endless fame,
Attend th' Almighty Father's name.
The Saviour Son be glorified,
Who for lost man's redemption died;
And equal adoration be,
Eternal Paraclete, to thee!

POPE.

MESSIAH.

Ye nymphs of Solyma! begin the song :
To heavenly themes sublimer strains belong.
The mossy fountains and the sylvan shades,
The dreams of Pindus and the Aonian maids,
Delight no more. O Thou my voice inspire,
Who touched Isaiah's hallowed lips with fire!

Rapt into future times, the bard begun ;
A Virgin shall conceive, a Virgin bear a son!
From Jesse's root behold a branch arise,
Whose sacred flower with fragrance fills the skies:
The ethereal Spirit o'er its leaves shall move,
And on its top descends the mystic dove.
Ye heavens ! from high the dewy nectar pour,
And in soft silence shed the kindly shower!
The sick and weak the healing plant shall aid,
From storms a shelter, and from heat a shade.
All crimes shall cease, and ancient frauds shall fail
Returning Justice lift aloft her scale :
Peace o'er the world her olive wand extend,
And white-robed Innocence from heaven descend

Swift fly the years, and rise the expected morn;
Oh, spring to light, auspicious Babe, be born!
See, Nature hastes her earliest wreaths to bring,
With all the incense of the breathing Spring:
See lofty Lebanon his head advance,
See nodding forests on the mountains dance:
See spicy clouds from lowly Sharon rise,
And Carmel's flowery top perfumes the skies!
Hark! a glad voice the lonely desert cheers;
Prepare the way! A God, a God appears!
A God, a God! the vocal hills reply;
The rocks proclaim the approaching Deity.
Lo, earth receives him from the bending skies!
Sink down, ye mountains; and ye valleys, rise!
With heads declined, ye cedars, homage pay!
Be smooth, ye rocks; ye rapid floods, give way!
The Saviour comes! by ancient bards foretold;
Hear him, ye deaf; and all ye blind, behold.
He from thick film shall purge the visual ray,
And on the sightless eyeball pour the day:
'Tis he the obstructed paths of sound shall clear,
And bid new music charm the unfolding ear:
The dumb shall sing, the lame his crutch forego,
And leap exulting, like the bounding roe.
No sigh, no murmur, the wide world shall hear;
From every face he wipes off every tear.
In adamantine chains shall death be bound,
And hell's grim tyrant feel the eternal wound.
As the good shepherd tends his fleecy care,
Seeks freshest pasture, and the purest air;
Explores the lost, the wandering sheep directs,
By day o'ersees them, and by night protects;

The tender lambs he raises in his arms,
Feeds from his hand, and in his bosom warms:
Thus shall mankind his guardian care engage,
The promised father of the future age.
No more shall nation against nation rise,
Nor ardent warriors meet with hateful eyes,
Nor fields with gleaming steel be covered o'er,
The brazen trumpets kindle rage no more;
But useless lances into scythes shall bend,
And the broad falchion in a ploughshare end.
Then palaces shall rise; the joyful son
Shall finish what his short-liv'd sire begun;
Their vines a shadow to their race shall yield,
And the same hand that sowed shall reap the field;
The swain in barren deserts with surprise
Sees lilies spring, and sudden verdure rise;
And starts among the thirsty wilds to hear
New falls of water murmuring in his ear.
On rifted rocks, the dragon's late abodes,
The green reed trembles, and the bulrush nods.
Waste, sandy valleys, once perplexed with thorn,
The spiry fir and shapely box adorn:
To leafless shrubs the flowery palm succeed,
And odorous myrtle to the noisome weed.
The lambs with wolves shall graze the verdant mead,
And boys in flowery bands the tiger lead.
The steer and lion at one crib shall meet,
And harmless serpents lick the pilgrim's feet.
The smiling infant in his hand shall take
The crested basilisk and speckled snake,
Pleased, the green lustre of the scales survey,
And with their forky tongues shall innocently play.

Rise, crowned with light, imperial Salem, rise!
Exalt thy towery head, and lift thine eyes!
See a long race thy spacious courts adorn;
See future sons, and daughters yet unborn,
In crowding ranks on every side arise,
Demanding life, impatient for the skies!
See barbarous nations at thy gates attend,
Walk in thy light, and in thy temple bend:
See thy bright altars thronged with prostrate kings,
And heaped with products of Sabean springs!
For thee Idumea's spicy forests blow,
And seeds of gold in Ophir's mountains glow.
See heaven its sparkling portals wide display,
And break upon thee in a flood of day!
No more the rising sun shall gild the morn,
Nor evening Cynthia fill her silver horn;
But lost, dissolved in thy superior rays,
One tide of glory, one unclouded blaze,
O'erflow thy courts: the Light himself shall shine
Revealed, and God's eternal day be thine!
The seas shall waste, the skies in smoke decay,
Rocks fall to dust, and mountains melt away;
But fixed his word, his saving power remains;
Thy realm for ever lasts, thy own Messiah reigns

FROM "THE RAPE OF THE LOCK"

Nor with more glories, in the ethereal plain,
The sun first rises o'er the purpled main,
Than, issuing forth, the rival of his beams
Launched on the bosom of the silver Thames.
Fair nymphs, and well-dressed youth around her shone
But every eye was fixed on her alone.

On her white breast a sparkling cross she wore,
Which Jews might kiss, and Infidels adore,
Her lively looks a sprightly mind disclose,
Quick as her eyes, and as unfixed as those:
Favours to none, to all she smiles extends:
Oft she rejects, but never once offends.
Bright as the sun, her eyes the gazers strike,
And, like the sun, they shine on all alike.
Yet, graceful ease, and sweetness void of pride,
Might hide her faults, if belles had faults to hide:
If to her share some female errors fall,
Look on her face, and you'll forget them all.

This nymph, to the destruction of mankind,
Nourished two locks, which graceful hung behind
In equal curls, and well conspired to deck
With shining ringlets the swooth ivory neck.
Love in these labyrinths his slaves detains,
And mighty hearts are held in slender chairs.
With hairy springes we the birds betray,
Slight lines of hair surprise the finny prey,
Fair tresses man's imperial race insnare,
And beauty draws us with a single hair.

9

FROM THE "ELEGY."

As into air the purest spirits flow,
And separate from their kindred dregs below;
So flew thy soul to its congenial place,
Nor left one virtue to redeem thy race.

But thou, false guardian of a charge too good,
Thou mean deserter of thy brother's blood!
See on these ruby lips the trembling breast,
These cheeks now fading at the blast of death;
Cold is that breath which warmed the world before,
And those love-darting eyes must roll no more.
Thus, if eternal justice rules the ball,
Thus shall your wives, and thus your children fall;
On all the line a sudden vengeance waits,
And frequent hearses shall besiege your gates;
There passengers shall stand, and pointing say,
(While the long funerals blacken all the way,)
Lo! these were they whose souls the furies steeled,
And cursed with hearts unknowing how to yield.
Thus unlamented pass the proud away,
The gaze of fools, and pageant of a day!
So perish all, whose breasts ne'er learned to glow
For others' good, or melt at others' wo.

What can atone, oh, ever injured shade,
Thy fate unpitied, and thy rites unpaid?
No friend's complaint, no kind domestic tear,
Pleased thy pale ghost, or graced thy mournful bier.
By foreign hands thy dying eyes were closed;
By foreign hands thy decent limbs composed:

PoPE.

By foreign hands thy humble grave adorned,
By strangers honoured, and by strangers mourned.
What though no friends in sable weeds appear,
Grieve for an hour, perhaps, then mourn a year,
And bear about the mockery of wo,
To midnight dances, and the public show?
What though no weeping loves thy ashes grace,
Nor polished marble emulate thy face?
What though no sacred earth allow thee room,
Nor hallowed dirge be muttered o'er thy tomb?
Yet shall thy grave with rising flowers be drest,
And the green turf lie lightly on thy breast:
There shall the morn her earliest tears bestow,
There the first roses of the year shall blow;
While angels with their silver wings o'ershade
The ground, now sacred by thy relics made.

So peaceful rests, without a stone, a name,
What once had beauty, titles, wealth, and fame.
How loved, how honoured once, avails thee not,
To whom related, or by whom begot;
A heap of dust alone remains of thee,
'Tis all thou art, and all the proud shall be;
Poets themselves must fall like those they sung,
Deaf the praised ear, and mute the tuneful tongue.
Even he, whose soul now melts in mournful lays,
Shall shortly want the generous tear he pays;
Then from his closing eyes thy form shall part,
And the last pang shall tear thee from his heart;
Life's idle business at one gasp be o'er,
The muse forgot, and thou beloved no more,

FROM THE "EPISTLE TO DR. ARBUTHNOT."

' Shut, shut the door, good John,' fatigued I said ;
 Tie up the knocker, say I'm sick, I'm dead !
The dog-star rages ! nay, 'tis past a doubt,
All Bedlam or Parnassus is let out :
Fire in each eye, and papers in each hand,
They rave, recite, and madden round the land.
What walls can guard me, or what shades can hide?
They pierce my thickets, through my grot they glide ;
By land, by water, they renew the charge,
They stop the chariot, and they board the barge.
No place is sacred, not the church is free,
Even Sunday shines no Sabbath-day to me :
Then from the mint walks forth the man of rhyme,
Happy to catch me just at dinner time.
Is there a parson much be-mused in beer,
A maudlin poetess, a rhyming peer,
A clerk, fore-doomed his father's soul to cross,
Who pens a stanza when he should engross ?
Is there who, locked from ink and paper, scrawls
With desperate charcoal round his darkened walls ?
All fly to Twickenham, and in humble strain
Apply to me to keep them mad or vain.
Arthur, whose giddy son neglects the laws,
Imputes to me and my damned works the cause :
Poor Cornus sees his frantic wife elope,
And curses wit, and poetry, and Pope.
Friend to my life, which did not you prolong,
The world had wanted many an idle song,

POPE.

What drop or nostrum can this plague remove ?
Or which must end me, a fool's wrath or love ?
O dire dilemma! either way I'm sped ;
If foes, they write ; if friends, they read me dead.
Siezed and tied down to judge, how wretched I !
Who can't be silent, and who will not lie.
To laugh were want of goodness and of grace,
And to be grave, exceeds all power of face.
I sit with sad civility, I read
With honest anguish and an aching head,
And drop at last, but in unwilling ears,
This saving counsel, ' Keep your piece nine years.'
' Nine years !' cries he, who, high in Drury Lane,
Lulled by soft zephyrs through the broken pane,
Rhymes ere he wakes, and prints before term ends,
Obliged by hunger and request of friends :
' The piece you think is incorrect ? why take it,
I'm all submission, what you'd have it, make it.'
Three things another's modest wishes bound ;
' My friendship, and a prologue, and ten pound.'
Pitholeon sends to me ; you know his grace,
I want a patron ; ask him for a place.
Pitholeon libelled me,—' But here's a letter
Informs you, Sir, 'twas when he knew no better.
Dare you refuse him ?   Curll invites to dine !
He'll write a journal, or he'll turn divine.'
Bless me ! a packet.—' 'Tis a stranger sues,
A virgin tragedy, an orphan muse.
If I dislike it, ' Furies, death, and rage ;'
If I approve, ' Commend it to the stage.'
There (thank my stars) my whole commission ends
The players and I are, luckily, no friends.

9*

Fired that the house rejects him, 'Sdeath, I'll print it,
And shame the fools,—your interest, sir, with Lintot.
Lintot, dull rogue, will think your price too much ;
' Not, sir, if you revise it and retouch.'
All my demurs but double his attacks ;
At last he whispers, ' Do, and we go snacks.'
Glad of a quarrel, straight I clap the door,
Sir, let me see your works and you no more !

Why did I write ?   What sin to me unknown
Dipped me in ink,—my parents', or my own ?
As yet a child, nor yet a fool to fame,
I lisped in numbers, for the numbers came :
I left no calling for this idle trade,
No duty broke, no father disobeyed :
The Muse but served to ease some friend, not wife,
To help me through this long disease, my life,
To second, Arbuthnot ! thy art and care,
And teach the being you preserved to bear.

THOMSON.

FROM "THE CASTLE OF INDOLENCE."

In lonely dale, fast by a river's side,
With woody hill o'er hill encompassed round,
A most enchanting wizard did abide,
Than whom a fiend more fell is no where found.
It was, I ween, a lovely spot of ground,
And there a season atween June and May,
Half prankt with spring, with summer half imbrowned
A listless climate made, where, sooth to say,
No living wight could work, ne cared even for play.

Was nought around but images of rest,
Sleep-soothing groves, and quiet lawns between,
And flowery beds that slumberous influence cast,
From poppies breathed, and beds of pleasant green,
Where never yet was creeping creature seen.
Meantime unnumbered glittering streamlets played,
And hurled every where their waters sheen;
That as they bickered through the sunny glade,
Tho' restless still themselves, a lulling murmur made.

Joined to the prattle of the purling rills,
Were heard the lowing herds along the vale,
And flocks loud bleating from the distant hills,
And vacant shepherds piping in the dale ;
And now and then sweet Philomel would wail,
Or stock-doves plain amid the forest deep,
That drowsy rustled to the sighing gale ;
And still a coil the grasshopper did keep :
Yet all these sounds yblent inclined all to sleep.

Full in the passage of the vale above,
A sable, silent, solemn forest stood ;
Where nought but shadowy forms were seen to move,
As Idless fancied in her dreaming mood :
And up the hills, on either side, a wood
Of blackening pines, ay waving to and fro,
Sent forth a sleepy horror through the blood ;
And where this valley winded out below,
The murm'ring main was heard, and scarcely heard to flow

A pleasing land of drowsy-head it was,
Of dreams that wave before the half-shut eye ;
And of gay castles in the clouds that pass,
For ever flushing round a summer sky :
There eke the soft delights that witchingly
Instil a wanton sweetness through the breast,
And the calm pleasures, always hovered nigh ;
But whate'er smacked of 'noyance, or unrest,
Was far, far off expelled from this delicious nest.

The landscape such, inspiring perfect ease,
Where Indolence (for so the wizard hight)
Close hid his castle 'mid embowering trees,
That half shut out the beams of Phœbus bright,
And made a kind of chequered day and night;
Meanwhile, unceasing at the massy gate,
Beneath a spacious palm, the wicked wight
Was placed; and, to his lute, of cruel fate
And labour harsh complained, lamenting man's estate.

   *   *   *   *   *   *   *

The doors, that knew no shrill alarming bell,
Ne cursed knocker, plied by villain's hand,
Self-opened into halls, where, who can tell
What elegance and grandeur wide expand;
The pride of Turkey and of Persia land?
Soft quilts on quilts, carpets on carpets spread,
And couches stretched around in seemly band
And endless pillows rise to prop the head;
So that each spacious room was one full swelling bed.

   *   *   *   *   *   *   *

Each sound too here to languishment inclined,
Lulled the weak bosom, and induced ease:
Aërial music in the warbling wind,
At distance rising oft, by small degrees,
Nearer and nearer came, till oe'r the trees
It hung, and breathed such soul-dissolving airs,
As did, alas! with soft perdition please:
Entangled deep in its enchanting snares,
The listening heart forgot all duties and all cares.

A certain music, never known before,
Here lulled the pensive, melancholy mind
Full easily obtained.   Behoves no more,
But sidelong, to the gentle waving wind,
To lay the well tuned instrument reclined ;
From which, with airy flying fingers light,
Beyond each mortal touch the most refined,
The god of winds drew sounds of deep delight :
Whence, with just cause, the harp of Æolus it hight

    * * * * - * * *

Near the pavilions where we slept, still ran
Soft tinkling streams, and dashing waters fell,
And sobbing breezes sighed, and oft began
(So worked the wizard) wintry storms to swell,
As heaven and earth they would together mell,
At doors and windows, threatening, seemed to call
The demons of the tempest growling fell,
Yet the least entrance found they none at all ;
Whence sweeter grew our sleep, secure in massy pall.

And hither Morpheus sent his kindest dreams,
Raising a world of gayer tint and grace ;
O'er which were shadowy cast elysian gleams,
That played, in waving lights, from place to place,
And shed a roseate smile on nature's face,
Not Titian's pencil e'er could so array,
So fleece with clouds the pure ethereal space ;
Ne could it e'er such melting forms display,
As loose on flowery beds all languishingly lay.

SUMMER IN THE TORRID ZONE.

There, sublimed
To fearless lust of blood, the savage race
Roam, licensed by the shading hour of guilt
And foul misdeed, when the pure day has shut
His sacred eye.   The tiger darting fierce
Impetuous on the prey his glance has doomed :
The lively-shining leopard, speckled oe'r
With many a spot, the beauty of the waste ;
And, scorning all the taming arts of man,
The keen hyena, fellest of the fell.
These, rushing from the inhospitable woods
Of Mauritania, or the tufted isles,
That verdant rise amid the Lybian wild,
Innumerous glare around their shaggy king,
Majestic, stalking o'er the printed sand ;
And, with imperious and repeated roars,
Demand their fated food.   The fearful flocks
Crowd near the guardian swain ; the nobler herds,
Where round their lordly bull, in rural ease,
They ruminating lie, with horror hear
The coming rage.   The awakened village starts ;
And to her fluttering breast the mother strains
Her thoughtless infant.   From the pirate's den,
Or stern Morocco's tyrant fang escaped,
The wretch half wishes for his bonds again.
While, uproar all, the wilderness resounds,
From Atlas eastward, to the frighted Nile.

Unhappy he ! who, from the first of joys,
Society, cut off, is left alone

Amid this world of death.   Day after day,
Sad, on the jutting eminence he sits,
And views the main that ever toils below ;
Still fondly forming in the farthest verge,
Where the round ether mixes with the wave,
Ships, dim-discovered, dropping from the clouds :
At evening, to the setting sun he turns
A mournful eye, and down his dying heart
Sinks helpless.

  Nor stop the terrors of these regions here.
Commissioned demons oft, angels of wrath,
Let loose the raging elements.   Breathed hot
From all the boundless furnace of the sky,
And the wide glittering waste of burning sand,
A suffocating wind the pilgrim smites
With instant death.   Patient of thirst and toil,
Son of the desert ! even the camel feels,
Shot through his withered heart, the fiery blast.
Or from the black-red ether, bursting broad,
Sallies the sudden whirlwind.   Straight the sands,
Conmoved around, in gathering eddies play.
Nearer and nearer still they darkening come ;
Till, with the general all-involving storm
Swept up, the whole continuous wilds arise,
And by their noon-day fount dejected thrown,
Or sunk at night in sad disastrous sleep,
Beneath ascending hills, the caravan
Is buried deep.   In Cairo's crowded streets
The impatient merchant, wondering, waits in vain,
And Mecca saddens at the long delay.

DEATH OF THE STAG.

The stag too, singled from the herd, where long
He ranged, the branching monarch of the shade,
Before the tempest drives.   At first, in speed
He, sprightly, puts his faith ; and, roused by fear,
Gives all his swift aërial soul to flight ;
Against the breeze he darts, that way the more
To leave the lessening murderous cry behind :
He bursts the thickets, glances through the glades,
And plunges deep into the wildest wood :
If slow, yet sure, adhesive to the track,
Hot-steaming, up behind him come again
The inhuman rout, and from the shady depth
Expel him, circling through his every shift.
He sweeps the forest oft, and sobbing sees
The glades, mild opening to the golden day ;
Where, in kind contest, with his butting friends
He wont to struggle, or his loves enjoy.
Oft in the full-descending flood he tries
To lose the scent, and lave his burning sides :
Oft seeks the herd ; the watchful herd, alarmed,
With selfish care avoid a brother's wo.
What shall he do ?   His once so vivid nerves,
So full of buoyant spirits, now no more
Inspire the course ; but fainting breathless toil,
Sick, seizes on his heart : he stands at bay ;
And puts his last weak refuge in despair.
The big round tears run down his dappled face ;
He groans in anguish ; while the growling pack,
Blood-happy, hang at his fair jutting chest,
And mark his beauteous chequered sides with gore,

10

WINTER SCENES.

The keener tempests rise : and fuming dun
From all the livid east, or piercing north,
Thick clouds ascend ; in whose capacious womb
A vapoury deluge lies, to snow congealed.
Heavy they roll their fleecy world along ;
And the sky saddens with the gathered storm.
Through the hushed air the whitening shower descends
At first thin wavering ; till at last the flakes
Fall broad, and wide, and fast, dimming the day
With a continual flow.   The cherished fields
Put on their winter robe of purest white.
'Tis brightness all ; save where the new snow melts
Along the mazy current.   Low the woods
Bow their hoar head ; and, ere the languid sun
Faint from the west emits his evening ray,
Earth's universal face, deep hid and chill,
Is one wide dazzling waste, that buries wide
The works of man.   Drooping, the labourer-ox
Stands covered o'er with snow, and then demands
The fruit of all his toil.   The fowls of heaven,
Tamed by the cruel season, crowd around
The winnowing store, and claim the little boon
Which Providence assigns them.   One alone,
The red-breast, sacred to the household gods,
Wisely regardful of the embroiling sky,
In joyless fields, and thorny thickets, leaves
His shivering mates, and pays to trusted man
His annual visit.   Half afraid, he first
Against the window beats ; then, brisk, alights

On the warm hearth; then, hopping o'er the floor,
Eyes all the smiling family askance,
And pecks, and starts, and wonders where he is:
Till, more familiar grown, the table-crumbs
Attract his slender feet.   The foodless wilds
Pour forth their brown inhabitants.   The hare,
Though timorous of heart, and hard beset
By death in various forms, dark snares, and dogs,
And more unpitying man, the garden seeks,
Urged on by fearless Want.   The bleating kind
Eye the bleak heaven, and next the glistening earth,
With looks of dumb despair; then, sad dispersed,
Dig for the withered herb through heaps of snow.

*   *   *   *   *   *   *

As thus the snows arise; and foul, and fierce,
All winter drives along the darkened air;
In his own loose revolving fields, the swain
Disastered stands: sees other hills ascend,
Of unknown joyless brow; and other scenes,
Of horrid prospect, shag the trackless plain:
Nor finds the river, nor the forest, hid
Beneath the formless wild: but wanders on
From hill to dale, still more and more astray;
Impatient flouncing through the drifted heaps,
Stung with the thoughts of home; the thoughts of home
Rush on his nerves, and call their vigour forth
In many a vain attempt.   How sinks the soul!
What black despair, what horror fills his heart!
When for the dusky spot, which fancy feigned
His tufted cottage rising through the snow

He meets the roughness of the middle waste,
Far from the track, and blessed abode of man,
While round him night resistless closes fast,
And every tempest howling o'er his head,
Renders the savage wilderness more wild.
Then throng the busy shapes into his mind,
Of covered pits, unfathomably deep,
A dire descent! beyond the power of frost;
Of faithless bogs; of precipices huge,
Smoothed up with snow; and, what is land unknown.
What water, of the still unfrozen spring,
In the loose marsh or solitary lake,
Where the fresh fountain from the bottom boils.
These check his fearful steps; and down he sinks
Beneath the shelter of the shapeless drift,
Thinking o'er all the bitterness of death,
Mixed with the tender anguish Nature shoots
Through the wrung bosom of the dying man,
His wife, his children, and his friends unseen.
In vain for him the officious wife prepares
The fire fair-blazing, and the vestment warm;
In vain his little children, peeping out
Into the mingling storm, demand their sire,
With tears of artless innocence.   Alas!
Nor wife, nor children, more shall he behold,
Nor friends, nor sacred home.   On every nerve
The deadly Winter seizes; shuts up sense;
And, o'er his inmost vitals creeping cold,
Lays him along the snows a stiffened corse,
Stretched out, and bleaching in the northern blast

*   *   *   *   *   *   *   *

But what is this? our infant Winter sinks,
Divested of his grandeur, should our eye
Astonished shoot into the frigid zone ;
Where, for relentless months, continual Night
Holds, o'er the glittering waste her starry reign.
There, through the prison of unbounded wilds,
Barred by the hand of nature from escape,
Wide roams the Russian exile. Nought around
Strikes his sad eye, but deserts lost in snow ;
And heavy loaded groves ; and solid floods,
That stretch athwart the solitary vast
Their icy horrors to the frozen main ;
And cheerless towns far distant, never blessed,
Save when its annual course the caravan
Bends to the golden coast of rich Cathay,
With news of human kind. Yet there life glows ;
Yet cherished there, beneath the shining waste,
The furry nations harbour ; tipt with jet,
Fair ermines, spotless as the snows they press ;
Sables of glossy black ; and dark embrowned ;
Or beauteous freaked with many a mingled hue,
Thousands besides, the costly pride of courts.
There, warm together pressed, the trooping deer,
Sleep on the new-fallen snows ; and scarce his head
Raised o'er the heapy wreath, the branching elk
Lies slumbering sullen in the white abyss.
The ruthless hunter wants nor dogs nor toils,
Nor with the dread of sounding bows he drives
The fearful flying race ; with ponderous clubs,
As weak against the mountain heaps they push
Their beating breast in vain, and piteous bray
10*

He lays them quivering in the ensanguined snows,
And with loud shouts rejoicing bears them home.
There through the piny forest half absorped,
Rough tenant of these shades, the shapeless bear,
With dangling ice all horrid, stalks forlorn ;
Slow-paced, and sourer as the storms increase,
He makes his bed beneath the inclement drift ;
And, with stern patience, scorning weak complaint,
Hardens his heart against assailing want.

     *   *   *   *   *   *   *

    Still pressing on, beyond Tornea's lake,
And Hecla flaming through a waste of snow,
And farthest Greenland, to the pole itself,
Where, failing gradual, life at length goes out,
The Muse expands her solitary flight ;
And, hovering o'er the wild stupendous scene,
Beholds new scenes beneath another sky.
Throned in his palace of cerulean ice,
Here Winter holds his unrejoicing court ;
And through his airy hall the loud misrule
Of driving tempest is forever heard :
Here the grim tyrant meditates his wrath ;
Here arms his winds with all-subduing frost ;
Moulds his fierce hail, and treasures up his snows,
With which he now oppresses half the globe.
Thence winding eastward to the Tartar's coast,
She sweeps the howling margin of the main ;
Where undissolving, from the first of time,
Snows swell on snows, amazing, to the sky ;
And icy mountains, high on mountains piled,

THOMSON.

Seem to the shivering sailor from afar,
Shapeless and white, an atmosphere of clouds.
Projected huge, and horrid o'er the surge,
Alps frown on Alps ; or, rushing hideous down,
As if old Chaos was again returned,
Wide rend the deep, and shake the solid pole.
Ocean itself no longer can resist
The binding fury ; but in all its rage
Of tempest, taken by the boundless frost,
Is many a fathom to the bottom chained,
And bid to roar no more : a bleak expanse,
Shagged o'er with wavy rocks, cheerless, and void
Of every life, that from the dreary months
Flies conscious southward.   Miserable they !
Who, here entangled in the gathering ice,
Take their last look of the descending sun ;
While full of death, and fierce with tenfold frost,
The long, long night, incumbent o'er their heads
Falls horrible.   Such was the Briton's fate,
As with first prow, (what have not Britons dared !)
He for the passage sought, attempted since
So much in vain, and seeming to be shut
By jealous Nature with eternal bars.
In these fell regions, in Arzina caught,
And to the stony deep his idle ship
Immediate sealed, he, with his hapless crew,
Each full exerted at his several task,
Froze into statues ; to the cordage glued
The sailor, and the pilot to the helm.

TO AMANDA.

Come, dear Amanda, quit the town,
  And to the rural hamlets fly ;
Behold ! the wintry storms are gone :
  A gentle radiance glads the sky.

The birds awake, the flowers appear,
  Earth spreads a verdant couch for thee ;
'Tis joy and music all we hear,
  'Tis love and beauty all we see.

Come, let us mark the gradual spring,
  How peeps the bud, the blossom blows ;
'Till Philomel begins to sing,
  And perfect May to swell the rose.

E'en so thy rising charms improve,
  As life's warm season grows more bright
And opening to the sighs of love,
  Thy beauties glow with full delight.

TO THE SAME.

Unless with my Amanda bless'd,
  In vain I twine the woodbine bower ;
Unless to deck her sweeter breast,
  In vain I rear the breathing flower.

Awaken'd by the genial year,
  In vain the birds around me sing ;
In vain the freshening fields appear :—
  Without my love there is no spring.

YOUNG

MIDNIGHT

TIRED Nature's sweet restorer, balmy sleep !
He, like the world, his ready visit pays
Where Fortune smiles ; the wretched he forsakes :
Swift on his downy pinion flies from wo,
And lights on lids unsullied with a tear.
    From short (as usual) and disturbed repose
I wake : how happy they who wake no more !
Yet that were vain, if dreams infest the grave.
I wake, emerging from a sea of dreams
Tumultuous ; where my wrecked desponding thought,
From wave to wave of fancied misery
At random drove, her helm of reason lost.
Though now restored, 'tis only change of pain,
(A bitter change !) severer for severe :
The day too short for my distress ; and night,
E'en in the zenith of her dark domain,
Is sunshine to the colour of my fate.
    Night, sable Goddess ! from her ebon throne,
In rayless majesty, now stretches forth
Her leaden sceptre o'er a slumbering world.

Silence how dead! and darkness how profound!
Nor eye, nor list'ning ear, an object finds;
Creation sleeps. 'Tis as the general pulse
Of life stood still, and Nature made a pause;
An awful pause! prophetic of her end.
And let her prophecy be soon fulfilled:
Fate! drop the curtain; I can lose no more.
 Silence and darkness! solemn sisters! twins
From ancient Night, who nurse the tender thought
To reason, and on reason build resolve,
(That column of true majesty in man,)
Assist me: I will thank you in the grave;
The grave, your kingdom: there this frame shall fall
A victim sacred to your dreary shrine.
But what are ye?—
 Thou, who didst put to flight
Primœval silence, when the morning star
Exulting, shouted o'er the rising ball:
O Thou! whose word from solid darkness struck
That spark, the sun, strike wisdom from my soul;
My soul, which flies to thee, her trust, her treasure,
As misers to their gold, while others rest.
Through this opaque of nature and of soul,
This double night, transmit one pitying ray,
To lighten and to cheer. O lead my mind,
(A mind that fain would wander from its wo,)
Lead it through various scenes of life and death,
And from each scene the noblest truths inspire.
Nor less inspire my conduct than my song;
Teach my best reason, reason; my best will
Teach rectitude; and fix my firm resolve
Wisdom to wed, and pay her long arrear:

Nor let the phial of thy vengeance, poured
On this devoted head, be poured in vain.
     The bell strikes one.   We take no note of time,
But from its loss : to give it then a tongue
Is wise in man.   As if an angel spoke,
I feel the solemn sound.   If heard aright,
It is the knell of my departed hours.
Where are they ?   With the years beyond the flood.
It is the signal that demands dispatch :
How much is to be done ?   My hopes and fears
Start up alarmed, and o'er life's narrow verge
Look down—on what ?   A fathomless abyss !
A dread eternity ! How surely mine !
And can eternity belong to me,
Poor pensioner on the bounties of an hour ?
How poor, how rich, how abject, how august,
How complicate, how wonderful is man !
How passing wonder He, who made him such !
Who centered in our make such strange extremes,
From different natures marvellously mixed,
Connexion exquisite of distant worlds !
Distinguished link in being's endless chain !
Midway from nothing to the Deity !
A beam ethereal, sullied, and absorpt !
Though sullied and dishonoured, still divine !
Dim miniature of greatness absolute !
An heir of glory ! a frail child of dust !
Helpless immortal ! insect infinite !
A worm ! a God !—I tremble at myself,
And in myself am lost   At home, a stranger,
Thought wanders up and down, surprised, aghast,
And wondering at her own.   How reason reels !

O what a miracle to man is man!
Triumphantly distressed!   What joy! what dread
Alternately transported and alarmed!
What can preserve my life! or what destroy!
An angel's arm can't snatch me from the grave;
Legions of angels can't confine me there.

PROCRASTINATION.

  Be wise to-day; 'tis madness to defer:
Next day the fatal precedent will plead;
Thus on, till wisdom is pushed out of life!
Procrastination is the thief of time;
Year after year it steals, till all are fled,
And to the mercies of a moment leaves
The vast concerns of an eternal scene.
If not so frequent, would not this be strange?
That 'tis so frequent, this is stranger still.
Of man's miraculous mistakes this bears
The palm, " That all men are about to live,"
For ever on the brink of being born:
All pay themselves the compliment to think
They one day shall not drivel, and their pride
On this reversion takes up ready praise;
At least their own; their future selves applaud
How excellent that life they ne'er will lead!
Time lodged in their own hands is Folly's vails;
That lodged in Fate's, to wisdom they consign;
The thing they can't but purpose, they postpone
'Tis not in folly not to scorn a fool;
And scarce in human wisdom to do more.

All promise is poor dilatory man,
And that through every stage.   When young, indeed,
In full content we sometimes nobly rest,
Unanxious for ourselves, and only wish,
As duteous sons, our fathers were more wise
At thirty, man suspects himself a fool ;
Knows it at forty, and reforms his plan ;
At fifty chides his infamous delay,
Pushes his prudent purpose to resolve ;
In all the magnanimity of thought
Resolves, and re-resolves ; then dies the same.
    And why ? because he thinks himself immortal.
All men think all men mortal but themselves ;
Themselves, when some alarming shock of Fate
Strikes through their wounded hearts the sudden dread :
But their hearts wounded, like the wounded air,
Soon close ; where, past the haft, no trace is found.
As from the wing no scar the sky retains,
The parted wave no furrow from the keel,
So dies in human hearts the thought of death ·
Even with the tender tear which nature sheds
O'er those we love, we drop it in their grave.

AKENSIDE.

FOR A STATUE OF CHAUCER, AT WOODSTOCK.

Such was old Chaucer. Such the placid mien
Of him who first with harmony informed
The language of our fathers. Here he dwelt
For many a cheerful day. 'These ancient walls
Have often heard him, while his legend blithe
He sang; of love, or knighthood, or the wiles
Of homely life: through each estate and age,
The fashions and the follies of the world,
With cunning hand pourtraying. Though perchance
From Blenheim's towers, O stranger, thou art come,
Glowing with Churchill's trophies; yet in vain
Dost thou applaud them, if thy breast be cold
To him, this other hero; who, in times
Dark and untaught, began with charming verse
To tame the rudeness of his native land.

MOURNFUL PLEASURES.

　　　　　Ask the faithful youth,
Why the cold urn of her whom long he loved,
So often fills his arms; so often draws
His lonely footsteps at the silent hour,
To pay the mournful tribute of his tears?
O! he will tell thee that the wealth of worlds
Should ne'er seduce his bosom to forego
That sacred hour, when stealing from the noise
Of care and envy, sweet remembrance soothes
With virtue's kindest looks his aching breast
And turns his tears to rapture.　Ask the crowd
Which flies impatient from the village walk,
To climb the neighbouring cliffs, when far below
The cruel winds have hurled upon the coast
Some helpless bark; while sacred pity melts
The general eye, or terror's icy hand
Smites their distorted limbs and horrent hair,
While every mother closer to her breast
Catches her child, and pointing where the waves
Foam through the shattered vessel, shrieks aloud,
As some poor wretch that spreads his piteous arms
For succour, swallowed by the roaring surge,
As now another, dashed against the rock,
Drops lifeless down.　O, deemest thou indeed
No kind endearment here by nature given
To mutual terror and compassion's tears?
No sweetly melting softness which attracts,
O'er all that edge of pain, the social powers,
To this their proper action and their end?

PLEASURES OF IMAGINATION.

Oh! blest of heaven, whom not the languid songs
Of luxury, the Syren! not the bribes
Of sordid wealth, nor all the gaudy spoils
Of pageant honour can seduce to leave
Those ever blooming sweets, which from the store
Of nature fair imagination culls
To charm the enlivened soul! What though not all
Of mortal offspring can attain the heights
Of envied life; though only few possess
Patrician treasures or imperial state;
Yet nature's care, to all her children just,
With richer treasures and an ampler state,
Endows at large whatever happy man
Will deign to use them.   His the city's pomp
The rural honours his.   Whate'er adorns
The princely dome, the column and the arch,
The breathing marble and the sculptured gold
Beyond the proud possessor's narrow claim,
His tuneful breast enjoys.   For him, the spring
Distils her dews, and from the silken gem
Its lucid leaves unfolds: for him, the hand
Of autumn tinges every fertile branch
With blooming gold, and blushes like the morn,
Each passing hour sheds tribute from her wings;
And still new beauties meet his lonely walk,
And loves unfelt attract him.   Not a breeze
Flies o'er the meadow, not a cloud imbibes
The setting sun's effulgence, not a strain
From all the tenants of the warbling shade   —

Ascends, but whence his bosom can partake
Fresh pleasure, unreproved.   Nor thence partakes
Fresh pleasure only ; for the attentive mind,
By this harmonious action on her powers,
becomes herself harmonious : wont so oft
in outward things to meditate the charm
Of sacred order, soon she seeks at home
To find a kindred order, to exert
Within herself this elegance of love,
This fair inspired delight : her tempered powers
Refine at length, and every passion wears
A chaster, milder, more attractive mien.

FOR A MONUMENT AT RUNNYMEDE.

Thou, who the verdant plain doth traverse here,
While Thames among his willows from thy view
Retires ; O stranger, stay thee, and the scene
Around contemplate well.   This is the place
Where England's ancient barons, clad in arms,
And stern in conquest, from their tyrant king
(Then rendered tame) did challenge and secure
The charter of thy freedom.   Pass not on,
Till thou hast blessed their memory, and paid
Those thanks which God appointed the reward
Of public virtue, and if chance thy home
Salute thee with a father's honoured name,
Go, call thy sons : instruct them what a debt
They owe their ancestors ; and make them swear
To pay it, by transmitting down entire
Those sacred rights to which themselves were born.

11*

FOR A STATUE OF SHAKESPEARE.

O youths and virgins : O declining eld :
O pale misfortune's slaves : O ye who dwell
Unknown with humble quiet ; ye who wait
In courts, or fill the golden seat of kings :
O sons of sport and pleasure : O thou wretch
That weepest for jealous love, or the sore wounds
Of conscious guilt, or death's rapacious hand
Which left thee void of hope : O ye who roam
In exile ; ye who through the embattled field
Seek bright renown ; or who for nobler palms
Contend, the leaders of a public cause ;
Approach, behold this marble.   Know ye not
The features ? Hath not oft his faithful tongue
Told you the fashion of your own estate,
The secrets of your bosom ? Here then, round
His monument with reverence while ye stand,
Say to each other, ' this was Shakespeare's form ;
Who walked in every path of human life ;
Felt every passion : and to all mankind
Doth now, will ever, that experience yield,
Which his own genius only could acquire.'

COLLINS

THE PASSIONS

WHEN Music, heavenly maid, was young
While yet in early Greece she sung,
The Passions oft, to hear her shell,
Thronged around her magic cell,
Exulting, trembling, raging, fainting,
Possessed beyond the Muse's painting ;
By turns they felt the glowing mind
Disturbed, delighted, raised, refined :
Till once, 'tis said, when all were fired,
Filled with fury, rapt, inspired,
From the supporting myrtles round,
They snatched her instruments of sound
And, as they oft had heard apart
Sweet lessons of her forceful art,
Each (for madness ruled the hour)
Would prove his own expressive power.

First Fear his hand, its skill to try,
   Amid the chords bewildered laid,
And back recoiled, he knew not why,
   Even at the sound himself had made.

Next Anger rushed; his eyes on fire,
   In lightnings owned his secret stings:
In one rude clash he struck the lyre,
   And swept with hurried hand the strings.

With woful measures wan Despair,
   Low, sullen sounds his grief beguiled;
solemn, strange, and mingled air;
   'Twas sad by fits, by starts 'twas wild.

But thou, O Hope, with eyes so fair,
   What was thy delighted measure?
Still it whispered promised pleasure,
   And bade the lovely scenes at distance hail!
Still would her touch the strain prolong;
   And from the rocks, the woods, the vale,
She called on echo still, through all the song,
   And, where her sweetest theme she chose,
   A soft responsive voice was heard at every close:
And Hope enchanted smiled, and waved her golden hair
And longer had she sung: but, with a frown,
   Revenge impatient rose:
He threw his blood-stained sword in thunder down
   And, with a withering look,
The war-denouncing trumpet took,
And blew a blast so loud and dread,
Were ne'er prophetic sounds so full of wo!

And ever and anon, he beat,
The doubling drum, with furious heat;
And though sometimes, each dreary pause between,
   Dejected Pity, at his side,
   Her soul subduing voice applied,
Yet still he kept his wild unaltered mien,
While each strained ball of sight seemed bursting from
   his head.

Thy numbers, Jealousy, to nought were fixed,
   Sad proof of thy distressful state:
Of differing themes the veering song was mixed;
   And now it courted Love, now raving called on Hate.

   With eyes up-raised, as one inspired,
   Pale Melancholy sat retired;
   And from her wild sequestered seat,
   In notes by distance made more sweet,
Poured through the mellow horn her pensive soul;
   And, dashing soft from rocks around,
   Bubbling runnels joined the sound;
Through glades and glooms the mingled measure stole:
   Or, o'er some haunted stream, with fond delay,
     Round an holy calm diffusing,
     Love of peace, and lonely musing,
   In hollow murmurs died away.

   But O! how altered was its sprightlier tone,
When Cheerfulness, a nymph of healthiest hue,
   Her bow across her shoulder flung,
Her buskins gemmed with morning dew;
   Blew an inspiring air, that d   ld thicket rung,

The hunter's call, to Faun and Dryad known.
The oak-crowned Sisters, and their chaste-eyed Queen,
   Satyrs and Sylvan boys were seen,
    Peeping forth from their alleys green:
Brown Exercise rejoiced to hear;
And Sport leaped up, and seized his beechen spear.

Last came Joy's ecstatic trial;
   He, with viny crown advancing,
  First to the lively pipe his hand addressed:
But soon he saw the brisk awakening viol,
  Whose sweet entrancing voice he loved the best:
They would have thought, who heard the strain,
   They saw, in Tempe's vale, her native maids,
   Amidst the festal sounding shades,
    To some unwearied minstrel dancing,
While, as his flying fingers kissed the strings,
Love framed with Mirth a gay fantastic round;
  Loose were her tresses seen, her zone unbound;
And he, amidst his frolic play,
  As if he would the charming air repay,
Shook thousand odours from his dewy wings.

   O Music! sphere-descended maid,
   Friend of Pleasure, Wisdom's aid!
   Why Goddess? why to us denied,
   Lays't thou thy ancient lyre aside?
   As in that loved Athenian bower,
   You learned an all-commanding power
   Thy mimic soul, O Nymph endeared,
   Can well recall what then it heard.

COLLINS.

Where is thy native simple heart,
Devote to Virtue, Fancy, Art?
Arise, as in that elder time,
Warm, energetic, chaste, sublime !
Thy wonders in that godlike age,
Fill thy recording Sister's page—
'Tis said and I believe the tale,
Thy humblest reed could more prevail,
Had more of strength, diviner rage,
Than all which charms this laggard age
E'en all at once together found,
Cecilia's mingled world of sound—
O bid our vain endeavours cease ;
Revive the just designs of Greece :
Return in all thy simple state !
Confirm the tales her sons relate !

EPITAPH.

How sleep the brave, who sink to rest,
By all their country's wishes blest !
When Spring, with dewy fingers cold,
Returns to deck their hallowed mould,
She there shall dress a sweeter sod
Than Fancy's feet have ever trod.

By fairy hands their knell is rung :
By forms unseen their dirge is sung ;
There Honour comes, a pilgrim gray,
To bless the turf that wraps their clay ;
And Freedom shall awhile repair,
To dwell a weeping hermit there.

ODE TO EVENING.

If aught of oaten stop, or pastoral song,
May hope, O pensive Eve, to soothe thine ear
    Like thy own modest springs,
    Thy springs, and dying gales ;

O nymph reserved, while now the bright-haired sun
Sits in yon western tent, whose cloudy skirts,
    With brede ethereal wove,
    O'erhang his wavy bed:

Now air is hushed, save where the weak-eyed bat,
With short shrill shriek flits by on leathern wing,
    Or where the beetle winds
    His small but sullen horn.

As oft he rises midst the twilight path,
Against the pilgrim borne in heedless hum ;
    Now teach me, maid composed,
    To breathe some softened strain,

Whose numbers stealing through thy darkening vale,
May not unseemly with its stillness suit ;
    As musing slow I hail
    Thy genial loved return !

For when thy folding star arising shows
His paly circlet, at his warning lamp
    The fragrant hours and elves
    Who slept in buds the day,

And many a nymph who wreathes her brows with sedge,
And sheds the freshening dew, and, lovelier still,
  The pensive pleasures sweet
  Prepare thy shadowy car.

Then let me rove some wild and heathy scene,
Or find some ruin midst its dreary dells,
  Whose walls more awful nod
  By thy religious gleams.

Or if chill blustering winds, or driving rain,
Prevent my willing feet, be mine the hut, .
  That from the mountain's side
  Views wilds and swelling floods,

And hamlets brown, and dim discovered spires,
And hears their simple bell, and marks o'er all
  Thy dewy fingers draw
  The gradual dusky veil.

While Spring shall pour his showers, as oft he wont,
And bathe thy breathing tresses, meekest Eve!
  While Summer loves to sport
  Beneath thy lingering light;

While sallow Autumn fills thy lap with leaves;
Or Winter yelling through the troublous air,
  Affrights thy shrinking train,
  And rudely rends thy robes;

So long, regardful of thy quiet rule,
Shall Fancy, Friendship, Science, smiling Peace,
  Thy gentlest influence own,
  And love thy favourite name!

DIRGE IN CYMBELINE.

To fair Fidele's grassy tomb
  Soft maids and village hinds shall bring
Each opening sweet, of earliest bloom,
  And rifle all the breathing spring.

No wailing ghost shall dare appear,
  To vex with shrieks this quiet grove,
But shepherd lads assemble here,
  And melting virgins own their love.

No withered witch shall here be seen,
  No goblins lead their nightly crew!
The female fays shall haunt the green,
  And dress thy grave with pearly dew!

The redbreast oft at evening hours,
  Shall kindly lend his little aid,
With hoary moss, and gathered flowers,
  To deck the ground where thou art laid.

When howling winds and beating rain,
  In tempests shake the sylvan cell,
Or midst the chace on every plain,
  The tender thought on thee shall dwell:

Each lonely scene shall thee restore,
  For thee the tear be duly shed;
Beloved, till life can charm no more;
  And mourned, till pity's self be dead.

ODE ON THE DEATH OF THOMSON

In yonder grave a Druid lies,
   Where slowly winds the stealing wave!
The year's best sweets shall duteous rise,
   To deck its poet's sylvan grave.

In yon deep bed of whispering reeds,
   His airy harp shall now be laid,
That he whose heart in sorrow bleeds,
   May love through life the soothing shade.

Then maids and youths shall linger here,
   And while its sounds at distance swell,
Shall sadly seem in pity's ear
   To hear the woodland pilgrim's knell.

Remembrance oft shall haunt the shore,
   When Thames in summer wreaths is drest,
And oft suspend the dashing oar,
   To bid his gentle spirit rest!

And oft as ease and health retire,
   To breezy lawn or forest deep,
The friend shall view yon whitening spire,
   And mid the varied landscape weep.

But thou who own'st that earthly bed,
   Ah! what will every dirge avail!
Or tears which love and pity shed,
   That mourn beneath the gliding sail!

Yet lives there one whose heedless eye
   Shall scorn thy pale shrine glimmering near!
With him, sweet bard! may fancy die,
   And joy desert the blooming year.

But thou lorn stream, whose sullen tide
   No sedge-crowned sisters now attend,
Now waft me from the green hill's side,
   Whose cold turf hides the buried friend!

And see the fairy valleys fade,
   Dun night has veiled the solemn view!
Yet once again, dear parted shade,
   Meek nature's child, again adieu!

The genial meads, assigned to bless
   Thy life, shall mourn thy early doom!
There hinds and shepherd girls shall dress
   With simple hands thy rural tomb.

Long, long thy stone and pointed clay
   Shall melt the musing Briton's eyes,
Oh! vales, and wild woods, shall he say,
   In yonder grave your Druid lies.

GRAY.

ELEGY WRITTEN IN A COUNTRY CHURCHYARD.

THE curfew tolls the knell of parting day,
  The lowing herd winds slowly o'er the lea,
The plowman homewards plods his weary way,
  And leaves the world to darkness and to me.

Now fades the glimmering landscape on the sight,
  · And all the air a solemn stillness holds,
Save where the beetle wheels his droning flight,
  And drowsy tinklings lull the distant folds.

Save that from yonder ivy-mantled tower,
  The moping owl does to the moon complain,
Of such as, wandering near her secret bower,
  Molest her ancient solitary reign.

Beneath those rugged elms, that yew tree's shade,
  Where heaves the turf in many a mouldering heap
Each in his narrow cell for ever laid,
  The rude forefathers of the hamlet sleep.

12*

The breezy call of incense-breathing morn,
   The swallow twittering from the straw-built shed,
The cock's shrill clarion, or the echoing horn,
   No more shall rouse them from their lowly bed.

For them no more the blazing hearth shall burn,
   Or busy housewife ply her evening care :
No children run to lisp their sire's return,
   Or climb his knees the envied kiss to share.

Oft did the harvest to their sickle yield,
   Their harrow oft the stubborn glebe has broke ;
How jocund did they drive their team a-field !
   How bowed the woods beneath their sturdy stroke .

Let not ambition mock their useful toil,
   Their homely joys, and destiny obscure ;
Nor grandeur hear with a disdainful smile,
   The short and simple annals of the poor.

The boast of heraldry, the pomp of power,
   And all that beauty, all that wealth e'er gave,
Await alike the inevitable hour.
   The paths of glory lead but to the grave.

Nor you, ye proud, impute to these the fault,
   If memory o'er their tomb no trophies raise,
Where through the long drawn aisle and fretted vault,
   The pealing anthem swells the notes of praise.

Can storied urn and animated bust
   Back to its mansion call the fleeting breath?
Can honour's voice provoke the silent dust,
   Or flattery soothe the dull cold ear of death?

Perhaps in this neglected spot is laid,
   Some heart once pregnant with celestial fire;
Hands, that the rod of empire might have swayed,
   Or waked to ecstacy the living lyre:

But knowledge to their eyes her ample page,
   Rich with the spoils of time, did ne'er unroll,
Chill penury repressed their noble rage,
   And froze the genial current of the soul.

Full many a gem of purest ray serene,
   The dark unfathomed caves of ocean bear:
Full many a flower is born to blush unseen,
   And waste its sweetness on the desert air.

Some village Hampden that with dauntless breast,
   The little tyrant of his fields withstood,
Some mute inglorious Milton here may rest,
   Some Cromwell, guiltless of his country's blood.

The applause of listening senates to command,
   The threat of pain and ruin to despise,
To scatter plenty o'er a smiling land,
   And read their history in a nation's eyes.

Their lot forbade : nor circumscribed alone
    Their growing virtues, but their crimes confined ;
Forbade to wade through slaughter to a throne,
    And shut the gates of mercy on mankind :

The struggling pangs of conscious truth to hide,
    To quench the blushes of ingenuous shame,
Or heap the shrine of luxury and pride,
    With incense kindled at the muse's flame.

Far from the maddening crowd's ignoble strife,
    Their sober wishes never learnt to stray ;
Along the cool sequestered vale of life,
    They kept the noiseless tenor of their way.

Yet even these bones from insult to protect,
    Some frail memorial still erected nigh,
With uncouth rhymes and shapeless sculptures deckt,
    Implores the passing tribute of a sigh.

Their name, their years spelt by th' unlettered Muse,
    The place of fame and elegy supply :
And many a holy text around she strews
    That teach the rustic moralist to die.

For who to dumb forgetfulness a prey,
    This pleasing, anxious being e'er resigned,
Left the warm precincts of the cheerful day,
    Nor cast one longing, lingering look behind ?

GRAY

On some fond breast the parting soul relies,
  Some pious drops the closing eye requires;
Even from the tomb the voice of nature cries,
  Even in our ashes live their wonted fires.

For thee, who mindful of th' unhonoured dead,
  Dost in these lines their artless tale relate;
If chance by lonely contemplation led,
  Some kindred spirit shall enquire thy fate:

Haply some hoary-headed swain may say,
  " Oft we have seen him at the peep of dawn,
Brushing with hasty steps the dews away,
  To meet the sun upon the upland lawn.

" There at the foot of yonder nodding beech
  That wreathes its old fantastic roots so high,
His listless length at noontide would he stretch,
  And pore upon the brook that babbles by.

" Hard by yon wood, now smiling as in scorn,
  Muttering his wayward fancies he would rove,
Now drooping woful wan, like one forlorn,
  Or craz'd with care, or crossed in hopeless love.

" One morn I miss'd him on the 'custom'd hill,
  Along the heath, and near his favourite tree,
Another came; nor yet beside the rill,
  Nor up the lawn, nor at the wood was he;

" The next with dirges due in sad array,
   Slow through the church-way path we saw him borne,
Approach and read, for thou canst read, the lay,
   Graved on the stone beneath yon aged thorn."

THE EPITAPH.

Here rests his head upon the lap of earth,
   A youth, to fortune and to fame unknown;
Fair science frowned not on his humble birth,
   And melancholy marked him for her own.

Large was his bounty and his soul sincere,
   Heaven did a recompense as largely send ;
He gave to misery, all he had, a tear ;
   He gain'd from heaven, 'twas all he wish'd a friend.

No farther seek his merits to disclose,
   Nor draw his frailties from their dread abode,
There they alike in trembling hope repose,
   The bosom of his father and his God.

ODE ON A DISTANT PROSPECT OF ETON COLLEGE

Ye distant spires, ye antique towers,
   That crown the watery glade,
Where grateful science still adores
   Her Henry's holy shade ;
And ye that from the stately brow
Of Windsor's heights the expanse below
   Of grove, of lawn, of mead survey,
Whose turf, whose shade, whose flowers among,
Wanders the hoary Thames along
   His silver-winding way ;

Ah, happy hills, ah pleasing shade,
   Ah, fields beloved in vain,
Where once my careless childhood strayed,
   A stranger yet to pain !
I feel the gales that from ye blow
A momentary bliss bestow,
   As waving fresh their gladsome wing,
My weary soul they seem to soothe,
And redolent of joy and youth,
   To breathe a second spring.

Say, father Thames, for thou hast seen
    Full many a sprightly race,
Disporting on thy margent green,
    The paths of pleasure trace,
Who foremost now delight to cleave,
With pliant arm thy glassy wave?
    The captive linnet which enthral?
What idle progeny succeed
To chase the rolling circle's speed,
    Or urge the flying ball?

While some on earnest business bent,
    Their murmuring labours ply,
'Gainst graver hours, that bring constraint
    To sweeten liberty;
Some bold adventurers disdain
The limits of their little reign,
    And unknown regions dare descry;
Still as they run they look behind,
They hear a voice in every wind,
    And snatch a fearful joy.

Gay hope is their's by fancy fed,
    Less pleasing when possest;
The tear forgot as soon as shed,
    The sunshine of the breast:
Their's buxom health, of rosy hue;
Wild wit, invention ever new;
    And lively cheer, of vigour born;
The thoughtless day, the easy night,
The spirits pure, the slumbers light,
    That fly the approach of morn.

Alas! regardless of their doom,
 The little victims play!
No sense have they of ills to come,
 Nor care beyond to-day;
Yet see how all around them wait
The ministers of human fate,
 And black misfortune's baleful train.
Ah! show them where in ambush stand,
To seize their prey, the murderous band,
 Ah! tell them they are men!

These shall the fury passions tear,
 The vultures of the mind,
Disdainful anger, pallid fear,
 And shame that skulks behind;
Or pining love shall waste their youth,
Or jealousy with rankling tooth,
 That inly gnaws the secret heart;
And envy wan, and faded care,
Grim visaged, comfortless despair,
 And sorrow's piercing dart.

Ambition this shall tempt to rise,
 Then whirl the wretch from high,
To bitter scorn a sacrifice,
 And grinning infamy.
The stings of falsehood, those shall try,
And hard unkindness' altered eye,
 That mocks the tear it forced to flow;
And keen remorse, with blood defiled,
And moody madness laughing wild,
 Amidst severest wo.

13

Lo, in the vale of years beneath
  A grisly troop are seen,
The painful family of death,
  More hideous than their queen :
'This racks the joints, this fires the veins,
That every labouring sinew strains,
  Those in the deeper vitals rage ;
Lo, poverty, to fill the band,
That numbs the soul with icy hand;
  And slow consuming age.

To each his sufferings ; all are men,
  Condemned alike to groan :
The tender for another's pain,
  The unfeeling for his own.
Yet ah ! why should they know their fate ?
Since sorrow never comes too late,
  And happiness too swiftly flies ;
Thought would destroy their paradise——
No more ;——where ignorance is bliss,
  'Tis folly to be wise.

HYMN TO ADVERSITY.

Daughter of Jove, relentless power,
   Thou tamer of the human breast,
Whose iron scourge and torturing hour,
   The bad affright, afflict the best !
Bound in thy adamantine chain,
The proud are taught to taste of pain,
And purple tyrants vainly groan,
With pangs unfelt before, unpitied and alone.

When first thy sire to send on earth,
   Virtue, his darling child, designed,
To thee he gave the heavenly birth,
   And bade to form her infant mind.
Stern rugged nurse ; thy rigid lore
With patience many a year she bore ;
What sorrow was, thou bad'st her know,
And from her own she learnt to melt at others' woe.

Scared at thy frown terrific, fly
   Self-pleasing folly's idle brood,
Wild laughter, noise, and thoughtless joy,
   And leave us leisure to be good.
Light they disperse, and with them go,
The summer friend, the flattering foe ;
By vain prosperity received,
To her they vow their truth, and are again believed.

Wisdom in sable garb arrayed,
   Immersed in rapturous thought profound,
And melancholy, silent maid,
   With leaden eye that loves the ground,
Still on thy solemn steps attend :
Warm charity, the general friend,
With justice, to herself severe,
And pity, dropping soft the sadly pleasing tear.

Oh, gently on thy suppliant's head,
   Dread goddess, lay thy chastening hand !
Not in thy gorgon terrors clad,
   Not circled with the vengeful band,
As by the impious thou art seen,
With thundering voice, and threatening mien,
With screaming horror's funeral cry,
Despair, and fell disease, and ghastly poverty.

Thy form benign, O goddess wear,
   Thy milder influence impart,
Thy philosophic train be there,
   To soften, not to wound the heart.
The generous spark extinct revive,
Teach me to love, and to forgive,
Exact my own defects to scan,
What others are, to feel, and know myself a man

JOHNSON.

FROM "THE VANITY OF HUMAN WISHES."

On what foundation stands the warrior's pride,
How just his hopes, let Swedish Charles decide;
A frame of adamant, a soul of fire,
No dangers fright him, and no labours tire;
O'er love, o'er fear, extends his wide domain,
Unconquered lord of pleasure and of pain,
No joys to him pacific sceptres yield,
War sounds the trump, he rushes to the field;
Behold surrounding kings their powers combine,
And one capitulate, and one resign;
Peace courts his hand, but spreads her charms in vain
" Think nothing gained," he cries, " till nought remain
On Moscow's walls till Gothic standards fly,
And all be mine beneath the polar sky."
The march begins in military state,
And nations on his eye suspended wait;

13*

Stern Famine guards the solitary coast,
And winter barricades the realms of Frost ;
He comes ; nor want nor cold his course delay,
Hide, blushing Glory, hide Pultowa's day :
The vanquished hero leaves his broken bands,
And shows his miseries in distant lands ;
Condemned a needy supplicant to wait,
While ladies interpose, and slaves debate.
But did not chance at length her error mend ?
Did no subverted empire mark his end ?
Did rival monarchs give the fatal wound ?
Or hostile millions press him to the ground ?
—His fall was destined to a barren strand,
A petty fortress, and a dubious hand ;
He left the name, at which the world grew pale,
To point a moral, or adorn a tale.

*   *   *   *   *   *   *

    Where then shall Hope and Fear their objects fir d
Must dull suspense corrupt the stagnant mind ?
Must helpless man, in ignorance sedate,
Roll darkling down the torrent of his fate ?
Must no dislike alarm, no wishes rise,
No cries invoke the mercies of the skies ?
Inquirer, cease ; petitions yet remain
Which Heaven may hear, nor deem religion vain.
Still raise for good the supplicating voice,
But leave to Heaven the measure and the choice.
Safe in his power whose eyes discern afar,
The secret ambush of a specious prayer ;

JOHNSON.

Implore his aid, in his decisions rest,
Secure, whate'er he gives, he gives the best.
Yet, when the sense of sacred presence fires,
And strong devotion to the skies aspires,
Pour forth thy fervours for a healthful mind,
Obedient passions, and a will resigned ;
For love, which scarce collective man can fill ;
For patience, sovereign o'er transmuted ill ;
For faith, that, panting for a happier seat,
Counts death kind Nature's signal of retreat :
These goods for man the laws of Heaven ordain,
These goods he grants, who grants the power to
With these celestial Wisdom calms the mind,
And makes the happiness she does not find.

GOLDSMITH.

FROM " THE TRAVELLER."

REMOTE, unfriended, melancholy, slow,
Or by the lazy Scheld, or wandering Po;
Or onward, where the rude Carinthian boor
Against the houseless stranger shuts the door;
Or where Campania's plain forsaken lies,
A weary waste expanding to the skies;
Where'er I roam, whatever realms to see,
My heart, untravelled, fondly turns to thee;
Still to my brother turns with ceaseless pain,
And drags at each remove a lengthening chain.
   Eternal blessings crown my earliest friend,
And round his dwelling guardian saints attend;
Blest be that spot, where cheerful guests retire
To pause from toil, and trim their evening fire;
Blest that abode, where want and pain repair,
And every stranger finds a ready chair;
Blest be those feasts with simple plenty crowned,
Where all the ruddy family around
Laugh at the jests or pranks that never fail,
Or sigh with pity at some mournful tale;

Or press the bashful stranger to his food,
And learn the luxury of doing good.
    But me, not destined such delights to share,
My prime of life in wandering spent and care;
Impelled with steps unceasing to pursue
Some fleeting good, that mocks me with the view;
That, like the circle bounding earth and skies,
Allures from far, yet, as I follow, flies;
My fortune leads to traverse realms alone,
And find no spot of all the world my own.
    E'n now, where Alpine solitudes ascend,
I sit me down a pensive hour to spend;
And, placed on high above the storm's career,
Look downward where a hundred realms appear:
Lakes, forests, cities, plains, extending wide,
The pomp of kings, the shepherd's humbler pride.
    When thus creation's charms around combine,
Amidst the store, should thankless pride repine?
Say, should the philosophic mind disdain
That good which makes each humbler bosom vain?
Let school-taught pride dissemble all it can,
These little things are great to little man;
And wiser he, whose sympathetic mind
Exults in all the good of all mankind.
Ye glittering towns, with wealth and splendour crowned,
Ye fields, where summer spreads profusion round;
Ye lakes, where vessels catch the busy gale;
Ye bending swains, that dress the flowery vale;
For me your tributary stores combine:
Creation's heir, the world, the world is mine.
    As some lone miser, visiting his store,
Bends at his treasure, counts, recounts it o'er;

Hoards after hoards his rising raptures fill,
Yet still he sighs, for hoards are wanting still :
Thus to my breast alternate passions rise,
Pleased with each good that Heaven to man supplies
Yet oft a sigh prevails, and sorrows fall,
To see the hoard of human bliss so small ;
And oft I wish, amidst the scene, to find
Some spot to real happiness consigned,
Where my worn soul, each wandering hope at rest,
May gather bliss, to see my fellows blest.
  But where to find that happiest spot below,
Who can direct, when all pretend to know ?
The shuddering tenant of the frigid zone
Boldly proclaims that happiest spot his own,
Extols the treasures of his stormy seas,
And his long nights of revelry and ease :
The naked negro, panting at the line,
Boasts of his golden sands, and palmy wine,
Basks in the glare, or stems the tepid wave,
And thanks his gods for all the good they gave.
Such is the patriot's boast, where'er we roam,
His first, best country, ever is at home.
And yet, perhaps, if countries we compare,
And estimate the blessings which they share,
Though patriots flatter, still shall wisdom find
An equal portion dealt to all mankind :
As different good, by art or nature given,
To different nations makes their blessings even.

          *   *   *   *   *   *   *

  Far to the right, where Appennine ascends,
Bright as the summer, Italy extends :

Its uplands, sloping, deck the mountain's side,
Woods over woods in gay theatric pride;
While oft some temple's mouldering tops between,
With memorable grandeur mark the scene.
    Could Nature's bounty satisfy the breast,
The sons of Italy were surely blest.
Whatever fruits in differing climes are found,
That proudly rise, or humbly court the ground;
Whatever blooms in torrid tracks appear,
Whose bright succession decks the varied year;
Whatever sweets salute the northern sky
With vernal lives, that blossom but to die;
These here disporting own the kindred soil,
Nor ask luxuriance from the planter's toil;
While seaborn gales their gelid wings expand,
To winnow fragrance round the smiling land.
    But small the bliss that sense alone bestows,
And sensual bliss is all the nation knows.
In florid beauty groves and fields appear,
Man seems the only growth that dwindles here.
Contrasted faults through all his manners reign;
Though poor, luxurious; though submissive, vain;
Though grave, yet trifling; zealous, yet untrue;
And e'en in penance planning sins anew.
All evils here contaminate the mind,
That opulence departed leaves behind;
For wealth was theirs: not far removed the date,
When commerce proudly flourished through the sta.e
At her command the palace learnt to rise,
Again the long-fallen column sought the skies;
The canvass glowed, beyond e'en nature warm,
The pregnant quarry teemed with human form;

Till, more unsteady than the northern gale,
Commerce on other shores displayed her sail ;
While nought remained of all that riches gave,
But towns unmanned, and lords without a slave :
And late the nation found, with fruitless skill,
Its former strength was but plethoric ill.
    Yet, still the loss of wealth is here supplied
By arts, the splendid wrecks of former pride ;
From these the feeble heart and long-fallen mind
An easy compensation seem to find.
Here may be seen, in bloodless pomp arrayed,
The pasteboard triumph and the cavalcade ;
Processions formed for piety and love,
A mistress or a saint in every grove.
By sports like these are all their cares beguiled,
The sports of children satisfy the child:
Each nobler aim, repressed by long control,
Now sinks at last, or feebly mans the soul :
While low delights, succeeding fast behind,
In happier meanness occupy the mind :
As in those domes, where Cæsars once bore sway,
Defaced by time, and tottering in decay,
There in the ruin, heedless of the dead,
The shelter-seeking peasant builds his shed ;
And, wondering man could want the larger pile,
Exults, and owns his cottage with a smile.
    My soul turn from them, turn we to survey
Where rougher climes a nobler race display ;
Where the bleak Swiss their stormy mansions tread,
And force a churlish soil for scanty bread.
No product here the barren hills afford,
But man and steel, the soldier and his sword ·

No vernal blooms their torpid rocks array,
But winter, lingering, chills the lap of May;
No zephyr fondly sues the mountain's breast,
But meteors glare, and stormy glooms invest.
    Yet still, even here, content can spread a charm,
Redress the clime, and all its rage disarm,
Though poor the peasant's hut, his feasts though small,
He sees his little lot the lot of all;
Sees no contiguous palace rear its head,
To shame the meanness of his humble shed;
No costly lord the sumptuous banquet deal,
To make him loathe his vegetable meal:
But calm, and bred in ignorance and toil,
Each wish contracting, fits him to the soil.
Cheerful at morn, he wakes from short repose,
Breathes the keen air, and carols as he goes:
With patient angle trolls the finny deep,
Or drives his venturous ploughshare to the steep;
Or seeks the den where snow-tracks mark the way,
And drags the struggling savage into day.
At night returning, every labour sped,
He sits him down the monarch of a shed;
Smiles by his cheerful fire, and round surveys
His children's looks, that brighten at the blaze;
While his loved partner, boastful of her hoard,
Displays her cleanly platter on the board:
And haply too some pilgrim thither led,
With many a tale repays the nightly bed.
    Thus every good his native wilds impart,
Imprints the patriot passion on his heart;
And even those hills that round his mansion rise,
Enhance the bliss his scanty fund supplies:

14

Dear is that shed to which his soul conforms,
And dear that hill which lifts him to the storms;
And as a child, when scaring sounds molest,
Clings close and closer to the mother's breast;
So the loud torrent, and the whirlwind's roar,
But bind him to his native mountains more.
     Such are the charms to barren states assigned;
Their wants but few, their wishes all confined:
Yet let them only share the praises due,
If few their wants, their pleasures are but few;
For every want that stimulates the breast,
Becomes a source of pleasure when redressed.
Whence from such lands each pleasing science flies,
That first excites desire, and then supplies;
Unknown to them when sensual pleasures cloy,
To fill the languid pause with finer joy;
Unknown those powers that raise the soul to flame,
Catch every nerve, and vibrate through the frame,
Their level life is but a smouldering fire,
Unquenched by want, unfanned by strong desire;
Unfit for raptures, or, if raptures cheer
On some high festival of once a year,
In wild excess the vulgar breast takes fire,
Till, buried in debauch, the bliss expire.
     But not their joys alone thus coarsely flow,
Their morals, like their pleasures, are but low,
For, as refinement stops, from sire to son,
Unaltered, unimproved, the manners run;
And love's and friendship's finely pointed dart,
Fall blunted from each indurated heart.
Some sterner virtues o'er the mountain's breast
May sit, like falcons cowering on the nest:

But all the gentler morals, such as play
Through life's more cultured walks, and charm the way,
These, far dispersed, on timorous pinions fly,
To sport and flutter in a kinder sky.
   To kinder skies, where gentler manners reign,
I turn; and France displays her bright domain.
Gay, sprightly land of mirth and social ease,
Pleased with thyself, whom all the world can p'ease
How often have I led thy sportive choir,
With tuneless pipe, beside the murmuring Loire !
Where shady elms along the margin grew,
And, freshened from the wave, the zephyr flew :
And haply, though my harsh touch faltering still ;
But mocked all tune, and marred the dancer's skill ;
Yet would the village praise my wondrous power,
And dance forgetful of the noontide hour.
Alike all ages: Dames of ancient days
Have led their children through the mirthful maze ;
And the gay grandsire, skilled in jestic lore,
Has frisked beneath the burden of threescore.
So blessed a life these thoughtless realms display,
Thus idly busy rolls their world awny :
Theirs are those arts that mind to mind endear,
For honour forms the social temper here :
Honour, that praise which real merit gains,
Or e'en imaginary worth obtains,
Here passes current ; paid from hand to hand,
It shifts, in splendid traffic, round the land :
From courts to camps, to cottages it strays,
And all are taught an avarice of praise ;
They please, are pleased, they give to get esteem,
Till, seeming blest, they grow to what they seem.

But while this softer art their bliss supplies,
It gives their follies also room to rise ;
For praise too dearly loved, or warmly sought,
Enfeebles all the internal strength of thought ;
And the weak soul, within itself unblest,
Leans for all pleasure on another's breast.
Hence ostentation here, with tawdry art,
Pants for the vulgar praise which fools impart ;
Here vanity assumes her pert grimace,
And trims her robes of frieze with copper lace ;
Here beggar pride defrauds her daily cheer,
To boast one splendid banquet once a year :
The mind still turns where shifting fashion draws,
Nor weighs the solid worth of self-applause.
    To men of other minds my fancy flies,
Embosomed in the deep where Holland lies.
Methinks her patient sons before me stand,
Where the broad ocean leans against the land,
And, sedulous to stop the coming tide,
Lift the tall rampire's artificial pride.
Onward methinks, and diligently slow,
The firm connected bulwark seems to grow ;
Spreads its long arms amidst the watery roar,
Scoops out an empire, and usurps the shore :
While the pent ocean rising o'er the pile,
Sees an amphibious world beneath him smile ;
The slow canal, the yellow-blossomed vale,
The willow-tufted bank, the gliding sail,
The crowded mart, the cultivated plain,
A new creation rescued from his reign.
    Thus, while around, the wave-subjected soil,
Impels the native to repeated toil,

Industrious habits in each bosom reign,
And industry begets a love of gain.
Hence all the good from opulence that springs,
With all those ills superfluous treasure brings,
Are here displayed.   Their much-loved wealth imparts
Convenience, plenty, elegance, and arts ;
But view them closer, craft and fraud appear,
E'en liberty itself is bartered here.
At gold's superior charms all freedom flies,
The needy sell it, and the rich man buys.
A land of tyrants, and a den of slaves,
Here wretches seek dishonourable graves,
And, calmly bent, to servitude conform,
Dull as their lakes that slumber in the storm,
    Heavens ! how unlike their Belgic sires of old !
Rough, poor, content, ungovernably bold ;
War in each breast, and freedom on each brow :
How much unlike the sons of Britain now !
    Fired at the sound, my genius spreads her wing,
And flies where Britain courts the western spring ;
Where lawns extend that scorn Arcadian pride,
And brighter streams than famed Hydaspes glide,
There all around the gentlest breezes stray,
There gentle music melts on every spray ;
Creation's mildest charms are there combined,
Extremes are only in the master's mind ;
Stern o'er each bosom reason holds her state,
With daring aims irregularly great :
Pride in their port, defiance in their eye,
I see the lords of humankind pass by ;
Intent on high designs, a thoughtful band,
By forms unfashioned, fresh from nature's hand,
14*

Fierce in their native hardiness of soul,
True to imagined right, above control,
While e'en the peasant boasts these rights to scan,
And learns to venerate himself as man.
  Thine, Freedom, thine, the blessings pictured here,
Thine are those charms that dazzle and endear ;
Too blest indeed were such without alloy,
But, foster'd e'en by Freedom, ills annoy ;
That independence Britons prize too high,
Keeps man from man, and breaks the social tie ;
The self-dependent lordlings stand alone,
All claims that bind and sweeten life unknown ;
Here, by the bonds of nature feebly held,
Minds combat minds, repelling and repelled ;
Ferments arise, imprisoned factions roar,
Repressed ambition struggles round her shore ;
Till, overwrought, the general system feels
Its motion stop, or frenzy fire the wheels.
  Nor this the worst. As nature's ties decay,
As duty, love, and honour fail to sway,
Fictitious bonds, the bonds of wealth and law,
Still gather strength, and force unwilling awe.
Hence all obedience bows to these alone,
And talent sinks, and merit weeps unknown ;
Till time may come, when, stripped of all her charms,
The land of scholars, and the nurse of arms,
Where noble stems transmit the patriot flame,
Where kings have toiled, and poets wrote, for fame,
One sink of level avarice shall lie,
And scholars, soldiers, kings, unhonoured die.

     *   *   *   *   *   *

Vain, very vain, my weary search to find
That bliss which only centres in the mind.
Why have I strayed from pleasure and repose,
To seek a good each government bestows?
In every government, though terrors reign,
Though tyrant kings or tyrant laws restrain,
How small, of all that human hearts endure,
That part which laws or kings can cause or cure;
Still to ourselves in every place consigned,
Our own felicity we make or find;
With secret course which no loud storms annoy,
Glides the smooth current of domestic joy;
The lifted axe, the agonizing wheel,
Luke's iron crown, and Damien's bed of steel,
To men remote from power but rarely known,
Leave reason, faith, and conscience, all our own.

FROM "THE DESERTED VILLAGE."

Sweet Auburn! loveliest village of the plain,
Where health and plenty cheered the labouring swain,
Where smiling spring its earliest visit paid,
And parting summer's lingering blooms delayed;
Dear lovely bowers of innocence and ease,
Seats of my youth, when every sport could please;
How often have I loitered o'er thy green,
Where humble happiness endeared each scene!
How often have I paused on every charm,
The sheltered cot, the cultivated farm,
The never-failing brook, the busy mill,
The decent church that topped the neighbouring hill,
The hawthorn bush, with seats beneath the shade,
For talking age and whispering lovers made!
How often have I blest the coming day,
When toil remitting lent its turn to play,
And all the village train, from labour free,
Led up their sports beneath the spreading tree!
While many a pastime circled in the shade,
The young contending as the old surveyed;
And many a gambol frolicked o'er the ground,
And sleights of art, and feats of strength went round;
And still, as each repeated pleasure tired,
Succeeding sports the mirthful band inspired.
The dancing pair that simply sought renown,
By holding out to tire each other down;
The swain, mistrustless of his smutted face,
While secret laughter tittered round the place;

The bashful virgin's side-long looks of love,
The matron's glance that would those looks reprove:
These were thy charms, sweet village! sports like these,
With sweet succession, taught e'en toil to please ;
These round thy bowers their cheerful influence shed,
These were thy charms—but all these charms are fled.
  Sweet smiling village, loveliest of the lawn,
Thy sports are fled, and all thy charms withdrawn ;
Amidst thy bowers the tyrant's hand is seen,
And Desolation saddens all thy green :
One only master grasps the whole domain,
And half a tillage stints thy smiling plain ;
No more thy glassy brook reflects the day,
But, choked with sedges, works its weedy way ;
Along thy glades, a solitary guest,
The hollow-sounding bittern guards its nest ;
Amidst thy desert walks the lapwing flies,
And tires their echoes with unvaried cries ;
Sunk are thy bowers in shapeless ruin all,
And the long grass o'ertops the mouldering wall,
And, trembling, shrinking from the spoiler's hand,
Far, far away thy children leave the land.
  Ill fares the land, to hastening ills a prey,
Where wealth accumulates, and men decay :
Princes and lords may flourish, or may fade ;
A breath can make them, as a breath has made :
But a bold peasantry, their country's pride,
When once destroyed, can never be supplied.
  A time there was, ere England's griefs began,
When every rood of ground maintained its man ;
For him light Labour spread her wholesome store,
Just gave what life required, but gave no more ;

His best companions, innocence and health;
And his best riches, ignorance of wealth.
  But times are altered; trade's unfeeling train
Usurp the land, and dispossess the swain;
Along the lawn, where scattered hamlets rose,
Unwieldy wealth and cumberous pomp repose;
And every want to luxury allied,
And every pang that folly pays to pride.
Those gentle hours that plenty bade to bloom,
Those calm desires that asked but little room,
Those healthful sports that graced the peaceful scene
Lived in each look, and brightened all the green;
These, far departing, seek a kinder shore,
And rural mirth and manners are no more.
  Sweet Auburn, parent of the blissful hour,
Thy glades forlorn confess the tyrant's power.
Here, as I take my solitary rounds,
Amidst thy tangling walks, and ruined grounds,
And, many a year elapsed, return to view
Where once the cottage stood, the hawthorn grew,
Remembrance wakes with all her busy train,
Swells at my breast, and turns the past to pain.
  In all my wanderings round this world of care,
In all my griefs—and God has given my share—
I still had hopes, my latest hours to crown,
Amidst these humble bowers to lay me down;
To husband out life's taper at the close,
And keep the flame from wasting by repose;
I still had hopes, for pride attends us still,
Amidst the swains to show my book-learned skill
Around my fire an evening group to draw,
And tell of all I felt, and all I saw:

And, as a hare whom hounds and horns pursue,
Pants to the place from whence at first she flew,
I still had hopes, my long vexations past,
Here to return—and die at home at last.
   O blest retirement, friend to life's decline,
Retreat from care, that never must be mine.
How happy he who crowns, in shades like these,
A youth of labour with an age of ease ;
Who quits a world where strong temptations try,
And, since 'tis hard to combat, learns to fly !
For him no wretches, born to work and weep,
Explore the mine, or tempt the dangerous deep ;
No surly porter stands in guilty state,
To spurn imploring famine from the gate ;
But on he moves to meet his latter end,
Angels around befriending virtue's friend ;
Sinks to the grave with unperceived decay,
While resignation gently slopes the way ;
And, all his prospects brightening to the last,
His heaven commences ere the world be past.
   Sweet was the sound when oft at evening's close,
Up yonder hill the village murmur rose ;
There, as I passed with careless steps and slow,
The mingling notes came softened from below ;
The swain responsive as the milk-maid sung,
The sober herd that lowed to meet their young,
The noisy geese that gabbled o'er the pool,
The playful children just let loose from school,
The watch-dog's voice that bay'd the whispering wind,
And the loud laugh that spoke the vacant mind ;
These all in sweet confusion sought the shade,
And filled each pause the nightingale had made.

But now the sounds of population fail,
No cheerful murmurs fluctuate in the gale,
No busy steps the grass-grown footway tread,
But all the blooming flush of life is fled :
All but yon widowed solitary thing,
That feebly bends beside the plashing spring ;
She, wretched matron, forced, in age, for bread,
To strip the brook with mantling cresses spread,
To pick her wintry faggot from the thorn,
To seek her nightly shed, and weep till morn ;
She only left of all the harmless train,
The sad historian of the pensive plain.
    Near yonder copse, where once the garden smiled,
And still where many a garden-flower grows wild,
There, where a few torn shrubs the place disclose,
The village preacher's modest mansion rose.
A man he was to all the country dear,
And passing rich with forty pounds a year ;
Remote from towns he ran his godly race,
Nor e'er had changed, nor wished to change his place
Unpractised he to fawn, or seek for power,
By doctrines fashioned to the varying hour ;
Far other aims his heart had learnt to prize,
More skilled to raise the wretched than to rise.
His house was known to all the vagrant train,
He chid their wanderings, but relieved their pain ;
The long-remembered beggar was his guest,
Whose beard descending swept his aged breast ;
The ruined spendthrift, now no longer proud,
Claimed kindred there, and had his claim allowed
The broken soldier, kindly bade to stay,
Sat by his fire, and talked the night away ;

Wept o'er his wounds, or, tales of sorrow done,
Shouldered his crutch, and showed how fields were won.
Pleased with his guest, the good man learned to glow,
And quite forgot their vices in their wo;
Careless their merits or their faults to scan,
His pity gave ere charity began.
  Thus to relieve the wretched was his pride,
And even his failings leaned to virtue's side;
But in his duty prompt at every call,
He watched and wept, he prayed and felt for all :
And, as a bird each fond endearment tries,
To tempt its new-fledged offspring to the skies,
He tried each art, reproved each dull delay,
Allured to brighter worlds, and led the way.
  Beside the bed where parting life was laid,
And sorrow, guilt, and pain by turns dismayed,
The reverend champion stood. At his control
Despair and anguish fled the struggling soul;
Comfort came down, the trembling wretch to raise,
And his last faltering accents whispered praise.
  At church, with meek and unaffected grace,
His looks adorned the venerable place;
Truth from his lips prevailed with double sway,
And fools, who came to scoff, remained to pray.
The service past, around the pious man,
With steady zeal, each honest rustic ran;
Even children followed, with endearing wile,
And plucked his gown, to share the good man's smile.
His ready smile a parent's warmth exprest,
Their welfare pleased him, and their cares distrest;
To them his heart, his love, his griefs were given,
But all his serious thoughts had rest in heaven.

15

As some tall cliff, that lifts its awful form,
Swells from the vale, and midway leaves the storm,
Though round its breast the rolling clouds are spread,
Eternal sunshine settles on its head.
   Beside yon straggling fence that skirts the way,
With blossomed furze, unprofitably gay,
There, in his noisy mansion, skilled to rule,
The village master taught his little school.
A man severe he was, and stern to view,
I knew him well, and every truant knew;
Well had the boding tremblers learned to trace
The day's disasters in his morning face;
Full well they laughed, with counterfeited glee,
At all his jokes, for many a joke had he;
Full well the busy whisper, circling round,
Conveyed the dismal tidings when he frowned:
Yet he was kind, or if severe in aught.
The love he bore to learning was in fault;
The village all declared how much he knew;
'Twas certain he could write, and cypher too;
Lands he could measure, terms and tides presage,
And even the story ran that he could gauge:
In arguing too, the parson owned his skill,
For even though vanquished, he could argue still;
While words of learned length, and thundering sound,
Amazed the gazing rustics ranged around;
And still they gazed, and still the wonder grew
That one small head could carry all he knew.
But passed is all his fame: the very spot,
Where many a time he triumphed, is forgot.
   Near yonder thorn, that lifts its head on high,
Where once the sign-post caught the passing eye,

Low lies that house, where nut-brown draughts inspired,
Where graybeard mirth, and smiling toil retired,
Where village statesmen talked with looks profound,
And news much older than their ale went round.
Imagination fondly stoops to trace
The parlour splendours of that festive place ;
The white-washed wall, the nicely sanded floor,
The varnished clock that clicked behind the door ;
The chest, contrived a double debt to pay,
A bed by night, a chest of drawers by day ;
The pictures, placed for ornament and use,
The twelve good rules, the royal game of goose ;
The hearth, except when winter chilled the day,
With aspen boughs, and flowers, and fennel gay ;
While broken teacups, wisely kept for show,
Ranged o'er the chimney, glistened in a row.
Vain transitory splendours ! could not all
Retrieve the tottering mansion from its fall !
Obscure it sinks, nor shall it more impart
An hour's importance to the poor man's heart.
Thither no more the peasant shall repair,
To sweet oblivion of his daily care ;
No more the farmer's news, the barber's tale,
No more the woodman's ballad shall prevail ;
No more the smith his dusky brow shall clear,
Relax his ponderous strength, and lean to hear ;
The host himself no longer shall be found,
Careful to see the mantling bliss go round ;
Nor the coy maid, half willing to be prest,
Shall kiss the cup to pass it to the rest.
Yes ! let the rich deride, the proud disdain,
These simple blessings of the lowly train,

To me more dear, congenial to my heart,
One native charm, than all the gloss of art;
Spontaneous joys, where nature has its play,
The soul adopts, and owns their first-born sway;
Lightly they frolic o'er the vacant mind,
Unenvied, unmolested, unconfined.
But the long pomp, the midnight masquerade,
With all the freaks of wanton wealth arrayed,
In these, ere triflers half their wish obtain,
The toiling pleasure sickens into pain;
And, even while fashion's brightest arts decoy,
The heart distrusting asks, if this be joy?
     Ye friends to truth, ye statesmen, who survey
The rich man's joys increase, the poor's decay,
'Tis yours to judge how wide the limits stand
Between a splendid and a happy land.
Proud swells the tide with loads of freighted ore,
And shouting Folly hails them from the shore;
Hoards e'en beyond the miser's wish abound,
And rich men flock from all the world around.
Yet count our gains.   This wealth is but a name
That leaves our useful products still the same.
Not so the loss.   The man of wealth and pride
Takes up a space that many poor supplied;
Space for his lake, his park's extended bounds,
Space for his horses, equipage, and hounds;
The robe that wraps his limbs in silken sloth
Has robbed the neighbouring fields of half their growth;
His seat, where solitary sports are seen,
Indignant spurns the cottage from the green;
Around the world each needful product flies,
For all the luxuries the world supplies:

GOLDSMITH.

While thus the land, adorned for pleasure all
In barren splendour feebly waits the fall.
 As some fair female, unadorned and plain,
Secure to please while youth confirms her reign,
Slights every borrowed charm that dress supplies,
Nor shares with art the triumph of her eyes ;
But when those charms are past, for charms are fi
When time advances, and when lovers fail,
She then shines forth, solicitous to bless,
In all the glaring impotence of dress :
Thus fares the land, by luxury betrayed,
In nature's simplest charms at first arrayed ;
But verging to decline, its splendours rise,
Its vistas strike, its palaces surprise ;
While, scourged by famine, from the smiling land
The mournful peasant leads his humble band :
And while he sinks, without one arm to save,
The country blooms—a garden and a grave.
 Where then, ah ! where shall poverty reside,
To 'scape the pressure of contiguous pride ?
If to some common's fenceless limits strayed,
He drives his flock to pick the scanty blade,
Those fenceless fields the sons of wealth divide,
And e'en the bare-worn common is denied.
 If to the city sped—what waits him there ?
To see profusion that he must not share :
To see ten thousand baleful arts combined
To pamper luxury, and thin mankind ;
To see each joy the sons of pleasure know,
Extorted from his fellow-creature's wo.
Here, while the courtier glitters in brocade,
There the pale artist plies the sickly trade ;
15*

Here, while the proud their long drawn pomp display,
There the black gibbet glooms beside the way;
The dome where pleasure holds her midnight reign,
Here, richly decked, admits the gorgeous train;
Tumultuous grandeur crowds the blazing square,
The rattling chariots clash, the torches glare.
Sure scenes like these no troubles e'er annoy!
Sure these denote one universal joy!
Are these thy serious thoughts?—Ah! turn thine eyes
Where the poor houseless shivering female lies:
She once, perhaps, in village plenty blessed.
Has wept at tales of innocence distressed;
Her modest looks the cottage might adorn,
Sweet as the primrose peeps beneath the thorn;
Now lost to all; her friends, her virtue fled,
Near her betrayer's door she lays her head.
And, pinched with cold, and shrinking from the shower
With heavy heart deplores that luckless hour
When idly first, ambitious of the town,
She left her wheel and robes of country brown
 Do thine, sweet AUBURN, thine, the loveliest train,
Do thy fair tribes participate her pain?
E'n now, perhaps, by cold and hunger led,
At proud men's doors they ask a little bread
 Ah, no. To distant climes, a dreary scene,
Where half the convex world intrudes between,
Through torrid tracts with fainting steps they go
Where wild Altama murmurs to their wo.
Far different there from all that charmed before,
The various terrors of that horrid shore;
Those blazing suns that dart a downward ray,
And fiercely shed intolerable day;

Those matted woods, where birds forget to sing,
But silent bats in drowsy clusters cling;
Those poisonous fields with rank luxuriance crowned,
Where the dark scorpion gathers death around:
Where at each step the stranger fears to wake
The rattling terrors of the vengeful snake;
Where crouching tigers wait their hapless prey,
And savage men more murderous still than they;
While oft in whirls the mad tornado flies,
Mingling the ravaged landscape with the skies:
Far different these from every former scene,
The cooling brook, the grassy vested green,
The breezy covert of the warbling grove,
That only sheltered thefts of harmless love.
  Good heaven ' what sorrows gloomed that parting day,
That called them from their native walks away;
When the poor exiles every pleasure passed,
Hung round their bowers, and fondly looked their last;
And took a long farewell, and wished in vain
For seats like these beyond the western main;
And, shuddering still to face the distant deep,
Returned and wept, and still returned to weep.
The good old sire, the first prepared to go
To new-found worlds, and wept for others' wo;
But for himself, in conscious virtue brave,
He only wished for worlds beyond the grave.
His lovely daughter, lovelier in her tears,
The fond companion of his helpless years,
Silent went next, neglectful of her charms,
And left a lover's for a father's arms.
With louder plaints the mother spoke her woes,
And blessed the cot where every pleasure rose;

And kissed her thoughtless babes with many a tear,
And clasped them close, in sorrow doubly dear ;
Whilst her fond husband strove to lend relief,
In all the silent manliness of grief.
   O Luxury ! thou curst by Heaven's decree,
How ill exchanged are things like these for thee !
How do thy potions, with insidious joy,
Diffuse their pleasures only to destroy !
Kingdoms by thee, to sickly greatness grown,
Boast of a florid vigour not their own ;
At every draught more large and large they grow,
A bloated mass of rank unwieldy wo ;
Till sapped their strength, and every part unsound,
Down, down they sink, and spread a ruin round.
   E'en now the devastation is begun,
And half the business of destruction done ;
E'en now, methinks, as pondering here I stand,
I see the rural virtues leave the land.
Down where yon anchoring vessel spreads the sail,
That idly waiting flaps with every gale,
Downward they move, a melancholy band,
Pass from the shore, and darken all the strand
Contented toil, and hospitable care,
And kind connubial tenderness are there ;
And piety with wishes placed above,
And steady loyalty, and faithful love.
And thou, sweet Poetry, thou loveliest maid,
Still first to fly where sensual joys invade ;
Unfit, in these degenerate times of shame,
To catch the heart, or strike for honest fame ;
Dear charming nymph, neglected and decried
My shame in crowds, my solitary pride ;

Thou source of all my bliss, and all my woe,
That found'st me poor at first, and keep'st me so;
Thou guide, by which the nobler arts excel,
Thou nurse of every virtue, fare thee well;
Farewell! and O! where'er thy voice be tried,
On Torno's cliffs, or Pambamarca's side,
Whether where equinoctial fervours glow,
Or winter wraps the polar world in snow,
Still let thy voice, prevailing over time,
Redress the rigours of the inclement clime,
Aid slighted Truth, with thy persuasive strain;
Teach erring man to spurn the rage of gain;
Teach him, that states of native strength possessed,
Though very poor, may still be very blessed;
That trade's proud empire hastes to swift decay,
As ocean sweeps the laboured mole away;
While self-dependent power can time defy,
As rocks resist the billows and the sky.

BRUCE.

FROM "AN ELEGY."

Now Spring returns; but not to me returns
   The vernal joy my better years have known;
Dim in my breast life's dying taper burns,
   And all the joys of life with health are flown.

Starting and shivering in th' inconstant wind,
   Meagre and pale, the ghost of what I was,
Beneath some blasted tree I lie reclined,
   And count the silent moments as they pass:

The winged moments, whose unstaying speed
   No art can stop, or in their course arrest;
Whose flight shall shortly count me with the dead,
   And lay me down in peace with them that rest

Oft morning dreams presage approaching fate;
   And morning dreams, as poets tell, are true;
Led by pale ghosts, I enter death's dark gate,
   And bid the realms of light and life adieu.

I hear the helpless wail, the shriek of wo;
  I see the muddy wave, the dreary shore,
The sluggish streams that slowly creep below,
  Which mortals visit and return no more.

Farewell, ye blooming fields! ye cheerful plains!
  Enough for me the churchyard's lonely mound,
Where Melancholy with still Silence reigns,
  And the rank grass waves o'er the cheerless ground.

There let me wander at the shut of eve,
  When sleep sits dewy on the labourer's eyes;
The world and all its busy follies leave,
  And talk with Wisdom where my Daphnis lies.

There let me sleep forgotten in the clay,
  When death shall shut these weary aching eyes;
Rest in the hopes of an eternal day,
  Till the long night is gone, and the last morn arise

LOGAN.

HYMN.

WHERE high the heavenly temple stands,
The house of God not made with hands,
A great High Priest our nature wears,
The Patron of Mankind appears.

He who for men in mercy stood,
And poured on earth his precious blood,
Pursues in heaven his plan of grace,
The Guardian God of human race.

Though now ascended up on high,
He bends on earth a brother's eye,
Partaker of the human name,
He knows the frailty of our frame

Our fellow-sufferer yet retains,
A fellow-feeling of our pains ;
And still remembers in the skies,
His tears, and agonies, and cries

LOGAN.

In every pang that rends the heart,
The Man of Sorrows had a part;
He sympathizes in our grief,
And to the sufferer sends relief.

With boldness, therefore, at the throne,
Let us make all our sorrows known,
And ask the aids of heavenly power,
To help us in the evil hour.

SIR WILLIAM JONES.

AN ODE.

WHAT constitutes a State ?
Not high-raised battlement or laboured mound,
   Thick wall or moated gate ;
Not cities proud with spires and turrets crowned ;
   Not bays and broad-armed ports,
Where, laughing at the storm, rich navies ride ;
   Not starred and spangled courts,
Where low-browed baseness wafts perfume to pride.
   No ;—men, high-minded men,
With powers as far above dull brutes endued
   In forest, brake, or den,
As beasts excel cold rocks and brambles rude ;
   Men, who their duties know,
But know their rights, and, knowing, dare maintain,
   Prevent the long-aimed blow,
And crush the tyrant while they rend the chain :
   These constitute a State,
And sovereign Law, that State's collected will,
   O'er thrones and globes elate

JONES.

Sits Empress, crowning good, repressing ill;
   Smit by her sacred frown
The fiend dissension like a vapour sinks,
   And e'en th' all dazzling crown
Hides his faint rays, and at her bidding shrinks.
   Such was this heaven-loved isle,
Than Lesbos fairer and the Cretan shore!
   No more shall Freedom smile?
Shall Britons languish, and be men no more?
   Since all must life resign,
Those sweet rewards which decorate the brave,
   'Tis folly to decline,
And steal inglorious to the silent grave.

BURN.

THE COTTER'S SATURDAY NIGHT.

My loved, my honoured, much respected friend,
   No mercenary bard his homage pays;
With honest pride, I scorn each selfish end,
   My dearest meed a friend's esteem and praise:
To you I sing, in simple Scotish lays,
   The lowly train in life's sequestered scene;
The native feelings strong, the guileless ways;
   What Aiken in a cottage would have been;
Ah! tho' his worth unknown, far happier there, I ween.

November chill blaws loud wi' angry sugh;
   The shortening winter-day is near a close
The miry beasts retreating frae the pleugh;
   The blackening trains o' craws to their repose:
The toil-worn Cotter frae his labour goes,
   This night his weekly moil is at an end,
Collects his spades, his mattocks, and his hoes,
   Hoping the morn in ease and rest to spend,
And weary o'er the moor, his course does hameward bend.

At length his lonely cot appears in view,
    Beneath the shelter of an aged tree ;
The expectant wee-things, toddlin, stacher through
    To meet their dad, wi' flictherin noise an' glee.
His wee-bit ingle, blinkin bonnily,
    His clean hearth-stane, his thriftie wifie's smile,
The lisping infant prattling on his knee,
    Does a' his weary carking cares beguile,
An' makes him quite forget his labour an' his toil.

Belyve the elder bairns come drappin in,
    At service out, amang the farmers roun' ;
Some ca' the pleugh, some herd, some tentie rin
    A cannie errand to a neebor-town :
Their eldest hope, their Jenny, woman grown,
    In youthful bloom, love sparkling in her e'e,
Comes hame, perhaps, to show a braw new gown,
    Or deposite her sair-won penny-fee,
To help her parents dear, if they in hardship be.

Wi' joy unfeigned brothers and sisters meet,
    An' each for other's welfare kindly speers :
The social hours, swift winged, unnoticed fleet ;
    Each tells the unco that he sees and hears ;
The parents, partial, eye their hopeful years ;
    Anticipation forward points the view ;
The mother, wi' her needle an' her shears,
    Gars auld claes look amaist as weel's the new,
The father mixes a' wi' admonition due.
16*

Their master's an' their mistress's command,
   The younkers a' are warned to obey ;
' An' mind the labours wi' an eydent hand,
   An' ne'er, though out o' sight, to jauk or play ;
An' O, be sure to fear the Lord alway !
   An' mind your duty, duly, morn an' night !
Lest in temptation's path ye gang astray,
   Implore his counsel and assisting might :
They never sought in vain that sought the Lord aright

But hark ! a rap comes gently to the door ;
   Jenny, wha kens the meaning o' the same,
Tells how a neebor-lad cam o'er the moor,
   To do some errands, and convoy her hame.
'. he wily mother sees the conscious flame
   Sparkle in Jenny's e'e, and flush her cheek ;
With heart-struck anxious care, inquires his name,
   While Jenny hafflins is afraid to speak ;   [rake.
Weel pleased, the mother hears, its nae wild, worthless

Wi' kindly welcome Jenny brings him ben ;
   A strappan youth ; he takes the mother's eye :
Blythe Jenny sees the visit's no ill ta'en ;
   The father cracks of horses, pleughs, and kye.
The youngster's artless heart o'erflows wi' joy,
   But blate and laithfu', scarce can weel behave ;
The mother, wi' a woman's wiles, can spy
   What makes the youth sae bashful an' sae grave ;
Weel pleased to think her bairn's respected like the lave.

O, happy love! where love like this is found!
   O, heartfelt raptures! bliss beyond compare!
I've paced much this weary mortal round,
   And sage experience bids me this declare——
If Heaven a draught of heavenly pleasure spare,
   One cordial in this melancholy vale,
'Tis when a youthful, loving, modest pair,
   In other's arms breath out the tender tale,   [gale.
Beneath the milk-white thorn that scents the evening

Is there, in human form, that bears a heart——
   A wretch! a villain! lost to love and truth——
That can, with studied, sly, ensnaring art,
   Betray sweet Jenny's unsuspecting youth?
Curse on his perjured arts! dissembling, smooth!
   Are honour, virtue, conscience, all exiled?
Is there no pity, no relenting ruth,
   Points to the parents fondling o'er their child?
That paints the ruined maid, and their distraction wild?

But now the supper crowns their simple board,
   The healsome parritch, chief o' Scotia's food;
The soupe their only hawkie does afford,
   That, yont the hallan snugly chows her cood:
The dame brings forth in complimental mood,
   To grace the lad, her weel hained hebbuck, fell,
An' aft he's prest, an' aft he ca's it gude;
   The frugal wifie, garrulous, will tell,
How 'twas a towmond auld, sin' lint was i' tne bell.

The cheerfu' supper done, wi' serious face,
   They, round the ingle, form a circle wide ;
The sire turns o'er, wi' patriarchal grace,
   The big ha' bible, ance his father's pride :
His bonnet reverently is laid aside,
   His lyart haffets wearing thin an' bare ;
Those strains that once did sweet in Zion glide,
   He wales a portion with judicious care ;
And, ' Let us worship God !' he says, with solemn air

They chant their artless notes in simple guise,
   They tune their hearts, by far the noblest aim ;
Perhaps Dundee's wild, warbling measures rise,
   Or plaintive Martyr's, worthy of the name,
Or noble Elgin beats the heaven-ward flame,
   The sweetest far of Scotia's holy lays ;
Compared with these, Italian trills are tame,
   The tickled ears no heart-felt raptures raise,
Nae unison hae they with our Creator's praise.

The priest-like father reads the sacred page,
   How Abram was the friend of God on high ;
Or, Moses bade eternal warfare wage
   With Amalek's ungracious progeny ;
Or, how the royal bard did groaning lie
   Beneath the stroke of heaven's avenging ire ;
Or, Job's pathetic plaint and wailing cry ;
   Or, rapt Isaiah's wild, seraphic fire ;
Or, other holy seers that tune the sacred lyre.

Perhaps the Christian volume is the theme,
  How guiltless blood for guilty man was shed ;
How He, who bore in heaven the second name,
  Had not on earth whereon to lay his head ;
How his first followers and servants sped ;
  The precepts sage they wrote to many a land ;
How he, who lone in Patmos banished,
  Saw in the sun a mighty angel stand ;
And heard great Babylon's doom pronounced by
    Heaven's command.

Then, kneeling down, to Heaven's eternal King
  The saint, the father, and the husband, prays :
Hope ' springs exulting on triumphant wing,'
  That thus they all shall meet in future days ;
There ever bask in uncreated rays,
  No more to sigh, or shed the bitter tear,
Together hymning their Creator's praise,
  In such society, yet still more dear ;
While circling time moves round in an eternal sphere

Compared with this, how poor religion's pride,
  In all the pomp of method and of art,
When men display to congregations wide,
  Devotion's every grace, except the heart !
The Power, incensed, the pageant will desert,
  The pompous train, the sacerdotal stole ;
But haply, in some cottage far apart
  May hear, well pleased, the language of the soul,
And in his book of life the inmates poor enrol.

Then homeward all take off their several way,
    The youngling-cottagers retire to rest ;
The parent pair their secret homage pay,
    And proffer up to heaven the warm request,
That HE who stills the raven's clamorous nest,
    And decks the lily fair in flowery pride,
Would, in the way his wisdom sees the best,
    For them and for their little ones provide ;
But, chiefly, in their heart with grace divine preside

From scenes like these old Scotia's grandeur springs,
    That makes her loved at home, revered abroad :
Princes and Lords are but the breath of Kings,
    ' An honest man's the noblest work of God :'
And, certes, in fair Virtue's heavenly road,
    The cottage leaves the palace far behind ;
What is the lordling's pomp ? a cumbrous load,
    Disguising oft the wretch of human kind,
Studied in arts of hell, in wickedness refined.

O Scotia ! my dear, my native soil !
    For whom my warmest wish to heaven is sent !
Long may thy hardy sons of rustic toil
    Be blest with health, and peace, and sweet content !
And, O ! may heaven their simple lives prevent,
    From luxury's contagion, weak and vile !
Then, howe'er crowns and coronets be rent,
    A virtuous populace may rise the while,
And stand a wall of fire around their much loved Isle

O Thou! who poured the patriotic tide,
   That streamed through Wallace's undaunted heart
Who dared to nobly stem tyrannic pride,
   Or nobly die—the second glorious part;
(The patriot's God, peculiarly thou art,
   His friend, inspirer, guardian, and reward!)
O never, never, Scotia's realm desert;
   But still the patriot, and the patriot bard,
In bright succession raise, her ornament and guard.

TO A MOUNTAIN DAISY.

Wee, modest, crimson-tipped flower,
Thou'st met me in an evil hour;
For I maun crush amang the stoure,
     Thy slender stem;
To spare thee now is past my power
     Thou bonnie gem.

Alas! its no thy neebor sweet,
The bonnie lark, companion meet;
Bending thee 'mang the dewy weet,
     Wi' speckled breast,
When upward-springing, blythe to greet
     The purpling east.

Cauld blew the bitter-biting north,
Upon thy early, humble birth;
Yet cheerfully thou glinted forth,
        Amid the storm,
Scarce reared above the parent earth
        Thy tender form.

The flaunting flowers our gardens yield,
High sheltering woods and wa's maun shield;
But thou beneath the random-bield,
        O' clod or stane:
Adorns the histie stibble field,
        Unseen, alane.

There, in thy scanty mantle clad,
Thy snawie bosom sun-ward spread;
Thou liftst thy unassuming head
        In humble guise;
But now the share uptears thy bed,
        And low thou lies.

Such is the fate of artless maid,
Sweet floweret of the rural shade!
By love's simplicity betrayed,
        And guileless trust;
Till she, like thee, all soiled, is laid
        Low i' the dust.

Such is the fate of simple bard,
On life's rough ocean luckless starred :
Unskilful he to note the card,
      Of prudent lore,
Till billows rage, and gales blow hard,
      And whelm him o'er.

Such fate to suffering worth is given,
Who long with wants and woes has striven ;
By human pride or cunning driven,
      To misery's brink !
Till wrenched of every stay but heaven,
      He, ruined, sink !

Even thou who mourn'st the daisy's fate,
That fate is thine—no distant date ;
Stern Ruin's ploughshare drives, elate,
      Full on thy bloom ;
Till crushed beneath the furrow's weight,
      Shall be thy doom.

SONG.

The gloomy night is gathering fast,
Loud roars the wild inconstant blast,
Yon murky cloud is foul with rain,
I see it driving o'er the plain ;
The hunter now has left the moor,
The scatter'd coveys meet secure,
While here I wander, prest with care,
Along the lonely banks of Ayr.

The autumn mourns her ripening corn
By early winter's ravage torn ;
Across her placid, azure sky,
She sees the scowling tempest fly :
Chill runs my blood to hear it rave,
I think upon the stormy wave,
Where many a danger I must dare,
Far from the bonnie banks of Ayr.

'Tis not the surging billow's roar,
'Tis not that fatal deadly shore ;
Though death in every shape appear,
The wretched have no more to fear :
But round my heart the ties are bound,
That heart transpierc'd with many a wound ;
These bleed afresh, those ties I tear,
To leave the bonnie banks of Ayr.

Farewell! Old Coila's hills and dales,
Her healthy moors and winding vales;
The scenes where wretched fancy roves,
Pursuing past, unhappy loves!
Farewell, my friends! Farewell, my foes
My peace with these, my love with those—
The bursting tears my heart declare;
Farewell, the bonnie banks of Ayr

COWPER

THE INFIDEL AND THE CHRISTIAN.

The path to bliss abounds with many a snare;
Learning is one, and wit, however rare.
The Frenchman, first in literary fame,
(Mention him if you please.   Voltaire?—The same.)
With spirit, genius, eloquence, supplied,
Lived long, wrote much, laughed heartily, and died.
The Scripture was his jest-book, whence he drew
Bon-mots to gall the Christian and the Jew;
An infidel in health, but what when sick?
O—then a text would touch him at the quick:
View him at Paris in his last career,
Surrounding throngs the demi-god revere;
Exalted on his pedestal of pride,
And fumed with frankincense on every side,
He begs their flattery with his latest breath,
And smothered in't at last, is praised to death.
Yon cottager, who weaves at her own door,
Pillow and bobbins all her little store;

Content though mean, and cheerful if not gay,
Shuffling her threads about the livelong day,
Just earns a scanty pittance, and at night
Lies down secure, her heart and pocket light ;
She, for her humble sphere by nature fit,
Has little understanding, and no wit.
Receives no praise ; but, though her lot be such,
(Toilsome and indigent) she renders much ;
Just knows, and knows no more, her Bible true,
A truth the brilliant Frenchman never knew ;
And in that charter reads with sparkling eyes
Her title to a treasure in the skies.
  O happy peasant ! O unhappy bard !
His the mere tinsel, her's the rich reward ;
He praised perhaps for ages yet to come,
She never heard of half a mile from home :
He lost in errors his vain heart prefers,
She safe in the simplicity of hers.

PORTRAIT OF WHITFIELD.

  Leuconomus (beneath well-sounding Greek
I slur a name a poet may not speak)
Stood pilloried on Infamy's high stage,
And bore the pelting scorn of half an age ;
The very butt of Slander, and the blot
For every dart that Malice ever shot.
The man that mentioned *him* at once dismissed
All mercy from his lips, and sneered and hissed ;
His crimes were such as Sodom never knew,
And Perjury stood up to swear all true ;
                  17*

His aim was mischief, and his zeal pretence,
His speech rebellion against common sense,
A knave, when tried on honesty's plain rule,
And when by that of reason, a mere fool;
The world's best comfort was, his doom was pas ed
Die when he might, he must be damned at last.
    Now, Truth, perform thine office; waft asid
The curtain drawn by Prejudice and Pride,
Reveal (the man is dead) to wondering eyes
This more than monster, in his proper guise.
    He loved the world that hated him: the tear
That dropped upon his Bible was sincere;
Assailed by scandal and the tongue of strife,
His only answer was a blameless life;
And he that forged, and he that threw the dart,
Had each a brother's interest in his heart.
Paul's love of Christ, and steadiness unbribed,
Were copied close in him, and well transcribed.
He followed Paul; his zeal a kindred flame,
His apostolic charity the same.
Like him, crossed cheerfully tempestuous seas,
Forsaking country, kindred, friends, and ease:
Like him he laboured, and like him content
To bear it, suffered shame where'er he went.
Blush, Calumny! and write upon his tomb,
If honest Eulogy can spare thee room,
Thy deep repentance of thy thousand lies,
Which aimed at him, has pierced the offended sk
And say, Blot out my sin, confessed, deplored,
Against thine image in thy saint, O Lord!

CHRISTIAN LIBERTY.

He is the freeman whom the truth makes free,
And all are slaves beside.   There's not a chain
That hellish foes confederate for his harm
Can wind around him, but he casts it off
With as much ease as Samson his green withes.
He looks abroad into the varied field
Of nature ; and though poor, perhaps, compared
With those whose mansions glitter in his sight,
Calls the delightful scenery all his own.
His are the mountains, and the valley his,
And the resplendent rivers.   His to enjoy
With a propriety that none can feel,
But who, with filial confidence inspired,
Can lift to heaven an unpresumptuous eye,
And smiling say—' My father made them all !'
Are they not his by a peculiar right,
And by an emphasis of interest his,
Whose eyes they fill with tears of holy joy,
Whose heart with praise, and whose exalted mind
With worthy thoughts of that unwearied love
That planned, and built, and still upholds, a world
So clothed with beauty, for rebellious man ?
Yes, ye may fill your garners, ye that reap
The loaded soil, and ye may waste much good
In senseless riot ; but ye will not find
In feast, or in the chace, in song or dance,
A liberty like his, who, unimpeached
Of usurpation, and to no man's wrong,

Appropriates nature as his Father's work,
And has a richer use of yours than you.
He is indeed a freeman.   Free by birth
Of no mean city, planned or e'er the hills
Were built, the fountains opened, or the sea
With all his roaring multitude of waves.
His freedom is the same in every state ;
And no condition of this changeful life,
So manifold in cares, whose every day
Bring its own evil with it, makes it less :
For he has wings that neither sickness, pain,
Nor penury can cripple or confine ;
No nook so narrow but he spreads them there
With ease, and is at large.   The oppressor holds
His body bound ; but knows not what a range
His spirit takes, unconscious of a chain ;
And that to bind him is a vain attempt,
Whom God delights in, and in whom he dwells.
    Acquaint thyself with God, if thou wouldst taste
His works.   Admitted once to his embrace,
Thou shalt perceive that thou wast blind before :
Thine eye shall be instructed ; and thine heart
Made pure, shall relish with divine delight,
Till then unfelt, what hands divine have wrought.
Brutes graze the mountain top with faces prone
And eyes intent upon the scanty herb
It yields them ; or, recumbent on its brow,
Ruminate, heedless of the scene outspread
Beneath, beyond, and stretching far away,
From inland regions to the distant main.
Man views it and admires, but rests content
With what he views.   The landscape has his praise

But not its Author.   Unconcerned who formed
The paradise he sees, he finds it such;
And, such well-pleased to find it, asks no more.
Not so the mind that has been touched from heaven,
And in the school of sacred wisdom taught
To read his wonders, in whose thought the world,
Fair as it is, existed ere it was.
Not for its own sake merely, but for his
Much more who fashioned it, he gives it praise;
Praise that from earth resulting, as it ought,
To earth's acknowledged Sovereign, finds at once
Its only just proprietor in Him.
The soul that sees him, or receives sublimed
New faculties, or learns at least to employ
More worthily the powers she owned before,
Discerns in all things what, with stupid gaze
Of ignorance, till then she overlooked,
A ray of heavenly light, gilding all forms
Terrestrial, in the vast and the minute,
The unambiguous footsteps of the God
Who gives its lustre to an insect's wing,
And wheels his throne upon the rolling worlds.
Much conversant with heaven, she often holds
With those fair ministers of light to man,
That fills the skies nightly with silent pomp,
Sweet conference! inquires what strains were they
With which heaven rang, when every star, in haste
To gratulate the new-created earth,
Sent forth a voice, and all the sons of God
Shouted for joy.—' Tell me, ye shining hosts,
That navigate a sea that knows no storms,
Beneath a vault unsullied with a cloud,

If from your elevation, whence ye view
Distinctly scenes invisible to man,
And systems, of whose birth no tidings yet
Have reached this nether world, ye spy a race
Favoured as ours, transgressors from the womb,
And hasting to a grave, yet doomed to rise,
And to possess a brighter heaven than yours?
As one who, long detained on foreign shores,
Pants to return, and when he sees afar
His country's weather-bleached and battered rocks,
From the green wave emerging, darts an eye
Radiant with joy towards the happy land;
So I with animated hopes behold,
And many an aching wish, your beamy fires,
That show like beacons in the blue abyss,
Ordained to guide th' embodied spirit home,
From toilsome life to never-ending rest.
Love kindles as I gaze.　I feel desires
That give assurance of their own success,
And that, infused from heaven, must thither tend.'
　　So reads he Nature, whom the lamp of truth
Illuminates: thy lamp, mysterious Word!
Which whoso sees, no longer wanders lost,
With intellects bemazed, in endless doubt,
But runs the road of wisdom.　Thou hast built
With means that were not, till by thee employed,
Worlds that had never been, hadst thou in strength
Been less, or less benevolent than strong.
They are thy witnesses, who speak thy power
And goodness infinite, but speak in ears
That hear not, or receive not their report,
In vain thy creatures testify of thee,

Till thou proclaim thyself. Theirs is indeed
A teaching voice ; but 'tis the praise of thine,
That whom it teaches it makes prompt to learn,
And with the boon gives talents for its use.
Till thou art heard, imaginations vain
Possess the heart, and fables false as hell,
Yet deemed oracular, lure down to death
The uninformed and heedless souls of men,
We give to chance, blind chance, ourselves as blind,
The glory of thy work, which yet appears
Perfect and unimpeachable of blame,
Challenging human scrutiny, and proved
Then skilful most when most severely judged.
But chance is not ; or is not where thou reign'st :
Thy providence forbids that fickle power
(If power she be, that works but to confound)
To mix her wild vagaries with thy laws.
Yet thus we dote, refusing while we can
Instruction, and inventing to ourselves
Gods such as guilt makes welcome, gods that sleep,
Or disregard our follies, or that sit
Amused spectators of this bustling stage.
Thee we reject, unable to abide
Thy purity, till pure as thou art pure,
Made such by thee, we love thee for that cause,
For which we shunned and hated thee before.
Then we are free : then liberty, like day,
Breaks on the soul, and by a flash from heaven
Fires all the faculties with glorious joy.
A voice is heard, that mortal ears hear not
Till thou hast touched them ; 'tis the voice of song—
A loud Hosanna sent from all thy works,

Which he that hears it with a shout repeats,
And adds his rapture to the general praise.
In that blest moment Nature, throwing wide
Her veil opaque, discloses with a smile
The author of her beauties, who, retired
Behind his own creation, works unseen
By the impure, and hears his power denied.
Thou art the source and centre of all minds,
Their only point of rest, eternal Word !
From thee departing they are lost, and rove
At random, without honour, hope, or peace.
From thee is all that soothes the life of man,
His high endeavour, and his glad success,
His strength to suffer, and his will to serve.
But O, thou bounteous Giver of all good,
Thou art of all thy gifts thyself the crown !
Give what thou canst, without thee we are poor
And with thee rich, take what thou wilt away.

COWPER.

ANTICIPATIONS OF PROPHECY

The groans of nature in this nether world,
Which heaven has heard for ages, have an end.
Foretold by prophets, and by poets sung,
Whose fire was kindled at the prophet's lamp,
The time of rest, the promised Sabbath, comes.
Six thousand years of sorrow have well nigh
Fulfilled their tardy and disastrous course
Over a sinful world; and what remains
Of this tempestuous state of human things,
Is merely as the workings of a sea
Before a calm, that rocks itself to rest.
For He, whose car the winds are, and the clouds
The dust that waits upon his sultry march,
When sin hath moved him, and his wrath is hot,—
Shall visit earth in mercy; shall descend
Propitious in his chariot paved with love;
And what his storms have blasted and defaced,
For man's revolt, shall with a smile repair.
    Sweet is the harp of prophecy; too sweet
Not to be wronged by a mere mortal touch;
Nor can the wonders it records be sung
To meaner music, and not suffer loss.
But when a poet, or when one like me,
Happy to rove among poetic flowers,
Though poor in skill to rear them, lights at last
On some fair theme, some theme divinely fair
Such is the impulse and the spur he feels,
To give it praise proportioned to its worth,

18

That not t' attempt it, arduous as he deems
The labour, were a task more arduous still.
   O scenes surpassing fable, and yet true,
Scenes of accomplished bliss! which who can see,
Though but in distant prospect, and not feel
His soul refreshed with foretaste of the joy?
Rivers of gladness water all the earth,
And clothe all climes with beauty; the reproach
Of barrenness is past. The fruitful field
Laughs with abundance; and the land, once lean,
Or fertile only in its own disgrace,
Exults to see its thistly curse repealed.
The various seasons woven into one,
And that one season an eternal spring,
The garden fears no blight, and needs no fence,
For there is none to covet, all are full.
The lion, and the libbard, and the bear,
Graze with the fearless flocks: all bask at noon
Together, or all gambol in the shade
Of the same grove, and drink one common stream.
Antipathies are none. No foe to man
Lurks in the serpent now; the mother sees,
And smiles to see, her infant's playful hand
Stretched forth to dally with the crested worm,
Or stroke his azure neck, or to receive
The lambent homage of his arrowy tongue.
All creatures worship man, and all mankind
One Lord, one Father: Error has no place;
That creeping pestilence is driven away;
The breath of Heaven has chased it. In the heart
No passion touches a discordant string,
But all is harmony and love. Disease

Is not: the pure and uncontaminate blood
Holds its due course, nor fears the frost of age.
One song employs all nations, and all cry,
" Worthy the Lamb, for he was slain for us !"
The dwellers in the vales and on the rocks
Shout to each other, and the mountain-tops
From distant mountains catch the flying joy:
Till, nation after nation taught the strain,
Earth rolls the rapturous hosanna round.
Behold the measure of the promise filled ;
See Salem built, the labour of a God !
Bright as a sun the sacred city shines ;
All kingdoms, and all princes of the earth
Flock to that light, the glory of all lands
Flows into her ; unbounded is her joy,
And endless her increase.   Thy rams are there,
Nebaioth, and the flocks of Kedar there ;
The looms of Ormus, and the mines of Ind,
And Saba's spicy groves, pay tribute there.
Praise is in all her gates ; upon her walls,
And in her streets, and in her spacious courts,
Is heard salvation.   Eastern Java there
Kneels with the native of the farthest west ;
And Ethiopia spreads abroad the hand,
And worships.   Her report has travelled forth
Into all lands.   From every clime they come
To see thy beauty, and to share thy joy,
O Sion ! an assembly such as earth
Saw never ; such as heaven stoops down to see.

SLAVERY.

O for a lodge in some vast wilderness,
Some boundless contiguity of shade,
Where rumour of oppression and deceit,
Of unsuccessful or successful war,
Might never reach me more.   My ear is pained,
My soul is sick, with every day's report
Of wrong and outrage, with which earth is filled.
There is no flesh in man's obdurate heart,
_t does not feel for man ; the natural bond
Of brotherhood is severed as the flax,
That falls asunder at the touch of fire.
He finds his fellow guilty of a skin
Not coloured like his own ; and having power
T' enforce the wrong, for such a worthy cause
Dooms and devotes him as his lawful prey.
Lands intersected by a narrow frith
Abhor each other.   Mountains interposed
Make enemies of nations, who had else
Like kindred drops been mingled into one.
Thus man devotes his brother, and destroys ;
And, worse than all, and most to be deplored
As human nature's broadest, foulest blot,
Chains him, and tasks him, and exacts his sweat
With stripes, that Mercy, with a bleeding heart
Weeps, when she sees inflicted on a beast.
Then what is man ?   And what man, seeing this,
And having human feelings, does not blush,
And hang his head, to think himself a man ?

I would not have a slave to till my ground,
To carry me, to fan me while I sleep,
And tremble when I wake, for all the wealth
That sinews bought and sold have ever earned.
No: dear as freedom is, and in my heart's
Just estimation prized above all price,
I had much rather be myself the slave,
And wear the bonds, than fasten them on him.
We have no slaves at home.——Then why abroad?
And they themselves once ferried o'er the wave
That parts us, are emancipate and loosed.
Slaves cannot breathe in England; if their lungs
Receive our air, that moment they are free;
They touch our country, and their shackles fall.
That's noble, and bespeaks a nation proud
And jealous of the blessing.   Spread it then,
And let it circulate through every vein
Of all your empire; that, where Britain's power
Is felt, mankind may feel her mercy too.

THE WINTER EVENING.

Hark! 'tis the twanging horn o'er yonder bridge,
That with its wearisome but needful length
Bestrides the wintry flood, in which the moon
Sees her unwrinkled face reflected bright;—
He comes, the herald of a noisy world,
With spattered boots, strapped waist, and frozen locks
News from all nations lumbering at his back:
True to his charge, the close packed load behind,
Yet careless what he brings; his one concern,
Is to conduct it to the destined inn;
And, having dropped the expected bag, pass on.
He whistles as he goes, light hearted wretch,
Cold and yet cheerful, messenger of grief
Perhaps to thousands, and of joy to some;
To him indifferent whether grief or joy.
Houses in ashes, or the fall of stocks;
Births, deaths, and marriages; epistles wet
With tears, that trickled down the writer's cheeks,
Fast as the periods from his fluent quill;
Or charged with amorous sighs of absent swains,
Or nymphs responsive; equally affect
His horse and him, unconscious of them all.
But O the important budget! ushered in
With such heart-shaking music; who can say
What are its tidings? Have our troops awaked?
Or do they still, as if with opium drugged,
Snore to the murmurs of the Atlantic wave?
Is India free? and does she wear her plumed

And jewelled turban with a smile of peace,
Or do we grind her still? The grand debate,
The popular harangue, the tart reply,
The logic, and the wisdom, and the wit,
And the loud laugh—I long to know them all;
I burn to set the imprisoned wranglers free,
And give them voice and utterance once again.
 Now stir the fire, and close the shutters fast,
Let fall the curtains, wheel the sofa round,
And while the bubbling and loud hissing urn
Throws up a steamy column, and the cups,
That cheer but not inebriate, wait on each,
So let us welcome peaceful evening in.
Not such his evening, who with shining face
Sweats in the crowded theatre, and squeezed
And bored with elbow points through both his sides
Out-scolds the ranting actor on the stage:
Nor his, who patient stands till his feet throb,
And his head thumps, to feed upon the breath
Of patriots, bursting with heroic rage;
Or placemen, all tranquillity and smiles.
This folio of four pages, happy work!
Which not e'en critics criticize; that holds
Inquisitive attention, while I read,
Fast bound in chains of silence, which the fair,
Though eloquent themselves, yet fear to break:—
What is it but a map of busy life,
Its fluctuations, and its vast concerns?
Here runs the mountainous and craggy ridge
That tempts ambition. On the summit see
The seals of office glitter in his eyes;
He climbs, he pants, he grasps them! At his heels.

Close at his heels, a demagogue ascends,
And with a dextrous jerk soon twists him down,
And wins them but to lose them in his turn.
Here rills of oily eloquence in soft
Meanders lubricate the course they take ;
'The modest speaker is ashamed and grieved
To engross a moment's notice, and yet begs,
Begs a propitious ear for his poor thoughts,
However trivial all that he conceives.
Sweet bashfulness ! it claims at least this praise,
The dearth of information and good sense
That it foretells us, always comes to pass.
Cataracts of declamation thunder here ;
There forests of no meaning spread the page,
In which all comprehension wanders lost ;
While fields of pleasantry amuse us there
With merry descants on a nation's woes
The rest appears a wilderness of strange
But gay confusion ; roses for the cheeks,
And lilies for the brows of faded age;
Teeth for the toothless, ringlets for the bald ;
Heaven, earth, and ocean plundered of their sweets ;
Nectareous essences, Olympian dews,
Sermons, and city feasts, and favourite airs ;
Ethereal journies, submarine exploits,
And Katterfelto with his hair on end
At his own wonders—wondering for his bread.
'Tis pleasant through the loopholes of retreat
To peep at such a world ; to see the stir
Of the great Babel, and not feel the crowd ;
To hear the roar she sends through all her gates
At a safe distance, where the dying sound

Falls a soft murmur on the uninjured ear.
Thus sitting, and surveying thus at ease
The globe and its concerns, I seem advanced
To some secure and more than mortal height,
That liberates and exempts me from them all.
It turns, submitted to my view ; turns round,
With all its generations : I behold
The tumult and am still.   The sound of war
Has lost its terrors ere it reaches me ;
Grieves, but alarms me not.   I mourn the pride
And avarice, that make man a wolf to man ;
Hear the faint echo of those brazen throats,
By which he speaks the language of his heart,
And sigh, but never tremble at the sound.
He travels and expatiates ; as the bee
From flower to flower, so he from land to land ;
The manners, customs, policy of all
Pay contribution to the store he gleans ;
He sucks intelligence in every clime,
And spreads the honey of his deep research
At his return—a rich repast for me.
He travels, and I too.   I tread his deck,
Ascend his topmast, through his peering eyes
Discover countries, with a kindred heart
Suffer his woes, and share in his escapes ;
While fancy, like the finger of a clock,
Runs the great circuit, and is still at home.

ON THE RECEIPT OF MY MOTHER'S PICTURE.

Oh that those lips had language ! Life has passed
With me but roughly since I heard thee last.
Those lips are thine,---thine own sweet smile I see.
The same that oft in childhood solaced me ;
Voice only fails, else how distinct they say,
' Grieve not, my child ; chase all thy fears away !
The meek intelligence of those dear eyes,
(Blest be the art that can immortalize,
The art that baffles time's tyrannic claim
To quench it,) here shines on me still the same.
    Faithful remembrancer of one so dear,
O welcome guest, though unexpected here !
Who bid'st me honour with an artless song,
Affectionate, a mother lost so long.
I will obey, not willingly alone,
But gladly, as the precept were her own :
And, while that face renews my filial grief,
Fancy shall weave a charm for my relief ;
Shall steep me in Elysian reverie,
A momentary dream, that thou art she.
    My mother ! when I learnt that thou wast dead,
Say wast thou conscious of the tears I shed ?
Hovered thy spirit o'er thy sorrowing son,
Wretch even then, life's journey just begun ?
Perhaps thou gavest me, though unfelt, a kiss ;
Perhaps a tear, if souls can weep in bliss.
Ah, that maternal smile ! it answers—Yes.

heard the bell tolled on thy burial day,
I saw the hearse that bore thee slow away,
And, turning from my nursery window, drew
A long, long sigh, and wept a last adieu!
But was it such? It was.——Where thou art gone,
Adieus and farewells are a sound unknown.
May I but meet thee on that peaceful shore,
The parting word shall pass my lips no more!
Thy maidens, grieved themselves at my concern,
Oft gave me promise of thy quick return:
What ardently I wished, I long believed,
And, disappointed still, was still deceived.
By expectation every day beguiled,
Dupe of to-morrow even from a child.
Thus many a sad to-morrow came and went,
Till, all my stock of infant sorrow spent,
I learned, at last, submission to my lot,
But though I less deplored thee, ne'er forgot.
    Where once we dwelt, our name is heard no more,
Children not thine have trod my nursery floor;
And where the gardener Robin, day by day,
Drew me to school along the public way,
Delighted with my bauble coach, and wrapt
In scarlet mantle warm, and velvet cap,
'Tis now become a history little known,
That once we called the pastoral house our own.
Short-lived possession! but the record fair,
That memory keeps of all thy kindness there,
Still outlives many a storm, that has effaced
A thousand other themes less deeply traced.
Thy nightly visits to my chamber made,
That thou mightst know me safe and warmly laid;

Thy morning bounties ere I left my home,
The biscuit or confectionary plum ;
The fragrant waters on my cheeks bestowed
By thy own hand, till fresh they shone and glowed :
All this, and more endearing still than all,
Thy constant flow of love, that knew no fall,
Ne'er roughened by those cataracts and breaks,
That humour interposed too often makes ;
All this still legible in memory's page,
And still to be so till my latest age,
Adds joy to duty, makes me glad to pay
Such honours to thee as my numbers may :
Perhaps a frail memorial, but sincere,
Not scorned in heaven, though little noticed here.
   Could Time, his flight reversed, restore the hours,
When, playing with thy vesture's tissued flowers,
The violet, the pink, and jessamine,
I pricked them into paper with a pin,
(And thou wast happier than myself the while,
Wouldst softly speak, and stroke my head, and smile)
Could those few pleasant hours again appear,
Might one wish bring them, would   wish them here
I would not trust my heart,——the dear delight
Seems so to be desired, perhaps I might.
But no——what here we call our life is such,
So little to be loved, and thou so much,
That I should ill requite thee to constrain
Thy unbound spirit into bonds again.
   Thou, as a gallant bark from Albion's coast,
The storms all weathered, and the ocean crossed
Shoots into port at some well-havened isle,
Where spices breathe, and brighter seasons smile

There sits quiescent on the floods that show
Her beauteous form reflected clear below,
While airs impregnated with incense play
Around her fanning light her streamers gay;
So thou, with sails how swift! hast reach'd the shore,
" Where tempests never beat nor billows roar,"
And thy lov'd consort on the dang'rous tide
Of life, long since has anchor'd by thy side.
But me, scarce hoping to attain that rest,
Always from port withheld, always distress'd
Me howling blasts drive devious, tempest-toss'd,
Sails ripp'd, seams op'ning wide, and compass lost,
And day by day some current's thwarting force
Sets me more distant from a prosp'rous course.
Yet O the thought, that thou art safe, and he!
That thought is joy, arrive what may to me.
My boast is not, that I deduce my birth
From loins enthroned, and rulers of the earth;
But higher far my proud pretensions rise—
The son of parents passed into the skies.
And now farewell—Time unrevoked hath run
His wonted course, yet what I wish'd is done,
By contemplation's help, not sought in vain,
I seem t' have lived my childhood o'er again;
To have renewed the joys that once were mine,
Without the sin of violating thine;
And while the wings of Fancy still are free,
And I can view this mimic show of thee,
Time has but half succeeded in his theft—
Thyself remov'd, thy pow'r to sooth me left

19

BENEFITS OF AFFLICTION

The path of sorrow, and that path alone,
Leads to the land where sorrow is unknown ;
No traveller ever reached that blessed abode,
Who found not thorns and briars in his road.
The World may dance along the flowery plain
Cheered as they go by many a sprightly strain ;
Where Nature has her mossy velvet spread,
With unshod feet they yet securely tread,
Admonished, scorn the caution and the friend,
Bent all on pleasure, heedless of its end.
But he, who knew what human hearts would prove
How slow to learn the dictates of his love,
That, hard by nature and of stubborn will,
A life of ease would make them harder still,
In pity to the souls his grace designed
To rescue from the ruin of mankind,
Called for a cloud to darken all their years,
And said, ' Go, spend them in the vale of tears.'
   O balmy gales of soul-reviving air !
O salutary streams that murmur there !
These, flowing from the fount of grace above ;
Those, breathed from lips of everlasting love ;
The flinty soil indeed their feet annoys,
Chill blasts of trouble nip their springing joys,
An envious world will interpose its frown
To mar delights superior to its own,
And many a pang, experience still within,
Reminds them of their hated inmate, Sin ;

But ills of every shape and every name,
Transformed to blessing, miss their cruel aim;
And every moment's calm that soothes the breast,
Is given in earnest of eternal rest.
  Ah, be not sad, although thy lot be cast
Far from the flock, and in a boundless waste!
No shepherds' tents within thy view appear,
But the chief Shepherd even there is near;
Thy tender sorrows and thy plaintive strain
Flow in a foreign land, but not in vain,
Thy tears all issue from a source divine,
And every drop bespeaks a Saviour thine—
So once in Gideon's fleece the dews were found,
And drought on all the drooping herbs around.

THE CASTAWAY.

Obscurest night involved the sky,
    The Atlantic billows roared,
When such a destined wretch as I,
    Washed headlong from on board,
Of friends, of hope, of all bereft,
His floating home forever left.

No braver chief could Albion boast,
    Than he with whom he went,
Nor ever ship left Albion's coast
    With warmer wishes sent:
He loved them both, but both in vain,
Nor him beheld, nor her again.

Not long beneath the whelming brine
    Expert to swim, he lay ;
Nor soon he felt his strength decline,
    Or courage die away ;
But waged with death a lasting strife,
Supported by despair of life.

He shouted : nor his friends had failed
    To check the vessel's course,
But so the furious blast prevailed,
    That, pitiless perforce,
They left their outcast mate behind,
And scudded still before the wind.

Some succour yet they could afford ;
    And, such as storms allow,
The cask, the coop, the floated cord,
    Delayed not to bestow.
But he, they knew, nor ship nor shore,
Whate'er they gave, should visit more.

Nor, cruel as it seemed, could he
    Their haste himself condemn,
Aware that flight, in such a sea,
    Alone could rescue them ;
Yet bitter felt it still to die
Deserted, and his friends so nigh

He long survives, who lives an hour
    In ocean, self-upheld :
And so long he, with unspent power,
    His destiny repelled :
And ever as the minutes flew,
Entreated help, or cried—" Adieu !"

At length, his transient respite past,
   His comrades, who before
Had heard his voice in every blast,
   Could catch the sound no more :
For then, by toil subdued, he drank
The stifling wave, and then he sank.

No poet wept him : but the page
   Of narrative sincere,
That tells his name, his worth, his age
   Is wet with Anson's tear :
And tears by bards or heroes shed
Alike immortalize the dead.

I therefore purpose not, or dream,
   Descanting on his fate,
To give the melancholy theme
   A more enduring date ;
But misery still delights to trace
Its semblance in another's case.

No voice divine the storm allayed,
   No light propitious shone,
When, snatched from all effectual aid,
   We perished each alone ;
But I beneath a rougher sea,
And whelmed in deeper gulfs than he.

TO MRS. UNWIN.

The twentieth year is well nigh past,
Since first our sky was overcast;
Ah, would that this might be the last!
       My Mary!

Thy spirits have a fainter flow,
I see thee daily weaker grow—
'Twas my distress that brought thee low,
       My Mary!

Thy needles, once a shining store,
For my sake restless heretofore,
Now rust disused, and shine no more;
       My Mary!

For though thou gladly wouldst fulfil
The same kind office for me still,
Thy sight now seconds not thy will,
       My Mary!

But well thou play'dst the housewife's part,
And all thy threads with magic art
Have wound themselves about this heart,
       My Mary

Thy indistinct expressions seem
Like language uttered in a dream;
Yet me they charm, whate'er the theme,
       My Mary!

Thy silver locks, once auburn bright,
Are still more lovely in my sight
Than golden beams of orient light,
      My Mary!

For could I view nor them nor thee,
What sight worth seeing could I see?
The sun would rise in vain for me,
      My Mary!

Partakers of thy sad decline,
Thy hands their little force resign;
Yet gently prest, press gently mine,
      My Mary!

Such feebleness of limbs thou prov'st,
That now at every step thou mov'st
Upheld by two; yet still thou lov'st,
      My Mary!

And still to love, though prest with ill,
In wintry age to feel no chill,
With me is to be lovely still,
      My Mary!

But ah! by constant heed I know,
How oft the sadness that I show,
Transform thy smiles to looks of wo,
      My Mary!

COWPER.

And should my future lot be cast,
With much resemblance of the past,
Thy worn-out heart will break at last,
        My Mary.

TO THE REV. MR. NEWTON.

That ocean you have late surveyed,
    Those rocks, I too have seen ;
But I, afflicted and dismayed,
    You, tranquil and serene.

You, from the flood-controlling steep,
    Saw stretched before your view,
With conscious joy, the threatening deep
    No longer such to you.

To me, the waves that ceaseless broke
    Upon the dangerous coast,
Hoarsely and ominously spoke,
    Of all my treasure lost.

Your sea of troubles you have passed,
    And found the peaceful shore ;
I, tempest-tossed and wrecked at last,
    Come home to port no more.

HUMAN FRAILTY.

Weak and irresolute is man ;
   The purpose of to-day,
Woven with pains into his plan,
   To-morrow rends away.

The bow well bent, and smart the spring,
   Vice seems already slain ;
But Passion rudely snaps the string,
   And it revives again.

Some foe to his upright intent
   Finds out his weaker part ;
Virtue engages his assent,
   But Pleasure wins his heart.

'Tis here the folly of the wise,
   Through all his art we view ;
And, while his tongue the charge denies,
   His conscience owns it true.

Bound on a voyage of awful length
   And dangers little known,
A stranger to superior strength,
   Man vainly trusts his own.

But oars alone can ne'er prevail,
   To reach the distant coast ;
The breath of heaven must swell the sail,
   Or all the toil is lost.

COWPER

RETIREMENT.

Far from the world, O Lord! I flee,
  From strife and tumult far ;
From scenes where Satan wages still
  His most successful war.

The calm retreat, the silent shade,
  With prayer and praise agree ;
And seem, by thy sweet bounty, made
  For those who follow thee.

There if thy spirit touch the soul,
  And grace her mean abode ;
Oh ! with what peace, and joy, and love,
  She communes with her God !

There like the nightingale, she pours
  Her solitary lays ;
Nor asks a witness of her song,
  Nor thirsts for human praise.

Author and guardian of my life,
  Sweet source of light divine ;
And, all harmonious names in one,
  My Saviour, thou art mine !

What thanks I owe thee, and what love,
  A boundless, endless store,
Shall echo through the realms above,
  When time shall be no more.

PROVIDENCE.

God moves in a mysterious way,
   His wonders to perform ;
He plants his footsteps in the sea,
   And rides upon the storm.

Deep in unfathomable mines
   Of never-failing skill,
He treasures up his bright designs,
   And works his sovereign will.

Ye fearful saints, fresh courage take,
   The clouds ye so much dread,
Are big with mercy, and shall break
   In blessings on your head.

Judge not the Lord by feeble sense,
   But trust him for his grace ;
Behind a frowning providence
   He hides a smiling face.

His purposes will ripen fast,
   Unfolding every hour ;
The bud may have a bitter taste,
   But sweet will be the flower.

Blind unbelief is sure to err,
   And scan his work in vain;
God is his own interpreter,
   And he will make it plain.

CRABBE.

THE MOURNER.

Yes! there are real mourners,—1 have seen
A fair sad girl, mild, suffering, and serene;
Attention (through the day) her duties claimed,
And to be useful as resigned she aimed;
Neatly she drest, nor vainly seemed t' expect
Pity for grief, or pardon for neglect;
But when her wearied parents sunk to sleep,
She sought her place to meditate and weep;
Then to her mind was all the past displayed,
That faithful memory brings to sorrow's aid:
For then she thought on one regretted youth,
Her tender trust, and his unquestioned truth;
In every place she wandered, where they'd been,
And sadly-sacred held the parting scene,
Where last for sea he took his leave; that place
With double interest would she nightly trace!

Happy he sailed, and great the cares he took,
That he should softly sleep and smartly look;
White was his better linen, and his check
Was made more trim than any on the deck;
And every comfort men at sea can know,
Was her's to buy, to make, and to bestow:
For he to Greenland sailed, and much she told,
How he should guard against the climate's cold;
Yet saw not danger; dangers he'd withstood,
Nor could she trace the fever in his blood.
His messmates smiled at flushings on his cheek,
And he too smiled, but seldom would he speak;
For now he found the danger, felt the pain,
With grievous symptoms he could not explain.
He called his friend, and prefaced with a sigh
A lover's message.——' Thomas, I must die:
Would I could see my Sally, and could rest
My throbbing temples on her faithful breast,
And gazing go!—if not, this trifle take,
And say, till death I wore it for her sake:
Yes! I must die—blow on, sweet breeze, blow on,
Give me one look before my life be gone,
Oh! give me that, and let me not despair,
One last fond look!—and now repeat the prayer.'
He had his wish, had more: I will not paint
The lovers' meeting; she beheld him faint,—
With tender fears, she took a nearer view,
Her terrors doubling as her hopes withdrew:
He tried to smile; and, half succeeding, said,
" Yes! I must die"—and hope forever fled.
Still long she nursed him; tender thoughts meantime
Were interchanged, and hopes and views sublime.
20

To her he came to die, and every day
She took some portion of the dread away ;
With him she prayed, to him his Bible read,
Soothed the faint heart, and held the aching head :
She came with smiles the hour of pain to cheer,
Apart she sighed ; alone, she shed the tear ;
Then, as if breaking from a cloud, she gave
Fresh light, and gilt the prospect of the grave.
　　One day he lighter seemed, and they forgot
The care, the dread, the anguish of their lot ;
They spoke with cheerfulness, and seemed to think,
Yet said not so——" Perhaps he will not sink."
A sudden brightness in his look appeared,
A sudden vigour in his voice was heard ;——
She had been reading in the Book of Prayer,
And led him forth, and placed him in his chair ;
Lively he seemed, and spake of all he knew,
The friendly many, and the favourite few ;
Nor one that day did he to mind recall,
But she has treasured, and she loves them all ;
When in her way she meets them, they appear
Peculiar people——death has made them dear.
He named his friend, but then his hand she prest,
And fondly whispered, " Thou must go to rest."
" I go," he said ; but as he spoke, she found
His hand more cold, and fluttering was the sound ;
Then gazed affrighted ; but she caught a last,
A dying look of love, and all was past !
　　She placed a decent stone his grave above,
Neatly engraved——an offering of her love :
For that she wrought, for that forsook her bed,
Awake alike to duty and the dead ;

She would have grieved, had friends presumed to spare
The least assistance—'twas her proper care.
Here will she come, and on the grave will sit,
Folding her arms, in long abstracted fit:
But if observer pass, will take her round,
And careless seem, for she would not be found ;
Then go again, and thus her hours employ,
While visions please her, and while woes destroy.

A MOTHER'S DEATH.

Then died lamented, in the strength of life,
A valued Mother and a faithful Wife ;
Called not away, when time had loosed each hold
On the fond heart, and each desire grew cold ;
But when to all that knit us to our kind,
She felt fast bound, as charity can bind ;—
Not when the ills of age, its pain, its care,
The drooping spirit for its fate prepare ;
And, each affection failing, leaves the heart
Loosed from life's charm, and willing to depart ;—
But ALL her ties the strong invader broke,
In all their strength, by one tremendous stroke :
Sudden and swift the eager pest came on,
And terror grew, till every hope was gone:
Still those around appeared for hope to seek !
But viewed the sick and were afraid to speak.
Slowly they bore, with solemn step, the dead :—
When grief grew loud and bitter tears were shed :—
My part began ; a crowd drew near the place,
Awe in each eye, alarm in every face :

So swift the ill, and of so fierce a kind,
That fear with pity, mingled in each mind;
Friends with the husband came, their griefs to blend
For good-man Frankford was to all a friend.
The last-born boy they held above the bier,
He knew not grief, but cries expressed his fear;
Each different age and sex revealed its pain,
In now a louder, now a lower strain:
While the meek father, listening to their tones,
Swelled the full cadence of the grief by groans
The elder sister strove her pangs to hide,
And soothing words to younger minds applied
" Be still, be patient," oft she strove to say;
But failed as oft, and weeping turned away.
    Curious and sad, upon the fresh-dug hill,
The village-lads stood melancholy still;
And idle children, wandering to-and-fro,
As nature guided, took the tone of wo
    Arrived at home, how then they gazed around,
In every place—where she, no more, was found;
The seat at table she was wont to fill;
The fire-side chair, still set, but vacant still;
The garden walks, a labour all her own;
The lattice bower with trailing shrubs o'ergrown;
The Sunday-pew, she filled with all her race;
Each place of her's, was now a sacred place,
That, while it called up sorrows in the eyes,
Pierced the full heart, and forced them still to rise

PHŒBE DAWSON.

Two summers since, I saw, at Lammas Fair,
The sweetest flower that ever blossomed there,
When Phœbe Dawson gaily crossed the green,
In haste to see, and happy to be seen:
Her air, her manners, all who saw, admired;
Courteous though coy, and gentle though retired;
The joy of youth and health her eyes displayed,
And ease of heart her every look conveyed;
A native skill her simple robes expressed,
As with untutored elegance she dressed:
The lads around admired so fair a sight,
And Phœbe felt, and felt she gave, delight;
Admirers soon of every age she gained,
Her beauty won them and her worth retained;
Envy itself could no contempt display,
They wished her well, whom yet they wished away.
Correct in thought, she judged a servant's place,
Preserved a rustic beauty from disgrace;
But yet on Sunday-eve in freedom's hour,
With secret joy she felt that beauty's power,
When some proud bliss upon the heart would steal,
That, poor or rich, a beauty still must feel.——
    At length, the youth, ordained to move her breast,
Before the swains with bolder spirit pressed;
With looks less timid made his passion known,
And pleased by manners, most unlike her own;
Loud though in love, and confident though young;
Fierce in his air, and voluble of tongue;
                    20*

By trade a tailor, though, in scorn of trade,
He served the Squire, and brushed the coat he made:
Yet now, would Phœbe her consent afford,
Her slave alone, again he'd mount the board;
With her should years of growing love be spent,
And growing wealth :——she sighed, and looked consent.
    Now, through the lane, up hill, and cross the green,
Seen by but few, and blushing to be seen,——
Dejected, thoughtful, anxious, and afraid,
Led by the lover, walked the silent maid :
Slow through the meadows roved they, many a mile
Toyed by each bank and trifled at each stile ;
Where, as he painted every blissful view,
And highly coloured what he strongly drew,
The pensive damsel, prone to tender fears,
Dimmed the false prospect with prophetic tears.——
Thus passed the allotted hours, till lingering late,
The lover loitered at the master's gate ;
There he pronounced adieu ! and yet would stay,
Till chidden——soothed——intreated——forced away ;
He would of coldness, though indulged, complain
And oft retire and oft return again ;
When, if his teasing vexed her gentle mind,
The grief assumed, compelled her to be kind !
For he would proof of plighted kindness crave,
That she resented first and then forgave,
And to his grief and penance yielded more,
Than his presumption had required before.——
Oh ! fly temptation, youth ; refrain ! refrain,
Each yielding maid and each presuming swain !

    Lo ! now with red rent cloak, and bonnet black,

And torn green gown loose hanging at her back,
One who an infant in her arms sustains,
And seems in patience striving with her pains;
Pinched are her looks, as one who pines for bread,
Whose cares are growing and whose hopes are fled;
Pale her parched lips, her heavy eyes sunk low,
And tears unnoticed from their channels flow;
Serene her manner, till some sudden pain
Frets the meek soul, and then she's calm again;—
Her broken pitcher to the pool she takes,
And every step with cautious terror makes;
For not alone that infant in her arms,
But nearer cause, her anxious soul alarms.
With water burdened, then she picks her way,
Slowly and cautious, in the clinging clay;
Till in mid green, she trusts a place unsound,
And deeply plunges in th' adhesive ground;
Thence, but with pain, her slender foot she takes,
While hope the mind, as strength the frame, forsakes.
For when so full the cup of sorrow grows,
Add but a drop, it instantly o'erflows.
And now her path but not her peace she gains,
Safe from her task, but shivering with her pains;
Her home she reaches, open leaves the door,
And placing first her infant on the floor,
She bares her bosom to the wind, and sits
And sobbing struggles with the rising fits:
In vain they come, she feels the inflating grief,
That shuts the swelling bosom from relief;
That speaks in feeble cries a soul distressed,
Or the sad laugh that cannot be repressed;
The neighbour-matron leaves her wheel and flies,

With all the aid her poverty supplies ;
Unfee'd the calls of Nature she obeys,
Not led by profit, nor allured by praise ;
And waiting long, till these contentions cease,
She speaks of comfort, and departs in peace.
Friend of distress ! the mourner feels thy aid,
She cannot pay thee, but thou wilt be paid.

But who this child of weakness, want, and care 1
'Tis Phœbe Dawson, pride of Lammas Fair ;
Who took her lover for his sparkling eyes,
Expressions warm, and love-inspiring lies :
     *   .*   *   *   *   *   *
The faithless flatterer soon his vows forgot,
A captious tyrant or a noisy sot ;
If present, railing, till he saw her pained ;
If absent, spending what their labours gained ;
Till that fair form in want and sickness pined,
And hope and comfort fled that gentle mind.

MISERIES OF VICE.

" What indeed I meant
At first was vengeance ; but I long pursued
The pair, and I at last their misery viewed
In that vile garret, which I cannot paint.—
The sight was loathsome, and the smell was faint ;
And there that wife,—whom I had loved so well,
And thought so happy, was condemned to dwell ;
The gay, the grateful wife, whom I was glad
To see in dress beyond our station clad,
And to behold among our neighbours fine,
More than perhaps became a wife of mine ;
And now among her neighbours to explore,
And see her poorest of the very poor !—
I would describe it, but I bore a part,
Nor can explain the feelings of my heart ;
Yet memory since has aided me to trace
The horrid features of that dismal place.
There she reclined unmoved, her bosom bare
To her companion's unimpassioned stare,
And my wild wonder !—Seat of virtue ! chaste
As lovely once ! O how wert thou disgraced !
Upon that breast, by sordid rags defiled,
Lay the wan features of a famished child ;—
That sin-born babe in utter misery laid,
Too feebly wretched e'en to cry for aid ;
The ragged sheeting o'er her person drawn,
Served for the dress that hunger placed in pawn.
At the bed's feet the man reclined his frame :
Their chairs were perished to support the flame

That warmed his agued limbs ; and, sad to see,
That shook him fiercely as he gazed on me.

I was confused in this unhappy view :
My wife ! my friend ! I could not think it true ;
My children's mother,—my Alicia,—laid
On such a bed : so wretched, so afraid !
And her gay, young seducer, in the guise
Of all we dread, abjure, defy, despise,
And all the fear and terror in his look,
Still more my mind to its foundation shook.

At last he spoke :—'Long since I would have died,
' But could not leave her, though for death I sighed,
' And tried the poisoned cup, and dropped it as I tried,
' She is a woman, and that famished thing
' Makes her to life, with all its evils, cling :
' Feed her, and let her breathe her last in peace,
' And all my sufferings with your promise cease !
Ghastly he smiled :—I knew not what I felt,
But my heart melted—hearts of flint would melt,
To see their anguish, penury, and shame,
How base, how low, how grovelling they became ;
I could not speak my purpose, but my eyes,
And my expression—bade the creature rise.

Yet, O ! that woman's look ! my words are vain
Her mixed and troubled feelings to explain ;
True there was shame and consciousness of fall,
But yet remembrance of my love withal,
And knowledge of that power which she would now recall.

"But still the more that she to memory brought,
The greater anguish in my mind was wrought;
The more she tried to bring the past in view,
She greater horror on the present threw;
So that, for love or pity, terror thrilled
My blood, and vile and odious thoughts instilled.
This war within, those passions in their strife.
If thus protracted, had exhausted life;
But the strong view of these departed years,
Caused a full burst of salutary tears,
And as I wept at large, and thought alone,
I felt my reason re-ascend her throne."

CHARLOTTE SMITH.

SONNET.

QUEEN of the silver bow, by thy pale beam
   Alone and pensive I delight to stray,
And watch thy shadow trembling in the stream,
   Or mark the floating clouds that cross thy way.
And while I gaze, thy mild and placid light
   Sheds a soft calm upon my troubled breast ;
And oft I think, fair planet of the night,
   That in thy orb the wretched may have rest ;
The sufferers of the earth perhaps may go,
   Released by death, to thy benignant sphere ;
And the sad children of despair and wo,
   Forget, in thee, their cup of sorrow here.
O ! that I soon may reach thy world serene,
   Poor wearied pilgrim—in this toiling scene.

SOUTHEY.

MOONLIGHT.

How calmly gliding through the dark-blue sky,
The midnight moon ascends!   Her placid beams
Through thinly scattered leaves and boughs grotesque,
Mottle with mazy shades the orchard slope;
Here, o'er the chesnut's fretted foliage gray,
And massy, motionless they spread; here shine
Upon the crags, deepening with blacker night
Their chasms; and there the glittering argentry
Ripples and glances on the confluent streams.
A lovelier, purer light than that of day
Rests on the hills; and oh how awfully
Into that deep and tranquil firmament,
The summits of Auseva rise serene!
The watchman on the battlements partakes

The stillness of the solemn hour ; he feels
The silence of the earth, the endless sound
Of flowing water soothes him, and the stars,
Which, in that brightest moonlight well nigh quenched,
Scarce visible, as in the utmost depth
Of yonder sapphire infinite, are seen,
Draw on with elevating influence
Toward eternity the attempered mind.
Musing on worlds beyond the grave he stands,
And to the Virgin Mother silently,
Breathes forth her hymn of praise.

PELAYO MADE KING.

                              Alone, advanced
Before the ranks, the Goth in silence stood,
While from all voices round, loquacious joy
Mingled its buzz continuous with the blast
Of horn, shrill pipe, and tinkling cymbals' clash,
And sound of deafening drum.   But when the Prince
Drew nigh, and Urban, with the cross upheld,
Stept forth to meet him, all at once were stilled
With instantaneous hush ; as when the wind,
Before whose violent gusts the forest oaks,
Tossing like billows their tempestuous heads,
Roar like a raging sea, suspends its force,
And leaves so dead a calm that not a leaf
Moves on the silent spray.   The passing air.
Bore with it from the woodland undisturbed
The ring-dove's wooing, and the quiet voice

Of waters warbling near.
                    Son of a race
Of Heroes and of Kings ! The Primate thus
Addressed him, Thou in whom the Gothic blood,
Mingling with old Iberia's, has restored
To Spain a ruler of her native line,—
Stand forth, and in the face of God and man
Swear to uphold the right, abate the wrong,
With equitable hand, protect the cross
Whereon thy lips this day shall seal their vow,
And underneath that hallowed symbol, wage
Holy and inextinguishable war
Against the accursed nation that usurps
Thy country's sacred soil !
                    So speak of me
Now and for ever, O my countrymen !
Replied Pelayo ; and so deal with me
Here and hereafter, thou, Almighty God,
In whom I put my trust ;
                    Lord God of Hosts,
Urban pursued, of Angels and of Men
Creator and Disposer, King of Kings,
Ruler of Earth and Heaven,—Look down this day
And multiply thy blessings on the head
Of this thy servant, chosen in thy sight !
Be thou his counsellor, his comforter,
His hope, his joy, his refuge, and his strength !
Crown him with justice, and with fortitude !
Defend him with thy all-sufficient shield,
Surround him every where with the right hand
Of thine all-present power ! and with the might

Of thine omnipotence ;—send in his aid
Thy unseen angels forth, that potently
And royally against all enemies,
He may endure and triumph !   Bless the land
O'er which he is appointed ; bless it with
The waters of the firmament, the springs
Of the low-lying deep, the fruits which sun
And moon mature for man, the precious stores
Of the eternal hills, and all the gifts
Of earth, its wealth and fulness !

         Then he took
Pelayo's hand, and on his finger placed
The mystic circlet.   With this ring, O Prince,
To our dear Spain, who like a widow now
Mourneth in desolation, I thee wed :
For weal or wo thou takest her, till death
Dispart the union.   Be it blest to her,
To thee, and to thy seed.

MEDITATION.

      Soothed by the strain
Of such discourse, Julian was silent then,
And sate contemplating.   Florinda too
Was calmed.   If sore experience may be thought
To teach the uses of adversity,
She said, alas ! who better learned than I
In that sad school ! Methinks if ye would know
How visitations of calamity
Affect the pious soul, 'tis shown ye there !

Look yonder at that cloud, which through the sky
Sailing alone, doth cross in her career
The rolling moon! I watched it as it came,
And deemed the deep opaque would blot her beams;
But, melting like a wreath of snow, it hangs
In folds of wavy silver round, and clothes
The orb with richer beauties than her own,
Then passing, leaves her in her light serene.
Thus having said, the pious sufferer sat,
Beholding with fixed eyes that lovely orb,
Till quiet tears confused in dizzy light
The broken moonbeams. They too by the toil
Of spirit, as by travail of the day
Subdued, were silent, yielding to the hour.
The silver cloud diffusing slowly past,
And now into its airy elements
Resolved is gone; while through the azure depth
Alone in heaven the glorious moon pursues
Her course, appointed, with indifferent beams
Shining upon the silent hills around,
And the dark tents of that unholy host,
Who, all unconscious of impending fate,
Take their last slumber there. The camp is still,
The fires have mouldered, and the breeze which stirs
The soft and snowy embers, just lays bare,
At times a red and evanescent light,
Or for a moment wakes a feeble flame,
They by the fountain hear the stream below,
Whose murmurs, as the wind arose or fell,
Fuller or fainter, reach the ear attuned.
And now the nightingale, not distant far,
Began her solitary song; and poured
21*

To the cold moon a richer, stronger strain,
Than that with which the lyric lark salutes
The new-born day.   Her deep and thrilling song
Seemed with its piercing melody to reach
The soul, and in mysterious unison
Blend with all thoughts of gentleness and love.
Their hearts were open to the healing power
Of nature ; and the splendour of the night,
The flow of waters, and that sweetest lay
Came to them like a copious evening dew,
Falling on vernal herbs which thirst for rain.

THE VALE OF COVADONGO

There was a stirring in the air, the sun
Prevailed, and gradually the brightening mist
Began to rise and melt.   A jutting crag
Upon the right projected o'er the stream,
Not farther from the cave than a strong hand
Expert, with deadly aim, might cast the spear,
Or a strong voice, pitched to full compass, make
Its clear articulation heard distinct.
A venturous dalesman, once ascending there
To rob the eagle's nest, had fallen, and hung
Among the heather, wondrously preserved :
Therefore had he with pious gratitude
Placed on that overhanging brow a cross,
Tall as the mast of some light fisher's skiff,
And from the vale conspicuous.   As the Moors
Advanced, the chieftain in the van was seen,
Known by his arms, and from the crag a voice

Pronounced his name—Alcahman, hoa! look up,
Alcahman!   As the floating mist drew up,
It had divided there, and opened round
The cross; part clinging to the rock beneath,
Hovering and waving part in fleecy folds,
A canopy of silver light, condensed
To shape and substance.   In the midst there stood
A female form, one hand upon the cross,
The other raised in menacing act: below
Loose flowed her raiment, but her breast was armed,
And helmeted her head.   The Moor turned pale;
For on the walls of Auria he had seen
That well-known figure, and had well believed
She rested with the dead.   What, hoa! she cried;
Alcahman!   In the name of all who fell
At Auria in the massacre, this hour
I summon thee before the throne of God,
To answer for the innocent blood!   This hour,
Moor, Miscreant, Murderer, Child of Hell, this hour
I summon thee to judgment!   In the name
Of God! for Spain and vengeance!
                              Thus she closed
Her speech; for, taking from the Primate's hand
That oaken cross, which at the sacring rites
Had served for crosier, at the cavern's mouth
Pelayo lifted it, and gave the word.
From voice to voice on either side it past
With rapid repetition—In the name
Of God! for Spain and vengeance! and forthwith
On either side, along the whole defile,
The Asturians shouting in the name of God,
Set the whole ruin loose! huge trunks and stones,

And loosened crags, down, down they rolled with rush
And bound, and thundering force.   Such was the fall,
As when some city, by the labouring earth
Heaved from its strong foundations is cast down,
And all its dwellings, towers, and palaces
In one wide desolation prostrated.
From end to end of that long strait, the crash
Was heard continuous, and commixt with sounds
More dreadful—shrieks of horror, and despair,
And death—the wild and agonizing cry
Of that whole host in one destruction whelmed.
Vain was all valour there, all martial skill;
The valiant arm is helpless now; the feet
Swift in the race, avail not now to save;
They perish, all their thousands perish there;
Horsemen and infantry, they perish all,—
The outward armour, and the bones within,
Broken, and bruised, and crushed.   Echo prolonged
The long uproar: a silence then ensued,
Through which the sound of Deva's stream was heard,
A lonely voice of waters, wild and sweet.
The lingering groan, the faintly-uttered prayer,
The louder curses of despairing death,
Ascended not so high.   Down from the cave
Pelayo hastes, the Asturians hasten down;
Fierce and unmitigable, down they speed
On all sides, and along the vale of blood
The avenging sword did mercy's work that hour.

POVERTY.

Aye, Idleness! the rich folks never fail
To find some reason why the poor deserve
Their miseries!—Is it idleness, I pray you,
That brings the fever or the ague fit?
That makes the sick one's sickly appetite
Turn at the dry bread and potato meal?
Is it idleness that makes small wages fail
For growing wants? Six years ago, these bells
Rung on my wedding-day, and I was told
What I might look for,—but I did not heed
Good counsel. I had lived in service, Sir,
Knew never what it was to want a meal;
Laid down without one thought to keep me sleepless,
Or trouble me in sleep; had for a Sunday
My linen gown, and when the pedlar came
Could buy me a new ribbon. And my husband,
A towardly young man and well to do.
He had his silver buckles and his watch;
There was not in the village one who looked
Sprucer on holidays. We married, Sir,
And we had children, but as wants increased
Wages did not. The silver buckles went,
So went the watch; and when the holiday coat
Was worn to work, no new one in its place.
For me—you see my rags! but I deserve them,
For wilfully, like this new-married pair,
I went to my undoing.

But the Parish—
Aye, it falls heavy there; and yet their pittance

Just serves to keep life in.   A blessed prospect,
To slave while there is strength, in age the workhouse,
A parish shell at last, and the little bell
Tolled hastily for a pauper's funeral!

   Is this your child?

                            Aye, Sir; and were he drest
And cleaned, he'd be as fine a boy to look on
As the Squire's young master.   These thin rags of his
Let comfortably in the summer wind ;
But when the winter comes, it pinches me
To see the little wretch !   I've three besides ;
And, God forgive me ! but I often wish
To see them in their coffins.

SLAVERY.

   'Tis night; the mercenary tyrants sleep
As undisturbed as Justice ! but no more
The wretched slave, as on his native shore,
Rests on his reedy couch : he wakes to weep!
Though through the toil and anguish of the day
No tear escaped him, not one suffering groan
Beneath the twisted thong, he weeps alone
In bitterness; thinking that far away
Though the gay Negroes join the midnight song,
Though merriment resounds on Niger's shore,
She whom he loves, far from the cheerful throng
Stands sad, and gazes from her lowly door
With dim-grown eye, silent and wo-begone,
And weeps for him who will return no more.

INSCRIPTION.

Pizarro here was born; a greater name
The list of glory boasts not.   Toil and pain,
Famine, and hostile elements, and hosts
Embattled, failed to check him in his course;
Not to be wearied, not to be deterred,
Not to be overcome.   A mighty realm
He overran, and with relentless arms
Slew or enslaved its unoffending sons,
And wealth, and power, and fame, were his rewards.
There is another world, beyond the grave,
According to their deeds where men are judged,
O Reader! if thy daily bread be earned
By daily labour,—yea, however low,
However wretched be thy lot assigned,
Thank thou, with deepest gratitude, the God
Who made thee, that thou art not such as he

COLERIDGE.

THE NIGHTINGALE.

No cloud, no relique of the sunken day
Distinguishes the West, no long thin slip
Of sullen light, no obscure trembling hues.
Come, we will rest on this old, mossy bridge !
You see the glimmer of the stream beneath,
But hear no murmuring : it flows silently
O'er its soft bed of verdure.   All is still,
A balmy night ! and tho' the stars be dim,
Yet let us think upon the vernal showers
That gladden the green earth, and we shall find
A pleasure in the dimness of the stars.
And hark ! the Nightingale begins its song,
" Most musical, most melancholy" Bird !
A melancholy Bird ?   Oh ! idle thought !
In nature there is nothing melancholy.
But some night-wandering man, whose heart was pie. ced
With the resemblance of a grievous wrong,
Or slow distemper, or neglected love,
'And so, poor wretch ! filled all things with himself

And made all gentle sounds tell back the tale
Of his own sorrow) he, and such as he,
First named these notes a melancholy strain :
And many a poet echoes the conceit ;
Poet who hath been building up the rhyme
When he had better far have stretched his limbs
Beside a brook in mossy forest-dell,
By sun or moon-light, to the influxes
Of shapes, and sounds, and shifting elements
Surrendering his whole spirit, of his song
And of his fame forgetful !   So his fame
Should share in Nature's immortality,
A venerable thing ! and so his song
Should make all Nature lovelier, and itself
Be loved like Nature ! But 'twill not be so ;
And youths and maidens most poetical,
Who lose the deepening twilights of the spring
In ball-rooms and hot theatres, they still
Full of meek sympathy must heave their sighs
O'er Philomela's pity-pleading strains.
My Friend, and thou, our Sister ! we have learnt
A different lore : we may not thus profane
Nature's sweet voices, always full of love
And joyance ! 'Tis the merry Nightingale
That crowds, and hurries, and precipitates
With fast thick warble his delicious notes,
As he were fearful that an April night
Would be too short for him to utter forth
His love-chaunt, and disburden his full soul
Of all its music !
         And I know a grove
Of large extent, hard by a castle huge,

Which the great lord inhabits not ; and so
This grove is wild with tangling underwood,
And the trim walks are broken up, and grass,
Thin grass and king-cups grow within the paths.
But never elsewhere-in one place I knew
So many Nightingales ; and far and near,
In wood and thicket, over the wide grove,
They answer and provoke each other's songs,
With skirmish and capricious passagings,
And murmurs musical and swift jug jug,
And one, low piping, sounds more sweet than all,
Stirring the air with such an harmony,
That should you close your eyes, you might almost
Forget it was not day! On moonlight bushes,
Whose dewy leafits are but half disclosed,
You may perchance behold them on the twigs,
Their bright, bright eyes, their eyes both bright and full
Glistening, while many a glow-worm in the shade
Lights up her love-torch.
      A most gentle Maid,
Who dwelleth in her hospitable home
Hard by the castle, and at latest eve
(Even like a lady vowed and dedicate
To something more than Nature in the grove)
Glides thro' the pathways ; she knows all their notes.
That gentle Maid! and oft a moment's space,
What time the Moon was lost behind a cloud,
Hath heard a pause of silence ; till the Moon
Emerging, hath awakened earth and sky
With one sensation, and these wakeful Birds
Have all burst forth in choral minstrelsy,
As if one quick and sudden gale had swept

An hundred airy harps!   And she hath watched
Many a Nightingale perch giddily,
On blos'my twig still swinging from the breeze,
And to that motion tune his wanton song
Like tipsy joy that reels with tossing head.

    Farewell, O Warbler! till to-morrow eve,
And you, my friends! farewell, a short farewell!
We have been loitering long and pleasantly,
And now for our dear homes.——That strain again?
Full fain it would delay me!   My dear babe,
Who, capable of no articulate sound,
Mars all things with his imitative lisp,
How he would place his hand beside his ear,
His little hand, the small forefinger up,
And bid us listen!   And I deem it wise
To make him Nature's play-mate.   He knows well
The evening-star; and once, when he awoke
In most distressful mood, (some inward pain
Had made up that strange thing, an infant's dream)
I hurried with him to our orchard-plot,
And he beheld the Moon, and, hushed at once,
Suspends his sobs, and laughs most silently,
While his fair eyes, that swam with undropt tears,
Did glitter in the yellow moon-beam!   Well!——
It is a father's tale : But if that Heaven
Should give me life, his childhood shall grow up
Familiar with these songs, that with the night
He may associate joy!   Once more farewell,
Sweet Nightingale!   Once more, my friends, farewell.

WORDSWORTH

THE OLD CUMBERLAND BEGGAR

I saw an aged Beggar in my walk ;
And he was seated, by the highway side,
On a low structure of rude masonry
Built at the foot of a huge hill, that they
Who lead their horses down the steep rough road
May thence remount at ease.   The aged Man
Had placed his staff across the broad smooth stone
That overlays the pile ; and, from a bag
All white with flour, the dole of village dames,
He drew his scraps and fragments, one by one;
And scanned them with a fixed and serious look
Of idle computation.   In the sun,
Upon the second step of that small pile,
Surrounded by those wild unpeopled hills,
He sat, and ate his food in solitude ;
And ever, scattered from his palsied hand,
That, still attempting to prevent the waste,
Was baffled still, the crumbs in little showers

Fell on the ground; and the small mountain-birds,
Not venturing yet to peck their destined meal,
Approached within the length of half his staff.

Him from my childhood have I known; and then
He was so old, he seems not older now;
He travels on, a solitary Man,
So helpless in appearance, that for him
The sauntering horseman-traveller does not throw
With careless hand his alms upon the ground,
But stops,—that he may safely lodge the coin
Within the old Man's hat; nor quits him so,
But still, when he has given his horse the rein,
Watches the aged Beggar with a look
Sidelong—and half reverted.   She who tends
The toll-gate, when in summer at her door
She turns her wheel, if on the road she sees
The aged Beggar coming, quits her work,
And lifts the latch for him that he may pass.
The post-boy, when his rattling wheels o'ertake
The aged Beggar in the woody lane,
Shouts to him from behind; and, if thus warned
The old Man does not change his course, the Boy
Turns with less noisy wheels to the road-side,
And passes gently by—without a curse
Upon his lips, or anger at his heart.
He travels on, a solitary Man;
His age has no companion.   On the ground
His eyes are turned, and, as he moves along,
They move along the ground; and, evermore,
Instead of common and habitual sight
Of fields with rural works, of hill and dale,
22*

And the blue sky, one little span of earth
Is all his prospect.   Thus, from day to day,
Bow-bent, his eyes for ever on the ground,
He plies his weary journey: seeing still,
And seldom knowing that he sees, some straw,
Some scattered leaf, or marks which, in one track
The nails of cart or chariot wheel have left
Impressed on the white road,—in the same line,
At distance still the same.   Poor Traveller!
His staff trails with him; scarcely do his feet
Disturb the summer dust; he is so still
In look and motion, and the cottage curs,
Ere he have passed the door, will turn away,
Weary of barking at him.   Boys and girls,
The vacant and the busy, Maids and Youths,
And Urchins newly breeched—all pass him by
Him even the slow paced wagon leaves behind.

But deem not this Man useless, Statesmen ye
Who are so restless in your wisdom, ye
Who have a broom still ready in your hands
To rid the world of nuisances; ye proud,
Heart-swoln, while in your pride ye contemplate
Your talents, power, and wisdom, deem him not
A burden of the earth! 'Tis nature's law
That none, the meanest of created things,
Of forms created the most vile and brute,
The dullest or most noxious, should exist
Divorced from good—a spirit and pulse of good,
A life and soul, to every mode of being
Inseparably linked.   While thus he creeps
From door to door, the villagers in him

WORDSWORTH.

Behold a record which together binds
Past deeds and offices of charity,
Else unremembered, and so keeps alive
The kindly mood in hearts which lapse of years,
And that half wisdom half experience gives,
Make slow to feel, and by sure steps resign
To selfishness and cold oblivious cares.
Among the farms and solitary huts,
Hamlets and thinly scattered villages,
Where'er the aged Beggar takes his rounds,
The mild necessity of use compels
To acts of love ; and habit does the work
Of reason ; yet prepares that after-joy,
Which reason cherishes.   And thus the soul,
By that sweet taste of pleasure unpursued,
Doth find itself insensibly disposed
To virtue and true goodness.   Some there are,
By their good works exalted, lofty minds
And meditative, authors of delight
And happiness, which to the end of time
Will live and spread and kindle : even such minds
In childhood, from this solitary Being,
Or from like Wanderer, haply have received
(A thing more precious far than all that books
Or the solicitudes of love can do !)
That first mild touch of sympathy and thought,
In which they found their kindred with a world
Where want and sorrow were.   The easy man
Who sits at his own door,——and like the pear
That overhangs his head from the green wall,
Feeds in the sunshine ; the robust and young,
The prosperous and unthinking, they who live,

Sheltered, and flourish in a little grove
Of their own kindred ;—all behold in him
A silent monitor, which on their minds
Must needs impress a transitory thought
Of self-congratulation, to the heart
Of each recalling his peculiar boons,
His charters and exemptions ; and perchance,
Though he to no one give the fortitude
And circumspection needful to preserve
His present blessings, and to husband up
The respite of the season, he, at least,
And 'tis no vulgar service, makes them felt.
Yet further.——Many, I believe, there are
Who live a life of virtuous decency,
Men, who can hear the Decalogue and feel
No self-reproach ; who of the moral law
Established in the land where they abide
Are strict observers ; and not negligent,
In acts of love to those with whom they dwell,
Their kindred and the children of their blood.
Praise be to such, and to their slumbers peace !
—But of the poor man ask, the abject poor :
Go, and demand of him, if there be here,
In this cold abstinence from evil deeds,
And these inevitable charities,
Wherewith to satisfy the human soul ?
No—Man is dear to Man ; the poorest poor
Long for some moments in a weary life
When they can know and feel that they have been,
Themselves, the fathers and the dealers-out
Of some small blessings ; have been kind to such
As needed kindness, for this single cause,

That we have all of us one human heart.
—Such pleasure is to one kind Being known,
My neighbour, when with punctual care, each week
Duly as Friday comes, though prest herself
By her own wants, she from her store of meal
Takes one unsparing handful for the scrip
Of this old Mendicant, and, from her door
Returning with exhilarated heart,
Sits by her fire, and builds her hope in Heaven

    Then let him pass, a blessing on his head!
And while in that vast solitude to which
The tide of things has borne him, he appears
To breathe and live but for himself alone,
Unblamed, uninjured, let him bear about
The good which the benignant law of Heaven
Has hung around him: and, while life is his,
Still let him prompt the unlettered villagers
To tender offices and pensive thoughts.
—Then let him pass, a blessing on his head!
And, long as he can wander, let him breathe
The freshness of the valleys; let his blood
Struggle with frosty air and winter snows;
And let the chartered wind that sweeps the heath
Beat his gray locks against his withered face.
Reverence the hope whose vital anxiousness
Gives the last human interest to his heart.
May never HOUSE, misnamed of INDUSTRY,
Make him a captive! for that pent-up din,
Those life consuming sounds that clog the air,
Be his the natural silence of old age!
Let him be free of mountain solitudes;

And have around him, whether heard or not,
The pleasant melody of woodland birds.
Few are his pleasures : if his eyes have now
Been doomed so long to settle on the earth
That not without some effort they behold
The countenance of the horizontal sun,
Rising or setting, *let* the light at least
Find a free entrance to their languid orbs.
And let him, *where* and *when* he will, sit down
Beneath the trees, or by the grassy bank
Of highway side, and with the little birds
Share his chance-gathered meal ; and, finally,
As in the eye of Nature he has lived,
So in the eye of Nature let him die !

THE FRENCH ARMY IN RUSSIA

HUMANITY, delighting to behold
  A fond reflection of her own decay,
Hath painted Winter like a Traveller—old,
  Propped on a staff—and, through the sullen day,
In hooded mantle, limping o'er the plain,
As though his weakness were disturbed by pain :
Or, if a juster fancy should allow
  An undisputed symbol of command,
The chosen sceptre is a withered bough,
  Infirmly grasped within a palsied hand.
These emblems suit the helpless and forlorn,
But mighty Winter the device shall scorn.

  For he it was—dread Winter ! who beset—
Flinging round van and rear his ghastly net—
That host,—when from the regions of the Pole
They shrunk, insane ambition's barren goal,
That Host, as huge and strong as e'er defied
Their God, and placed their trust in human pride.
As fathers persecute rebellious sons,
He smote the blossoms of their warrior youth ;
He called on Frost's inexorable tooth
Life to consume in manhood's firmest hold ;
Nor spared the reverend blood that feebly runs ,
For why, unless for liberty enrolled
And sacred home, ah ! why should hoary Age be bold ,

Fleet the Tartar's reinless steed,
But fleeter far the pinions of the Wind,
Which from Siberian caves the Monarch freed,
And sent him forth, with squadrons of his kind,
And bade the Snow their ample backs bestride,
       And to the battle ride.
No pitying voice commands a halt,
No courage can repel the dire assault ;
Distracted, spiritless, benumbed, and blind,
Whole legions sink—and, in one instant, find
Burial and death : look for them—and descry,
When morn returns, beneath the clear blue sky
A soundless waste, a trackless vacancy!

LUCY.

Three years she grew in sun and shower,
Then Nature said "A lovelier flower
   On earth was never sown ;
This Child I to myself will take ;
She shall be mine, and I will make
   A Lady of my own.

Myself will to my darling be
Both law and impulse : and with me,
   The Girl, in rock and plain,
In earth and heaven, in glade and bower,
Shall feel an overseeing power,
   To kindle or restrain.

She shall be sportive as the Fawn
That wild with glee across the lawn
   Or up the mountain springs ;
And hers shall be the breathing balm,
And hers the silence and the calm,
   Of mute insensate things.

The floating Clouds their state shall lend
To her ; for her the willow bend ;
   Nor shall she fail to see,
Even in the motions of the Storm
Grace that shall mould the Maiden's form
   By silent sympathy.
    23

The stars of midnight shall be dear
To her; and she shall lean her ear
　　In many a secret place,
Where rivulets dance their wayward round,
And beauty born of murmuring sound
　　Shall pass into her face.

And vital feelings of delight
Shall rear her form to stately height,
　　Her virgin bosom swell;
Such thoughts to Lucy I will give,
While she and I together live
　　Here in this happy dell."

Thus Nature spake—The work was done—
How soon my Lucy's race was run!
　　She died, and left to me
This heath, this calm, and quiet scene;
The memory of what has been,
　　And never more will be.

TO A LADY.

Dear Child of Nature, let them rail !
—There is a nest in a green dale,
 A harbour and a hold,
Where thou, a Wife and Friend, shall see
Thy own delightful days, and be
 A light to young and old.

There healthy as a shepherd-boy,
And treading among flowers of joy,
 That at no season fade,
Thou, while thy Babes around thee cling,
Shalt show us how divine a thing
 A Woman may be made.

Thy thoughts and feelings shall not die,
Nor leave thee when gray hairs are nigh
 A melancholy slave ;
But an old age serene and bright,
And lovely as a Lapland night,
 Shall lead thee to thy grave.

SCOTT.

THE LAST MINSTREL.

THE way was long, the wind was cold,
The Minstrel was infirm and old;
His withered cheek, and tresses gray,
Seemed to have known a better day;
The harp, his sole remaining joy,
Was carried by an orphan boy;
The last of all the Bards was he,
Who sung of Border chivalry.
For, well   ay! their date was fled,
His tuneful brethren all were dead;
And he, neglected and oppressed, -
Wished to be with them, and at rest.
No more on prancing palfrey borne,
He carolled, light as lark at morn,
No longer courted and caressed,
High placed in hall, a welcome guest,
He poured, to lord and lady gay,
The unpremeditated lay:

SCOTT.

Old times were changed, old manners gone,
A stranger filled the Stuarts' throne ;
The bigots of the iron time,
Had called his harmless art a crime,
A wandering Harper, scorned and poor,
He begged his bread from door to door ;
And tuned to please a peasant's ear,
The harp, a king had loved to hear.

He passed where Newark's stately tower
Looks out from Yarrow's birchen bower :
The Minstrel gazed with wistful eye—
No humbler resting-place was nigh.
With hesitating step, at last,
The embattled portal-arch he passed,
Whose ponderous grate and massy bar
Had oft rolled back the tide of war,
But never closed the iron door
Against the desolate and poor.
The duchess marked his weary pace,
His timid mein, and reverend face,
And bade her page the menials tell,
That they should tend the old man well ;
For she had known adversity,
Though born in such a high degree ;
In pride of power, in beauty's bloom,
Had wept o'er Monmouth's bloody tomb !

When kindness had his wants supplied,
And the old man was gratified,
Began to rise his minstrel pride :
And he began to talk anon,

Of good earl Francis, dead and gone,
And of earl Walter, rest him God !
A braver ne'er to battle rode :
And how, full many a tale he knew,
Of the old warriors of Buccleugh ;
And, would the noble duchess deign
To listen to an old man's strain,
Though stiff his hand, his voice though weak,
He thought even yet, the sooth to speak,
That, if she loved the harp to hear,
He could make music to her ear.

The humble boon was soon obtained,
The aged minstrel audience gained.
But, when he reached the room of state
Where she, with all her ladies, sate,
Perchance he wished his boon denied ?
For, when to tune his harp he tried,
His trembling hand had lost the ease,
Which marks security to please ;
And scenes, long past, of joy and pain,
Came wildering o'er his aged brain——
He tried to tune his harp in vain.
The pitying duchess praised its chime,
And gave him heart, and gave him time
Till every string's according glee
Was blended into harmony.
And then, he said, he would full fain
He could recall an ancient strain,
He never thought to sing again.
It was not framed for village churls,
But for high dames and mighty earls ;

SCOTT.

He had played it to King Charles the Good,
When he kept court at Holyrood ;
And much he wished, yet feared, to try
The long forgotten melody.
—

    Amid the strings his fingers strayed,
And an uncertain warbling made,
And oft he shook his hoary head.
But when he caught the measure wild,
The old man raised his face, and smiled ;
And lightened up his faded eye,
With all a poet's ecstacy !
In varying cadence, soft or strong,
He swept the sounding chords along
The present scene, the future lot,
His toils, his wants, were all forgot :
Cold diffidence, and age's frost,
In the full tide of song were lost :
Each blank, in faithless memory void,
The poet's glowing thought supplied ;
And, while his harp responsive rung,
'Twas thus the latest minstrel sung.

THE TOMB OF MICHAEL SCOTT.

By a steel-clenched postern door,
    They entered now the chancel tall;
The darkened roof rose high aloof
    On pillars, lofty, and light, and small:
The key-stone that locked each ribbed aisle
Was a fleur-de-lys, or a quatre feuille;
The corbels were carved grotesque and grim,
And the pillars with clustered shafts so trim,
With base and with capital flourished around,
Seemed bundles of lances which garlands had bound.

Full many a scutcheon and banner, riven,
Shook to the cold night-wind of heaven,
    Around the screened altar's pale;
And there the dying lamps did burn,
Before thy low and lonely urn,
O gallant chief of Otterburne,
    And thine, dark knight of Liddesdale!
O fading honours of the dead!
O high ambition, lowly laid!

The moon on the east oriel shone,
Through slender shafts of shapely stone,
    By foliage tracery combined;
Thou wouldst have thought some fairy's hand
'Twixt poplars straight the ozier wand,
    In many a freakish knot, had twined;
Then framed a spell, when the work was done
And changed the willow wreaths to stone.

The silver light so pale and faint,
Showed many a prophet, and many a saint,
Whose image on the glass was dyed ;
Full in the midst his cross of red
Triumphant Michael brandished
    And trampled the apostate's pride.
The moon-beam kissed the holy pane,
And threw on the pavement a bloody stain.

They sate them down on a marble stone,
    A Scottish monarch slept below ;
Thus spoke the monk, in solemn tone :—
    " I was not always a man of wo ;
For Paynim countries I have trod,
And fought beneath the Cross of God ;
Now, strange to mine eyes thine arms appear,
And their iron clang sounds strange to my ear.

" In these fair climes, it was my lot
To meet the wondrous Michael Scott ;
    A wizard of such dreaded fame,
That when, in Salamanca's cave,
Him listed his magic wand to wave,
    The bells would ring in Notre Dame !
Some of his skill he taught to me ;
And, warrior, I could say to thee
The words that cleft Eildon hills in three,
    And bridled the Tweed with a curb of stone :
But to speak them were a deadly sin :
And for having but thought them my heart within,
    A treble penance must be done.

" When Michael lay on his dying bed,
His conscience was awakened ;
He bethought him of his sinful deed,
And he gave me a sign to come with speed .
I was in Spain when the morning rose,
But I stood by his bed ere evening close.
The words may not again be said,
That he spoke to me, on death-bed laid ;
They would rend this abbaye's massy nave,
And pile it in heaps above his grave.

" I swore to bury his Mighty Book,
That never mortal might therein look ;
And never to tell where it was hid,
Save at his chief of Branksome's need ;
And when that need was passed and o'er,
Again the volume to restore.
I buried him on St. Michael's night,
When the bell tolled one, and the moon was bright
And I dug his chamber among the dead,
When the floor of the chancel was stained red,
That his patron's cross might over him wave,
And scare the fiends from the wizard's grave.
* *

" It was a night of wo and dread,
When Michael in the tomb I laid !
Strange sounds around the chancel past,
The banners waved without a blast !"—
—Still spoke the monk, when the bell tolled one !
   I tell you that a braver man,
Than William of Deloraine, good at need,
Against a foe ne'er spurred a steed :

Yet somewhat was he chilled with dread,
And his hair did bristle upon his head.

"Lo, warrior! now the Cross of Red,
Points to the grave of the mighty dead;
Within it burns a wonderous light,
To chase the spirits that love the night:
That lamp shall burn unquenchably,
Until the eternal doom shall be!"
Slow moved the monk to the broad flag-stone,
Which the bloody cross was traced upon:
He pointed to a secret nook;
An iron bar the warrior took;
And the monk made a sign with his withered hand,
The grave's huge portal to expand.

With beating heart to the task he went,
His sinewy frame o'er the grave-stone bent;
With bar of iron heaved amain,
Till the toil-drops fell from his brows, like rain.
It was by dint of passing strength,
That he moved the massy stone at length,
I would you had been there to see
How the light broke forth so gloriously,
Streamed upward to the chancel roof,
And through the galleries far aloof!
No earthly flame blazed e'er so bright;
It shone like heaven's own blessed light;
And issuing from the tomb,
Showed the monk's cowl, and visage pale,
Danced on the dark-browed warrior's mail,
And kissed his waving plume.

Before their eyes the wizard lay,
As if he had not been dead a day ;
His hoary beard in silver rolled,
He seemed some seventy winters old ;
  A palmer's amice wrapped him round,
  With a wrought Spanish baldric bound,
    Like a pilgrim from beyond the sea :
His left hand held his Book of Might,
A silver cross was in his right ;
    The lamp was placed beside his knee :
High and majestic was his look,
At which the fellest fiends had shook,
And all unruffled was his face :
They trusted his soul had gotten grace.

Often had William of Deloraine
Rode through the battle's bloody plain,
And trampled down the warriors slain,
  And neither known remorse or awe ;
Yet now remorse and awe he owned ;
His breath came thick, his head swam round,
  When this strange scene of death he saw,
Bewildered and unnerved he stood,
And the priest prayed fervently and loud ;
With eyes averted prayed he ;
He might not endure the sight to see,
Of the man he had loved so brotherly.

And when the priest his death-prayer had prayed,
Thus unto Deloraine he said :——
" Now, speed thee what thou hast to ao,
Or warrior, we may dearly rue ;

For those thou mayest not look upon,
Are gathering fast round the yawning stone!"
Then Deloraine, in terror, took
From the cold hand, the mighty Book,
With iron clasped, and with iron bound:
He thought as he took it the dead man frowned:
But the glare of the sepulchral light,
Perchance had dazzled the warrior's sight.

When the huge stone sunk o'er the tomb,
The night returned in double gloom;
For the moon had gone down and the stars were few;
And, as the knight and the priest withdrew,
With wavering steps and dizzy brain,
They hardly might the postern gain.
'Tis said, as through the aisles they passed,
They heard strange noises on the blast;
And through the cloister-galleries small,
Which at mid-height thread the chancel wall,
Loud sobs, and laughter louder, ran,
And voices unlike the voice of man;
As if the fiends kept holiday,
Because these spells were brought to day.
I cannot tell how the truth may be;
I say the tale as 'twas said to me.

THE TRIAL OF CONSTANCE.

While round the fire such legends go,
Far different was the scene of wo,
Where, in a secret aisle beneath,
Council was held of life and death.
  It was more dark and lone that vault,
    Than the worst dungeon cell;
  Old Colwulf built it for his fault
    In penitence to dwell,
When he, for cowl and beads, laid down,
The Saxon battle-axe and crown.
This den, which, chilling every sense
  Of feeling, hearing, sight,
Was called the vault of Penitence,
  Excluding air and light,
Was, by the prelate Sexhelm, made
A place of burial, for such dead
As, having died in mortal sin,
Might not be laid the church within.
'Twas now a place of punishment;
Whence if so loud a shriek was sent,
  As reached the upper air,
The hearers blessed themselves, and said,
The spirits of the sinful dead
  Bemoaned their torments there.

But though, in the monastic pile,
Did of this penitential aisle
  Some vague tradition go;

Few only, save the abbot, knew
Where the place lay; and still more few
Were those, who had from him the clew,
  To that dread vault to go.
Victim and executioner
Were blindfold when transported there.
In low dark rounds the arches hung,
From the rude rock, the side walls sprung,
The grave-stones rudely sculptured o'er,
Half sunk in earth, by time half wore,
Were all the pavement of the floor;
The mildew drops fell one by one,
With tinkling flash, upon the stone.
A cresset, in an iron chain,
Which served to light this drear domain,
With damp and darkness seemed to strive,
As if it scarce might keep alive;
And yet it dimly served to show
The awful conclave met below.

There met to doom in secrecy,
Were placed the heads of convents three,
All servants of Saint Benedict,
The statutes of whose order strict,
  On iron table lay;
In long black dress, on seats of stone,
Behind were these three judges shown,
  By the pale cresset's ray:
The abbess of Saint Hilda's, there,
Sat for a space with visage bare,
Until, to hide her bosom's swell,
And tear drops that for pity fell.

SCOTT.

She closely drew her veil.
Yon shrouded figure, as I guess,
By her proud mein, and flowing dress,
Is Tynemouth's haughty prior's ;
And she with awe looks pale :
And he, that ancient man, whose sight
Has long been quenched by age's night,
Upon whose wrinkled brow alone,
Nor ruth, nor mercy's trace is shown,
   Whose look is hard and stern ;
Saint Cuthbert's abbot is his style ;
For sanctity called, through the isle,
   The saint of Lindisfarn.

Before them stood a guilty pair ;
But, though an equal fate they share,
Yet one alone deserves our care.
Her sex a page's dress belied ;
The cloak and doublet loosely tied,
Obscured her charms, but could not hide.
   Her cap down o'er her face she drew,
      And, on her doublet breast,
   She tried to hide the badge of blue,
      Lord Marmion's falcon crest.
But at the prioress' command,
A monk undid the silken band,
That tied her tresses fair,
And raised the bonnet from her head,
And down her slender form they spread,
In ringlets rich and rare.
Constance de Beverley they know
Sister professed of Fontevraud

SCOTT.

Whom the church numbered with the dead,
For broken vows and convent fled.
When thus her face was given to view,
(Although so pallid was her hue,
It did a ghastly contrast bear
To those bright ringlets glistening fair,)
Her look composed, and steady eye,
Bespoke a matchless constancy;
And there she stood, so calm and pale,
That, but her breathing did not fail,
And motion slight of eye and head,
And of her bosom warranted,
That neither sense nor pulse she lacks,
You might have thought a form of wax,
Wrought to the very life was there;—
So still she was, so pale, so fair!

Her comrade was a sordid soul,
    Such as does murder for a meed;
Who, but of fear, knows no control,
Because his conscience, seared and foul,
    Feels not the import of his deed;
One, whose brute-feeling ne'er aspires
Beyond his own more brute desires.
Such tools the tempter ever needs,
To do the savagest of deeds:
For them no visioned terrors daunt,
Their nights no fancied spectres haunt;
One fear with them, of all most base,
The fear of death,—alone finds place.
This wretch was clad in frock and cowl,
And shamed not loud to moan and how
24*

His body on the floor to dash,
And crouch, like hound beneath the lash;
While his mute partner, standing near,
Waited her doom without a tear.

Yet well the luckless wretch might shriek,
Well might her paleness terror speak !
For there were seen in that dark wall,
Two niches, narrow, deep, and tall ;—
Who enters at such grisly door,
Shall ne'er, I ween, find exit more !
In each a slender meal was laid,
Of roots, of water, and of bread :
By each, in Benedictine dress,
Two haggard monks stood motionless ,
Who, holding high a blazing torch,
Showed the grim entrance of the porch :
Reflecting back the smoky beam,
The dark-red walls and arches gleam.
Hewn stones and cement were displayed,
And building tools in order laid.

These executioners were chose,
As men who were with mankind foes,
And, with despite and envy fired,
Into the cloister had retired ;
Or who, in desperate doubt of grace,
Strove by deep penance to efface
         Of some foul crime the stain :
For as the vassals of her will,
Such men the church selected still,
As either joyed in doing ill. .

Or thought more grace to gain,
If, in her cause, they wrestled down
Feelings their nature strove to own.
By strange device were they brought there,
They knew not how, and knew not where.

And now that blind old abbot rose,
    To speak the chapter's doom,
On those the wall was to inclose,
    Alive, within the tomb ;
But stopped, because that woful maid,
Gathering her powers, to speak essayed.
Twice she essayed, and twice in vain,
Her accents might no utterance gain ;
Nought but imperfect murmurs slip
From her convulsed and quivering lip :
"Twixt each attempt all was so still,
You seemed to hear a distant rill,
    'Twas ocean's swells and falls ;
For though this vault of sin and fear,
Was to the sounding surge so near,
A tempest there you scarce could hear,
    So massive were the walls.

At length, an effort sent apart
The blood that curdled to her heart,
    And light came to her eye,
And colour dawned upon her cheek,
A hectic and a fluttered streak,
Like that left on the Cheviot peak,
    By Autumn's stormy sky ;
And when her silence broke at length.

SCOTT.

Still as she spoke, she gathered strength,
   And armed herself to bear;——
It was a fearful sight to see
Such high resolve and constancy,
In form so soft and fair.

" I speak not to implore your grace;
Well know I, for one minute's space,
   Successless might I sue:
Nor do I speak your prayers to gain;
For if a death of lingering pain,
To cleanse my sins, be penance vain,
   Vain are your masses too.——
I listened to a traitor's tale,
I left the convent and the veil,
For three long years I bowed my pride,
A horse-boy in his train to ride;
And well my folly's meed he gave,
Who forfeited, to be his slave,
All here, and all beyond the grave.——
He saw young Clara's face more fair;
He knew her of broad lands the heir,
Forgot his vows, his faith forswore,
And, Constance was beloved no more.——
'Tis an old tale, and often told;
   But, did my fate and wish agree,
Ne'er had been read, in story old,
Of maiden true betrayed for gold,
   That loved, or was avenged, like me!

" The king approved his favourite's aim
In vain a rival barred his claim.

Whose fate with Clare's was plight,
For he attaints that rival's fame
With treason's charge—and on they came,
  In mortal lists to fight.
Their oaths are said,
Their prayers are prayed,
Their lances in the rest are laid,
  They meet in mortal shock ;
And hark ! the throng, with thundering cry,
Shout ' Marmion, Marmion,' to the sky ;
  ' De Wilton to the block !'
Say ye, who preach heaven shall decide,
When in the lists two champions ride,
  Say, was heaven's justice here ?
When, loyal in his love and faith,
Wilton found overthrow or death,
  Beneath a traitor's spear?
How false the charge, how true he fell,
This guilty packet best can tell."—
Then drew a packet from her breast,
Paused, gathered voice, and spoke the rest.

" Still was false Marmion's bridal staid ;
To Whitby's convent fled the maid,
  The hated match to shun.
' Ho ! shifts she thus?' King Henry cried,
' Sir Marmion, she shall be thy bride,
  If she were sworn a nun.'
One way remained—the king's command
Sent Marmion to the Scottish land;
I lingered here, and rescue planned
  For Clara and for me:

This caitiff monk, for gold, did swear,
He would to Whitby's shrine repair,
And, by his drugs, my rival fair,
    A saint in heaven should be.
But ill the dastard kept his oath,
Whose cowardice hath undone us both.

    " And now my tongue the secret tells,
Not that remorse my bosom swells,
But to assure my soul, that none
Shall ever wed with Marmion.
Had fortune my last hope betrayed,
This packet to the king conveyed,
Had given him to the headsman's stroke,
Although my heart that instant broke.——
Now, men of death, work forth your will,
For I can suffer, and be still;
And come he slow, or come he fast,
It is but Death that comes at last.

    " Yet dread me, from my living tomb,
Ye vassal slaves of bloody Rome !
If Marmion's late remorse should wake,
Full soon such vengeance will he take,
That you shall wish the fiery Dane
Had rather been your guest again.
Behind, a darker hour ascends !
The altars quake, the crosier bends,
The ire of a despotic king,
Rides forth upon destruction's wing.
Then shall these vaults, so strong and deep,
Burst open to the sea-wind's sweep ;

Some traveller then shall find my bones,
Whitening amid disjointed stones,
And ignorant of priests' cruelty,
Marvel such relics here should be."

Fixed was her look, and stern her air;
Back from her shoulders streamed her hair,
The locks, that wont her brow to shade,
Stared up erectly from her head;
Her figure seemed to rise more high;
Her voice, despair's wild energy
Had given a tone of prophecy.
Appalled the astonished conclave sate;
With stupid eyes, the men of fate
Gazed on the light inspired form,
And listened for the avenging storm:
The judges felt the victim's dread;
No hand was moved, no word was said,
Till thus the abbot's doom was given,
Raising his sightless balls to heaven:—
" Sister, let thy sorrows cease;
Sinful brother, part in peace !"—
From that dire dungeon, place of doom.
Of execution too, and tomb,
    Paced forth the judges three;
Sorrow it were, and shame, to tell
The butcher-work that there befel,
When they had glided from the cell
    Of sin and misery.

An hundred winding steps convey
That conclave to the upper day;

But, ere they breathed thy fresher air,
'They heard the shriekings of despair,
   And many a stifled groan :
With speed their upward way they take,
Such speed as age and fear can make,
And crossed themselves for terror's sake,
   As hurrying, tottering on :
Even in the vesper's heavenly tone,
They seemed to hear a dying groan,
And bade the passing knell to toll
For welfare of a parting soul.
Slow o'er the midnight wave it swung,
Northumbrian rocks in answer rung :
To Warkworth cell the echoes rolled,
His beads the wakeful hermit told ;
The Bamborough peasant raised his head
But slept ere half a prayer he said ;
So far was heard the mighty knell,
The stag sprung up on Cheviot Fell,
Spread his broad nostril to the wind,
Listed before, aside, behind,
Then couched him down beside the hind,
And quaked among the mountain fern,
To hear that sound so dull and stern.

SONG.—THE CAVALIER

While the dawn on the mountain was misty and gray,
My true love has mounted his steed and away,
Over hill, over valley, o'er dale, and o'er down;
Heaven shield the brave gallant that fights for the crown!

He has doffed the silk doublet the breast-plate to bear,
He has placed the steel-cap o'er his long flowing hair,
From his belt to his stirrup his broadsword hangs down,—
Heaven shield the brave gallant that fights for the crown!

For the rights of fair England that broadsword he draws,
Her king is his leader, her church is his cause;
His watch-word is honour, his pay is renown,—
God strike with the gallant that strikes for the crown!

They may boast of their Fairfax, their Waller, and all
The roundheaded rebels of Westminster-hall;
But tell these bold traitors of London's proud town,
That the spears of the north have encircled the crown.

There's Derby and Cavendish, dread of their foes;
There's Erin's high Ormond, and Scotland's Montrose!
Would you match the base Skippon, and Massy, and
    Brown,
With the barons of England who fight for the crown?

Now joy to the crest of the brave cavalier?
Be his banner unconquered, resistless his spear,
Till in peace and in triumph his toils he may drown,
In a pledge to fair England, her church, and her crown!
25

MONTGOMERY.

THE DEATH OF ADAM.

THE sun went down amidst an angry glare
Of flushing clouds, that crimsoned all the air ;
The winds brake loose ; the forest boughs were torn,
And dark aloof the eddying foliage borne ;
Cattle to shelter scudded in affright ;
The florid evening vanished into night ;
Then burst the hurricane upon the vale,
In peals of thunder, and thick vollied hail ;
Prone rushing rains with torrents whelmed the land,
Our cot amidst a river seemed to stand ;
Around its base, the foamy-crested streams
Flashed through the darkness to the lightning's gleams
With monstrous throes an earthquake heaved the ground,
The rocks were rent, the mountains trembled round !
Never since Nature into being came,
Had such mysterious motion shook her frame ;
We thought, ingulpht in floods, or wrapt in fire,
The world itself would perish with our Sire.

Amidst this war of elements, within
More dreadful grew the sacrifice of sin,
Whose victim on his bed of torture lay,
Breathing the slow remains of life away
Erewhile, victorious faith sublimer rose
Beneath the pressure of collected woes :
But now his spirit wavered, went and came,
Like the loose vapour of departing flame,
Till at the point, when comfort seemed to die,
For ever in his fixed unclosing eye,
Bright through the smouldering ashes of the man,
The saint broke forth, and Adam thus began !

"—O ye, that shudder at this awful strife,
This wrestling agony of death and life,
Think not that He, on whom my soul is cast,
Will leave me thus forsaken to the last ;
Nature's infirmity alone you see ;
My chains are breaking, I shall soon be free ;
Though firm in God the spirit holds her trust,
The flesh is frail, and trembles into dust.
Horror and anguish seize me ;—'tis the hour
Of darkness, and I mourn beneath its power ;
The Tempter plies me with his direst art,
I feel the Serpent coiling round my heart ;
He stirs the wound he once inflicted there,
Instils the deadening poison of despair !
Belies the truth of God's delaying grace,
And bids me curse my Maker to his face.
I will not curse Him, though his grace delay ;
I will not cease to trust Him, though he slay ;

Full on his promised mercy I rely,
For God hath spoken—God, who cannot lie.
—Thou, of my faith the Author and the End !
Mine early, late, and everlasting Friend !
The joy, that once thy presence gave, restore,
Ere I am summoned hence, and seen no more:
Down to the dust returns this earthly frame,
Receive my spirit, Lord ! from whom it came ;
Rebuke the Tempter, show thy power to save,
O let thy glory light me to the grave,
That these, who witness my departing breath,
May learn to triumph in the grasp of death."

He closed his eyelids with a tranquil smile,
And seemed to rest in silent prayer awhile :
Around his couch with filial awe we kneeled,
When suddenly a light from heaven revealed
A Spirit, that stood within the unopened door ;—
The sword of God in his right hand he bore ;
His countenance was lightning, and his vest
Like snow at sun-rise on the mountain's crest ;
Yet so benignly beautiful his form,
His presence stilled the fury of the storm ;
At once the winds retire, the waters cease,
His look was love, his salutation, ' Peace !'

Our mother first beheld him, sore amazed,
But terror grew to transport while she gazed ;
—' 'Tis He, the Prince of Seraphim, who drove
Our banished feet from Eden's happy grove ;
Adam, my life, my spouse, awake !' she cried ;
' Return to Paradise; behold thy guide !'

'O let me follow in this dear embrace!'
She sunk, and on his bosom hid her face.
Adam looked up; his visage changed its hue,
Transformed into an angel's at the view:
'I come!' he cried, with faith's full triumph fired,
And in a sigh of ecstacy expired.
The light was vanished, and the vision fled;
We stood alone, the living with the dead;
The ruddy embers, glimmering round the room,
Displayed the corse amidst the solemn gloom;
But o'er the scene a holy calm reposed,
The gate of heaven had opened there, and closed.

Eve's faithful arm still clasped her lifeless spouse
Gently I shook it, from her trance to rouse;
She gave no answer; motionless and cold,
It fell like clay from my relaxing hold;
Alarmed, I lifted up the locks of gray
That hid her cheek; her soul had passed away;
A beauteous corse she graced her partner's side,
Love bound their lives, and death could not divide.

Trembling astonishment of grief we felt,
Till Nature's sympathies began to melt;
We wept in stillness through the long dark night,
—And O how welcome was the morning light.

ODE.

O for the death of those
Who for their country die,
Sink on her bosom to repose,
And triumph where they die!

How beautiful in death
The WARRIOR's corse appears,
Embalmed by fond Affection's breath,
And bathed in WOMAN's tears!

Their loveliest native earth
Enshrines the fallen brave;
In the dear land that gave them birth,
They find their tranquil grave.

——But the wild waves shall sweep
BRITANNIA's foes away,
And the blue monsters of the deep
Be surfeited with prey.——

——Thus vanish BRITAIN's foes
From her consuming eye;
But rich be the reward of those,
Who conquer,——those who die.

MONTGOMERY.

2

O'er-shadowing laurels deck,
The living hero's brows;
But lovelier wreaths entwine his neck,
His children and his spouse.

Exulting o'er his lot,
The dangers he has braved,
He clasps the dear one, hails the cot,
Which his own valour saved.

DAUGHTERS OF ALBION, weep:
On this triumphant plain,
Your fathers husbands, brethren sleep,
For you and freedom. slain.

O gently close the eye
That loved to look on you;
O seal the lip whose earliest sigh,
Whose latest breath was true:

With knots of sweetest flowers
Their winding-sheet perfume;
And wash their wounds with true-love showers,
And dress them for the tomb.

For beautiful in death
The WARRIOR'S corse appears,
Embalmed by fond Affection's breath
And bathed in WOMAN'S tears.

———Give me the death of those
Who for their country die ;
And O be mine like their repose,
When cold and low they lie !

Their loveliest mother Earth
Entwines the fallen brave,
In her sweet lap who gave them birth
They find their tranquil grave.

THE DIAL

This shadow on the Dial's face,
   That steals from day to day,
With slow, unseen, unceasing pace,
   Moments, and months, and years away ;—
This shadow, which, in every clime,
   Since light and motion first began,
Hath held its course sublime ;—
   What is it ?———Mortal Man !
It is the scythe of TIME :
—A shadow only to the eye ;
   Yet, in its calm career,
It levels all beneath the sky !
   And still through each succeeding year,
Right onward, with resistless power,
Its stroke shall darken every hour,
   Till Nature's race be run,
And 'Time's last shadow shall eclipse the sun

Nor only o'er the Dial's face,
   This silent phantom, day by day,
With slow, unseen, unceasing pace,
   Steals moments, months, and years away;
From hoary rock and aged tree,
   From proud Palmyra's mouldering walls
From Teneriffe, towering o'er the sea,
   From every blade of grass, it falls;
For still where'er a shadow sleeps
   The scythe of time destroys,
And man at every footstep weeps
   O'er evanescent joys;
Like flowerets glittering with the dews of morn,
Fair for a moment, then for ever shorn:
—Ah! soon, beneath the inevitable blow,
I too shall lie in dust and darkness low.

Then TIME, the Conqueror, will suspend
   His scythe, a trophy, o'er my tomb,
Whose moving shadow shall portend -
   Each frail beholder's doom.
O'er the wide earth's illumined space,
   Though TIME's triumphant flight be shown,
The truest index on its face
   Points from the churchyard stone.

ON THE DEATH OF A FRIEND.

Friend after friend departs;
  Who hath not lost a friend?
There is no union here of hearts
  That finds not here an end;
Were this frail world our final rest,
Living or dying none were blest.

Beyond the flight of time,—
  Beyond the reign of death,—
There surely is some blessed clime
  Where life is not a breath;
Nor life's affections, transient fire,
Whose sparks fly upwards and expire!

There is a world above,
  Where parting is unknown;
A long eternity of love,
  Formed for the good alone;
And faith beholds the dying, here,
Translated to that glorious sphere!

Thus star by star declines,
  Till all are past away:
As morning high and higher shines,
  To pure and perfect day:
Nor sink those stars in empty night,
But hide themselves in heaven's own light.

CAMPBELL.

ODE.

Ye Mariners of England !
That guard our native seas ;
Whose flag has braved, a thousand years,
The battle, and the breeze !
Your glorious standard launch again
To match another foe,
And sweep through the deep,
While the stormy tempests blow ;
While the battle rages loud and long,
And the stormy tempests blow.

The spirits of your fathers
Shall start from every wave !—
For the deck it was their field of fame,
And Ocean was their grave :
Where Blake and mighty Nelson fell,
Your manly hearts shall glow,

As ye sweep through the deep,
While the stormy tempests blow ;
While the battle rages loud and long,
And the stormy tempests blow.

Britannia needs no bulwark,
No towers along the steep ;
Her march is o'er the mountain waves,
Her home is on the deep.
With thunders from her native oak,
She quells the floods below——
As they roar on the shore,
When the stormy tempests blow ;
When the battle rages loud and long,
And the stormy tempests blow.

The meteor flag of England
Shall yet terrific burn ;
Till danger's troubled night depart
And the star of peace return.
Then, then, ye ocean-warriors !
Our song and feast shall flow
To the fame of your name,
When the storm has ceased to blow ;
When the fiery fight is heard no more,
And the storm has ceased to blow.

CAMPBELL.

HOHENLINDEN.

On Linden, when the sun was low,
All bloodless lay the untrodden snow,
And dark as winter was the flow
Of Iser, rolling rapidly.

But Linden saw another sight,
When the drum beat, at dead of night,
Commanding fires of death to light
The darkness of her scenery.

By torch and trumpet fast arrayed,
Each horseman drew his battle blade,
And furious every charger neighed,
To join the dreadful revelry.

Then shook the hills with thunder riven,
Then rushed the steed to battle driven,
And louder than the bolts of heaven,
Far flashed the red artillery.

But redder yet that light shall glow,
On Linden hills of stained snow,
And bloodier yet the torrent flow
Of Iser, rolling rapidly.

Tis morn, but scarce yon lurid sun
Can pierce the war-clouds, rolling dun,
Where furious Frank, and fiery Hun,
Shout in their sulphurous canopy.

The combat deepens.   On ! ye brave,
Who rush to glory, or the grave !
Wave, Munich ! all thy banners wave !
And charge with all thy chivalry !

Few, few, shall part where many meet
The snow shall be their winding sheet,
And every turf beneath their feet
Shall be a soldier's sepulchre.

THE SOLDIER'S DREAM.

Our bugles sang truce—for the night-cloud had lowered,
  And the sentinel stars set their watch in the sky ;
And thousands had sunk on the ground overpowered,
  The weary to sleep, and the wounded to die.

When reposing that night on my pallet of straw,
  By the wolf-scaring faggot that guarded the slain ;
At the dead of the night a sweet vision I saw,
  And thrice ere the morning I dreamt it again.

Methought from the battle-field's dreadful array,
  Far, far I had roamed on a desolate track ;
'Twas autumn—and sunshine arose on the way
  To the home of my fathers, that welcomed me back.

I flew to the pleasant fields traversed so oft
  In life's morning march, when my bosom was young ;
I heard my own mountain-goats bleating aloft,
  And knew the sweet strain that the corn-reapers sung.

Then pledged we the wine cup, and fondly I swore,
  From my home and my weeping friends never to part ;
My little ones kissed me a thousand times o'er,
  And my wife sobbed aloud in her fulness of heart.

'Stay, stay with us—rest, thou art weary and worn ;'—
  And fain was their war-broken soldier to stay,
But sorrow returned with the dawning of morn,
  And the voice in my dreaming ear melted away.

ROGERS.

FOSCARI.

Let us lift up the curtain, and observe
What passes in that chamber.   Now a sigh,
And now a groan is heard.   Then all is still.
Twenty are sitting as in judgment there;
Men who have served their country, and grown gray
In governments and distant embassies,
Men eminent alike in war and peace;
Such as in effigy shall long adorn
The walls of Venice—to show what she has been.
Their garb is black, and black the arras is,
And sad the general aspect.   Yet their looks
Are calm, are cheerful; nothing there like grief,
Nothing or harsh, or cruel.   Still that noise,
That low and dismal moaning.

                      Half withdrawn,
A little to the left sits one in crimson,
A venerable man, fourscore and upward.

Cold drops of sweat stand on his furrowed brow.
His hands are clenched ; his eyes half shut and glazed ;
His shrunk and withered limbs rigid as marble.
'Tis FOSCARI, the Doge.   And there is one,
A young man, lying at his feet, stretched out
In torture.   'Tis his son, his only one ;
'Tis GIACOMO, the blessing of his age,
(Say, has he lived for this ?) accused of murder,
The murder of the Senator Donato.
Last night the proofs, if proofs they are, were dropt
Into the lion's mouth, the mouth of brass,
That gapes and gorges ; and the Doge himself,
('Tis not the first time he has filled this office)
Must sit and look on a beloved son
Suffering the question.

                   Twice, to die in peace,
To save a falling house, and turn the hearts
Of his fell adversaries, those who now,
Like hell hounds in full cry, are running down
His last of four, twice did he ask their leave
To lay aside the Crown, and they refused him,
An oath exacting, never more to ask it ;
And there he sits, a spectacle of we,
By them, his rivals in the state, compelled,
Such the refinement of their cruelty,
To keep the place he sighed for.

                       Once again
The screw is turned, and as it turns, the Son
Looks up, and in a faint and broken accent,
Murmurs " My Father !"   The old man shrinks back.
              26*

And in his mantle muffles up his face.
" Art thou not guilty ?" says a voice, that once
Would greet the sufferer long before they met,
And on his ear strike like a pleasant music,
" Art thou not guilty ?"—" No ! indeed I am not."
But all is unavailing.   In that court
Groans are confessions ; Patience, Fortitude,
The work of magic ; and released, upheld,
For condemnation, from his Father's lips
He hears the sentence, " Banishment to CANDIA.
Death if he leaves it."

                  And the bark sets sail ;
And he is gone from all he loves—for ever !
His wife, his boys, and his disconsolate parents !
Gone in the dead of night—unseen of any—
Without a word, a look of tenderness,
To be called up, when, in his lonely hours
He would indulge in weeping.

                  Like a ghost,
Day after day, year after year, he haunts
An ancient rampart, that o'erhangs the sea ;
Gazing on vacancy, and hourly starting
To answer to the watch—Alas, how changed
From him the mirror of the youth of Venice,
In whom the slightest thing, or whim, or chance,
Did he but wear his doublet so and so,
All followed : at whose nuptials, when at length
He won that maid at once the fairest, noblest,
A daughter of the House of Contarini,
That house as old as VENICE, now among

Its ancestors in monumental brass,
Numbering eight Doges—to convey her home,
The Bucentaur went forth, and thrice the Sun
Shone on the Chivalry, that, front to front,
And blaze on blaze reflecting, met and ranged
To tourney in St. Marks.

                              But lo, at last,
Messengers come.   He is recalled : his heart
Leaps at the tidings.   He embarks : the boat
Springs to the oar, and back again he goes,
Into that very chamber ! there to lie
In his old resting-place, the bed of torture ;
And thence look up (Five long, long years of grief
Have not killed either) on his wretched Sire,
Still in that seat—as though he had not left it,
Immoveable, enveloped in his mantle.
But now he comes, convicted of a crime
Great by the laws of VENICE.   Night and day,
Brooding on what he had been, what he was,
'Twas more than he could bear.   His longing fits
Thickened upon him.   His desire for home
Became a madness ; and, resolved to go,
If but to die, in his despair he writes
A letter to Francesco, Duke of MILAN,
Soliciting his influence with the State,
And drops it to be found.—" Would ye know all—
I have transgressed, offended wilfully ;
And am prepared to suffer as I ought.
But let me, let me, if but for an instant,
Ye must consent—for all of you are sons,
Most of you husbands, fathers, let me first,

Indulge the natural feelings of a man,
And, ere I die, if such my sentence be,
Press to my heart ('tis all I ask of you)
My wife, my children—and my aged mother—
Say, is she yet alive?"

                              He is condemned
To go ere set of sun, go whence he came,
A banished man—and for a year to breathe
The vapour of a dungeon.——But his prayer
(What could they less?) is granted.

                              In a hall
Open and crowded by the common rabble,
'Twas there a trembling Wife and her four Sons
Yet young, a Mother, borne along, bedridden,
And an old Doge, mustering up all his strength,
That strength how small, assembled now to meet
One so long lost, long mourned, one who for them
Had braved so much—death, and yet worse than death—
To meet him, and to part with him for ever!

    Time and their heavy wrongs had changed them all,
Him most!   Yet when the Wife, the Mother looked
Again, 'twas he himself, 'twas Giacomo,
Their only hope, and trust, and consolation!
And all clung round him, weeping bitterly;
Weeping the more, because they wept in vain.

    Unnerved, unsettled in his mind from long
And exquisite pain, he sobs aloud and cries,
Kissing the old Man's cheek, " Help me, my Father!

Let me, I pray thee, live once more among you :
Let me go home !"—" My Son," returns the Doge,
Mastering awhile his grief, " if I may still
Call thee my Son, if thou art innocent,
As I would fain believe ;" but as he speaks,
He falls, " submit without a murmur."

Night,
That to the World brought revelry, to them
Brought only food for sorrow : Giacomo
Embarked—to die, sent to an early grave
For thee, Erizzo, whose death-bed confession,
" He is most innocent ! "Twas I who did it !"
Came when he slept in peace. The ship, that sailed
Swift as the winds with his recall to honour,
Bore back a lifeless corpse. Generous as brave,
Affection, kindness, the sweet offices
Of love and duty were to him as needful
As was his daily bread ;—and to become
A by-word in the meanest mouths of Venice,
Bringing a stain on those who gave him life,
On those, alas, now worse than fatherless—
To be proclaimed a ruffian, a night-stabber,
He on whom none before had breathed reproach—
He lived but to disprove it. That hope lost,
Death followed. From the hour he went, he spoke not;
And in his dungeon, when he laid him down,
He sunk to rise no more. Oh, if there be
Justice in heaven, and we are assured there is,
A day must come of ample Retribution !

Then was thy cup, old Man, full to o'erflowing.

But thou wert yet alive ; and there was one,
The soul and spring of all that enmity,
Who would not leave thee ; fastening on thy flank,
Hungering and thirsting, still unsatisfied :
One of a name illustrious as thine own !
One of the Ten ! one of the Invisible Three !
'Twas Loredano.

    When the whelps were gone
He would dislodge the Lion from his den ;
And, leading on the pack he long had led,
The miserable pack that ever howled
Against fallen greatness, moved that Foscari
Be Doge no longer ; urging his great age,
His incapacity and nothingness ;
Calling a Father's sorrows in his chamber
Neglect of duty, anger, contumacy.
" I am most willing to retire," said Foscari :
" But I have sworn, and cannot of myself.
" Do with me as ye please."

    He was deposed
He, who had reigned so long and gloriously ;
His ducal bonnet taken from his brow,
His robes stript off, his ring, that ancient symbol,
Broken before him. But now nothing moved
The meekness of his soul. All things alike.
Among the six that came with the decree,
Foscari saw one he knew not, and inquired
His name. " I am the son of Marco Memmo."
" Ah," he replied, " thy father was my friend."
And now he goes. It is the hour and past.

"I have no business here." But wilt thou not
Avoid the gazing crowd? That way is private.
"No! as I entered, so will I retire."
And leaning on his staff, he left the palace,
His residence for four and thirty years,
By the same staircase he came up in splendour—
The staircase of the giants. Turning round,
When in the court below, he stopt and said,
"My merits brought me hither; I depart,
Driven by the malice of my enemies."
Then through the crowd withdrew, poor as he came,
And in his gondola went off, unfollowed
But by the sighs of them that dared not speak.
This journey was his last. When the bell rung
Next day, announcing a new Doge to Venice,
It rung his knell.

           But whence the deadly hate
That caused all this—the hate of Loredano?
It was a legacy his father left him,
Who, but for Foscari, had reigned in Venice,
And, like the venom in the serpent's bag,
Gathered and grew! Nothing but turned to venom!
In vain did Foscari sue for peace, for friendship,
Offering in marriage his fair Isabel:
He changed not; with a dreadful piety,
Studying revenge; listening alone to those
Who talked of vengeance; grasping by the hand
Those in their zeal (and none, alas, were wanting)
Who came to tell him of another wrong,
Done or imagined. When his father died,
'Twas whispered in his ear, "He died by poison."

He wrote it on the tomb, ('tis there in marble,)
And in his leger-book, among the debtors,
Entered the name, " Francesco Foscari ;"
And added, " For the murder of my father:"
Leaving a blank to be filled up hereafter.
When Foscari's noble heart at length gave way,
He took the volume from the shelf again
Calmly, and with his pen filled up the blank,—
Inscribing, " He has paid me."

GENEVRA.

If ever you should come to Modena,
Stop at a palace near the Reggio-gate,
Dwelt in of old by one of the ORSINI.
Its noble gardens, terrace above terrace,
And rich in fountains, statues, cypresses,
Will long detain you,—but, before you go,
Enter the house—forget it not I pray you,
And look awhile upon a picture there.

'Tis of a lady in her earliest youth,
The last of that illustrious family ;
Done by ZAMPIERI—but by whom I care not.
He who observes it, ere he passes on,
Gazes his fill, and comes and comes again,
That he may call it up, when far away.

She sits, inclining forward as to speak,
Her lips half open, and her finger up,
As though she said, " Beware !" her vest of gold,
Broidered with flowers, and clasped from head to foot,
An emerald-stone in every golden clasp ;
And on her brow, fairer than alabaster,
A coronet of pearls

                        But then her face,
So lovely, yet so arch, so full of mirth,
The overflowings of an innocent heart—
It haunts me still, though many a year has fled,
Like some wild melody.

                        Alone it hangs
Over a mouldering heir-loom, its companion,
An oaken chest, half eaten by the worm,
But richly carved by Antony of Trent,
With Scripture stories from the Life of Christ.
A chest that came from Venice and had held
The ducal robes of some old ancestor—
That by the way—it may be true or false—
But don't forget the picture ; and you will not,
When you have heard the tale they told me there.

    She was an only child—her name GENEVRA,
The joy, the pride of an indulgent father ;
And in her fifteenth year became a bride,
Marrying an only son, FRANCESCO DORIA,
Her playmate from her birth, and her first love.

    Just as she looks there in her bridal dress,
She was all gentleness, all gaiety,
                        27

Her pranks the favourite theme of every tongue.
But now the day was come, the day, the hour;
Now, frowning, smiling for the hundredth time,
The nurse, that ancient lady, preached decorum,
And, in the lustre of her youth, she gave
Her hand, with her heart in it, to Francesco.

 Great was the joy; but at the nuptial feast,
When all sat down, the bride herself was wanting.
Nor was she to be found! Her father cried,
" 'Tis but to make a trial of our love!"
And filled his glass to all; but his hand shook,
And soon from guest to guest the panic spread.
'Twas but that instant she had left Francesco,
Laughing and looking back, and flying still,
Her ivory tooth imprinted on his finger.
But now, alas! she was not to be found;
Nor from that hour could any thing be guessed,
But that she was not!

      Weary of his life,
Francesco flew to Venice, and, embarking,
Flung it away in battle with the Turk!
Orsini lived—and long might you have seen
An old man wandering as in quest of something,
Something he could not find, he knew not what.
When he was gone, the house remained awhile,
Silent and tenantless;—then went to strangers.

 Full fifty years were past, and all forgotten,
When on an idle day, a day of search
Mid the old lumber in the gallery.

That mouldering chest was noticed; and 'twas said
By one as young, as thoughtless as Genevra,
' Why not remove it from its lurking place ?'
'Twas done as soon as said; but on the way
It burst, it fell; and lo, a skeleton,
With here and there a pearl, an emerald stone,
A golden clasp, clasping a shred of gold.
All else had perished——save a wedding ring,
And a small seal, her mother's legacy,
Engraven with a name, the name of both,
" GENEVRA,"

       There then had she found a grave !
Within that chest had she concealed herself,
Fluttering with joy, the happiest of the happy ;
When a spring lock, that lay in ambush there,
Fastened her down for ever !

ROGERS.

THE WISH.

Mine be a cot beside the hill ;
   A bee-hive's hum shall soothe my ear ;
A willowy brook, that turns a mill,
   With many a fall shall linger near.

The swallow oft, beneath my thatch,
   Shall twitter from her clay-built nest ;
Oft shall the pilgrim lift the latch,
   And share my meal, a welcome guest.

Around my ivied porch shall spring,
   Each fragrant flower that drinks the dew ;
And Lucy at her peals shall sing,
   In russet gown and apron blue.

The village-church among the trees,
   Where first our marriage vows were given,
With merry peals shall swell the breeze,
   And point with taper spire to heaven.

MOORE.

AWAKENED CONSCIENCE.

CHEERED by this hope she bends her thither;—
   Still laughs the radiant eye of Heaven,
   Nor have the golden bowers of Even
In the rich West begun to wither,—
When, o'er the vale of BALBEC winging
   Slowly, she sees a child at play,
Among the rosy wild flowers singing,
   As rosy and as wild as they ;
Chasing, with eager hands and eyes,
The beautiful blue damsel-flies,
That fluttered round the jasmine stems,
Like winged flowers or flying gems :—
And, near the boy, who tired with play,
Now nestling mid the roses lay,
She saw a wearied man dismount,
   From his hot steed, and on the brink
Of a small imaret's rustic fount
   Impatient fling him down to drink.
Then swift his haggard brow he turned

To the fair child, who fearless sat,
Though never yet hath day-beam burned
Upon a brow more fierce than that,——
Sullenly fierce,——a mixture dire,
Like thunder-clouds of gloom and fire !
In which the Peri's eye could read
Dark tales of many a ruthless deed ;
The ruined maid——the shrine profaned——
Oaths broken——and the threshold stained
With blood of guests ! there written all,
Black as the damning drops that fall
From the denouncing Angel's pen,
Ere Mercy weeps them out again !
Yet tranquil now, that man of crime
(As if the balmy evening time
Softened his spirit) looked and lay,
Watching the rosy infant's play :——
Though still, whene'er his eye by chance
Fell on the boy's, its lurid glance
Met that unclouded, joyous gaze,
As torches that have burnt all night,
Through some impure and godless rite,
Encounter morning's glorious rays.

But hark ! the vesper-call to prayer,
    As slow the orb of daylight sets,
Is rising sweetly on the air,
    From SYRIA's thousand minarets !
The boy has started from the bed
Of flowers, where he had laid his head,
And down upon the fragrant sod
Kneels, with his forehead to the south,

Lisping the eternal name of God
From Purity's own cherub mouth,
And looking, while his hands and eyes
Are lifted to the glowing skies,
Like a stray babe of Paradise,
Just lighted on that flowery plain,
And seeking for its home again!
Oh 'twas a sight—that Heaven—that child—
A scene, which might have well beguiled
Even haughty EBLIS of a sigh
For glories lost and peace gone by!

  And how felt *he*, the wretched Man,
Reclining there,—while memory ran
O'er many a year of guilt and strife,
Flew ô'er the dark flood of his life,
Nor found one sunny resting-place,
Nor brought him back one branch of grace
" There *was* a time," he said in mild
Heart-humbled tones, " thou blessed child,
" When young and haply pure as thou,
" I looked and prayed like thee—but now"—
He hung his head,—each nobler aim,
  And hope, and feeling, which had slept,
From boyhood's hour, that instant came
  Fresh o'er him, and he wept—he wept!

Blest tears of soul-felt penitence!
  In whose benign, redeeming flow
Is felt the first, the only sense
  Of guiltless joy that guilt can know

MOORE.

FROM THE LIGHT OF THE HARAM.

Alas!——how light a cause may move
Dissension between hearts that love!
Hearts that the world in vain had tried,
And sorrow but more closely tied;
That stood the storm, when waves were rou[ ]
Yet in a sunny hour fall off,
Like ships that have gone down at sea,
When heaven was all tranquillity!
A something, light as air,——a look,
A word unkind, or wrongly taken——
Oh! love, that tempests never shook,
A breath, a touch like this hath shaken.

And ruder words will soon rush in
To spread the breach that words begin;
And eyes forget the gentle ray
They wore in courtship's smiling day;
And voices lose the tone that shed
A tenderness round all they said;
Till fast declining, one by one,
The sweetnesses of love are gone,
And hearts so lately mingled, seem
Like broken clouds,——or like the stream,
That smiling left the mountain's brow,
As though its waters ne'er could sever,
Yet, ere it reach the plain below,
Breaks into floods. that part for ever.

Oh, you, that have the charge of Love,
  Keep him in rosy bondage bound,
As in the fields of bliss above,
  He sits, with flowerets fettered round ;—
Loose not a tie that round him clings,
Nor ever let him use his wings ;
For even an hour, a minute's flight
Will rob the plumes of half their light.
Like that celestial bird, whose nest
Is found beneath far eastern skies,
Whose wings, though radiant when at rest,
Lose all their glory when he flies !

SONG.

Fly to the desert, fly with me,
Our Arab tents are rude for thee ;
But, oh ! the choice what heart can doubt
Of tents with love, or thrones without !

Our rocks are rough, but smiling there
The acacia waves her yellow hair,
Lonely and sweet, nor loved the less
For flowering in a wilderness.

Our sands are bare, but down their slope
The silvery-footed antelope
As gracefully and gaily springs
As o'er the marble courts of kings.

Then come,—thy Arab maid will be
The loved and lone acacia-tree,
The antelope, whose feet shall bless
With their light sound thy loneliness.

Oh! there are looks and tones that dart
An instant sunshine through the heart,—
As if the soul that minute caught
Some treasure it through life had sought;

As if the very lips and eyes
Predestined to have all our sighs,
And never be forgot again,
Sparkled and spoke before us then!

So came thy every glance and tone,
When first on me they breathed and shone
New, as if brought from other spheres,
Yet welcome as if loved for years!

Then fly with me,—if thou hast known
No other flame, nor falsely thrown
A gem away, that thou hast sworn
Should ever in thy heart be worn.

Come, if the love thou hast for me
Is pure and fresh as mine for thee,—
Fresh as the fountain under ground,
When first 'tis by the lapwing found.

MOORE.

But if for me thou dost forsake
Some other maid, and rudely break
Her worshipped image from its base,
To give to me the ruined place ;——

Then, fare thee well,——I'd rather make
My bower upon some icy lake,
When thawing suns begin to shine,
Than trust to love so false as thine.

MY BIRTH-DAY.

" My birth-day"——what a different sound
    That word had in my youthful ears!
And how, each time the day comes round,
    Less and less white its mark appears !

When first our scanty years are told,
It seems like pastime to grow old ;
And, as Youth counts the shining links,
    That Time around him binds so fast,
Pleased with the task, he little thinks
    How hard that chain will press at last.

MOORE.

Vain was the man, and false as vain,
   Who said—" Were he ordained to run
" His long career of life again,
   " He would do all that he had done."—
Ah, 'tis not thus the voice, that dwells
   In sober birth-days, speaks to me,
Far otherwise—of time it tells,
   Lavished unwisely, carelessly—
Of counsel mocked—of talents, made
   Haply for high and pure designs,
But oft, like Israel's incense, laid
   Upon unholy, earthly shrines,—
Of nursing many a wrong desire,—
   Of wandering after Love too far,
And taking every meteor fire,
   That crossed my pathway, for his star!
All this it tells, and, could I trace
   Th' imperfect picture o'er again,
With power to add, retouch, efface,
   The light and shades,—the joy and pain,
How little of the past would stay !
How quickly all should melt away—
   All,—but that freedom of the mind,
   Which hath been more than wealth to me
Those friendships in my boyhood twined,
   And kept till now unchangingly ;
And that dear home, that saving ark,
   Where love's true light at last I've found
Cheering within when all grows dark,
   And comfortless, and stormy round !

SONG

Oft in the stilly night,
Ere slumber's chain has bound me,
  Fond memory brings the light
Of other days around me.

  The smiles, the tears of boyhood's years,
The words of love then spoken,
  The eyes that shone, now dimmed and gone,
The cheerful hearts now broken!

  When I remember all
'The friends so linked together,
  I've seen around me fall,
Like leaves in wintry weather,

  I feel like one, who treads alone
Some banquet-hall deserted,
  Whose lights are fled, whose garlands dead,
And all but he departed!

  Thus in the stilly night,
Ere slumber's chain has bound me,
  Fond memory brings the light
Of other days around me.

ON ROUSSEAU.

'Tis too absurd—'tis weakness, shame,
This low prostration before Fame—
This casting down, beneath the car
Of Idols, whatsoe'er they are,
Life's purest, holiest decencies,
To be careered o'er, as they please.
No,—let triumphant Genius have
All that his loftiest wish can crave.
If he be worshipped, let it be
    For attributes, his noblest, first,—
Not with that base idolatry,
    Which sanctifies his last and worst.

I may be cold—may want that glow
Of high romance, which bards should know
That holy homage, which is felt
In treading where the great have dwelt—
This reverence, whatso'er it be,
    I fear, I feel I have it not,
For here, at this still hour, to me
    The charms of this delightful spot—
Its calm seclusion from the throng,
    From all the heart would fain forget—
This narrow valley, and the song
    Of its small murmuring rivulet—
The flitting, to and fro, of birds,
    Tranquil and tame as they were once

MOORE.

In Eden, ere the startling words
  Of Man disturbed their orisons !——
Those little, shadowy paths, that wind
Up the hill side, with fruit-trees lined,
And lighted only by the breaks
The gay wind in the foliage makes,
Or vistas, here and there, that ope
  Through weeping-willows, like the snatches
Of far-off scenes of light, which Hope
  Even through the shade of sadness catches !
All this, which——would I once but lose
  The memory of those vulgar ties,
Whose grossness all the heavenliest hues
  Of Genius can no more disguise,
Than the sun's beam can do away
The filth of fens o'er which they play,——
This scene, which would have filled my heart
  With thoughts of all that happiest is——
Of Love, where self hath only part,
  As echoing back another's bliss——
Of solitude, secure and sweet,
Beneath whose shade the Virtues meet ;
Which, while it shelters, never chills
  Our sympathies with human wo,
But keeps them, like sequestered rills,
  Purer and fresher in their flow——
Of happy days, that share their beams
  'Twixt quiet mirth and wise employ——
Of tranquil nights, that give, in dreams,
  The moonlight of the morning's joy !——
All this my heart could dwell on here,
But for those hateful memories near,

Those sordid truths, that cross the track
Of each sweet thought, and drive them back
Full into all the mire, and strife,
And vanities of that man's life,
Who, more than all that e'er have glowed
  With Fancy's flame (and it was *his*,
If ever given to mortal) showed
  What an imposter Genius is—
How, with that strong mimetic art,
  Which is its life and soul, it takes
All shapes of thought, all hues of heart,
  Nor feels, itself, one throb it wakes :—
How like a gem its light may smile
  O'er the dark path, by mortals trod,
Itself as mean a worm, the while,
  As crawls along the sullying sod ;
What sensibility may fall
  From its false lip, what plans to bless,
While home, friends, kindred, country, all,
  Lie waste beneath its selfishness.

How, with the pencil hardly dry
  From colouring up such scenes of love
And beauty, as make young hearts sigh,
  And dream, and think through heaven they rove.
They, who can thus describe and move,
  The very workers of these charms,
Nor seek, nor ask a heaven, above
  Some Maman's or Theresa's arms !

How all, in short, that make the boast
Of their false tongues, they want the most :

MOORE

And, while with Freedom on their lips,
   Sounding her timbrels, to set free
This bright world, labouring in th' eclipse
   Of priestcraft and of slavery,
They may, themselves, be slaves as low
   As ever Lord or Patron made,
To blossom in his smile, or grow,
   Like stunted brushwood in the shade!

Out on the craft,—I'd rather be
   One of those hinds, that round me tread,
With just enough of sense to see
   The noon-day sun that's o'er my head,
Than thus, with high-built genius curst,
   That hath no heart for its foundation,
Be all, at once, that's brightest—worst—
   Sublimest—meanest in creation!

BYRON.

THE DYING GLADIATOR.

I see before me the Gladiator lie :
He leans upon his hand—his manly brow
Consents to death, but conquers agony,
And his drooped head sinks gradually low—
And through his side the last drops, ebbing slow
From the red gash, fall heavy, one by one,
Like the first of a thunder-shower ; and now
The arena swims around him—he is gone,
Ere ceased the inhuman shout which hailed the wretch
    who won.

He heard it, but he heeded not—his eyes
Were with his heart, and that was far away ;
He recked not of the life he lost nor prize,
But where his rude hut by the Danube lay,
There were his young barbarians all at play,
There was their Dacian mother—he, their sire
Butchered to make a Roman holiday—
All this rushed with his blood—Shall he expire
And unrevenged ?—Arise ! ye Goths, and glut your ire

WATERLOO.

There was a sound of revelry by night,
And Belgium's capital had gathered then
Her beauty and her chivalry, and bright
The lamps shone o'er fair women and brave men ;
A thousand hearts beat happily, and when
Music arose with its voluptuous swell,
Soft eyes looked love to eyes which spake again,
And all went merry as a marriage-bell ;
But hush ! hark ! a deep sound strikes like a rising knell

Did ye not hear it ?   No ; 'twas but the wind,
Or the car rattling o'er the stony street ;
On with the dance ! let joy be unconfined ;
No sleep till morn, when Youth and Pleasure meet
To chase the glowing hours with flying feet—
But, hark !—that heavy sound breaks in once more,
As if the clouds its echo would repeat ;
And nearer, clearer, deadlier than before !
Arm ! Arm ! it is—it is—the cannon's opening roar !

Within a windowed niche of that high hall
Sat Brunswick's fated chieftain ; he did hear
That sound the first amid the festival,
And caught its tone with death's prophetic ear ;
And when they smiled because he deemed it near,
His heart more truly knew that peal too well
Which stretched his father on a bloody bier,
And roused the vengeance blood alone would quell
He rushed into the field, and, foremost fighting, fell.

Ah ! then and there was hurrying to and fro,
And gathering tears, and tremblings of distress,
And cheeks all pale, which but an hour ago —
Blushed at the praise of their own loveliness ;
And there were sudden partings, such as press
The life from out young hearts, and choking sighs
Which ne'er might be repeated ; who could guess
If ever more should meet those mutual eyes,
Since upon nights so sweet such awful morn could rise !

And there was mounting in hot haste : the steed,
The mustering squadron, and the clattering car,
Went pouring forward with impetuous speed,
And swiftly forming in the ranks of war ;
And the deep thunder peal on peal afar ;
And near the beat of the alarming drum,
Roused up the soldier ere the morning star ;
While thronged the citizens with terror dumb,
Or whispering, with white lips—" The foe ! They come,
       they come !"

And wild and high the " Cameron s gathering" rose !
The war-note of Lochiel, which Albyn's hills
Have heard, and heard, too, have her Saxon foes :—
How in the noon of night that pibroch thrills,
Savage and shrill !   But with the breath which fills
Their mountain-pipe, so fill the mountaineers
With the fierce native daring which instils
The stirring memory of a thousand years,
And Evans, Donald's fame rings in each clansman's ears !

And Ardennes waves above them her green leaves,
Dewy with nature's tear-drops, as they pass,
Grieving, if aught inanimate e'er grieves,
Over the unreturning brave,—alas!
Ere evening to be trodden like the grass
Which now beneath them, but above shall grow,
In its next verdure, when this fiery mass
Of living valour, rolling on the foe,
And burning with high hope, shall moulder cold and low.

Last noon beheld them full of lusty life,
Last eve in beauty's circle proudly gay,
The midnight brought the signal sound of strife,
The morn the marshalling in arms,—the day
Battle's magnificently stern array!
The thunder-clouds close o'er it, which when rent,
The earth is covered thick with other clay,
Which her own clay shall cover, heaped and pent,
Rider and horse,—friend, foe,—in one red burial blent!

DRACHENFELLS.

The castled crag of Drachenfells
Frowns o'er the wide and winding Rhine,
Whose breast of waters broadly swells
Between the banks which bear the vine,
And hills all rich with blossomed trees,
And fields which promise corn and wine,
And scattered cities crowning these,
Whose far white walls along them shine,
Have strewed a scene, which I should see
With double joy wert *thou* with me!

BYRON.

And peasant girls, with deep blue eyes,
And hands which offer yearly flowers,
Walk smiling o'er this paradise ;
Above, the frequent feudal towers
Through green leaves lift their walls of gray,
And many a rock which steeply lowers,
And noble arch in proud decay,
Look o'er this vale of vintage borders ;
But one thing want these banks of Rhine,
Thy gentle hand to clasp in mine.

I send the lilies given to me ;
Though long before thy hand they touch,
I know that they must withered be,
But yet reject them not as such ;
For I have cherished them as dear,
Because they yet may meet thine eye,
And guide thy soul to mine ev'n here,
When thou beholdst them drooping nigh,
And knowest them gathered by the Rhine,
And offered from my heart to thine !

The river nobly foams and flows,
The charm of this enchanted ground,
And all its thousand turns disclose
Some fresher beauty varying round ;
The haughtiest breast its wish might bound
Through life to dwell delighted here ;
Nor could on earth a spot be found
To nature and to me so dear,
Could thy dear eyes in following mine
Still sweeten more these banks of Rhine.

AN ALPINE STORM.

The sky is changed!—and such a change! Oh night,
And storm, and darkness, ye are wondrous strong,
Yet lovely in your strength, as is the light
Of a dark eye in woman! Far along,
From peak to peak, the rattling crags among
Leaps the live thunder! Not from one lone cloud,
But every mountain now hath found a tongue,
And Jura answers, through her misty shroud,
Back to the joyous Alps, who call to her aloud!

And this is in the night:—Most glorious night!
Thou wert not sent for slumber! let me be
A sharer in thy fierce and far delight,—
A portion of the tempest and of thee!
How the lit lake shines, a phosphoric sea,
And the big rain comes dancing to the earth!
And now again 'tis black,—and now, the glee
Of the loud hills shakes with its mountain-mirth,
As if they did rejoice o'er a young earthquake's birth.

Now where the swift Rhone cleaves his way between
Heights which appear as lovers who have parted
In hate, whose mining depths so intervene,
That they can meet no more, though broken-hearted;
Though in their souls, which thus each other thwarted,
Love was the very root of the fond rage
Which blighted their life's bloom, and then departed:—
Itself expired, but leaving them an age
Of years all winters,—war within themselves to wage.

Now, where the quick Rhone thus has cleft his way,
The mightiest of the storms hath ta'en his stand :
For here, not one, but many, make their play,
And fling their thunder-bolts from hand to hand,
Flashing and cast around : of all the band,
The brightest through these parted hills hath forked
His lightnings,—as if he did understand,
That in such gaps as desolation worked,
There the hot shaft should blast whatever therein lurked.

Sky, mountains, rivers, winds, lake, lightnings ! ye !
With night, and clouds, and thunder, and a soul
To make these felt and feeling, well may be
Things that have made me watchful ; the far roll
Of your departing voices, is the knoll
Of what in me is sleepless,—if I rest.
But where of ye, oh tempests ! is the goal ?
Are ye like those within the human breast ?
Or do ye find, at length, like eagles, some high nest

FAREWELL TO ENGLAND.

" Adieu, adieu ! my native shore
   Fades o'er the waters blue ;
The Night-winds sign, the breakers roar
   And shrieks the wild seamew.
Yon Sun that sets upon he sea
   We follow in his flight ;
Farewell awhile to him and thee,
   My native Land—Good night !

" A few short hours and He will rise
  To give the morrow birth ;
And I shall hail the main and skies.
· But not my mother earth.
Deserted is my own good hall,
  Its hearth is desolate ;
Wild weeds are gathering on the wall ;
  My dog howls at the gate.

*   *   *   *   *   *

" And now I'm in the world alone,
  Upon the wide, wide sea :
But why should I for others groan,
  When none will sigh for me ?
Perchance my dog will whine in vain,
  Till fed by stranger hands ;
But long ere I come back again,
  He'd tear me where he stands.

" With thee, my bark, I'll swiftly go
  Athwart the foaming brine ;
Nor care what land thou bear'st me to,
  So not again to mine.
Welcome, welcome ye dark-blue waves !
  And when you fail my sight,
Welcome, ye deserts, and ye caves !
  My native Land—Good Night !"

AN ITALIAN SUNSET

'The moon is up and yet it is not night—
Sunset divides the sky with her—a sea
Of glory streams along the Alpine height
Of blue Friuli's mountains ; Heaven is free
From clouds, but of all colours seems to be
Melted to one vast Iris of the West,
Where the day joins the past eternity ;
While, on the other hand, meek Dian's crest
Floats through the azure air—an island of the blest !

A single star is at her side, and reigns
With her o'er half the lovely heaven ; but still
Yon sunny sea heaves brightly, and remains
Rolled o'er the peak of the far Rhætian hill,
As day and night contending were, until
Nature reclaimed her order :—gently flows
The deep-dyed Brenta, where their hues instil
The odorous purple of a new-born rose,
Which streams upon her stream, and glassed within it
    glows,

Filled with the face of heaven, which, from afar,
Comes down upon the waters ; all its hues,
From the rich sunset to the rising star,
Their magical variety diffuse :
And now they change ; a paler shadow strews
Its mantle o'er the mountains ; parting day
Dies like the dolphin, whom each pang imbues
With a new colour as it gasps away
The last still loveliest, till—'tis gone—and all is gray

THE OCEAN.

Roll on, thou deep and dark blue ocean—roll!
Ten thousand fleets sweep over thee in vain ;
Man marks the earth with ruin—his control
Stops with the shore ;—upon the watery plain
The wrecks are all thy deed, nor doth remain
A shadow of man's ravage, save his own,
When, for a moment, like a drop of rain,
He sinks into thy depths with bubbling groan,
Without a grave, unknelled, uncoffined, and unknown.

The armaments which thunderstrike the walls
Of rock-built cities, bidding nations quake,
And monarchs tremble in their capitals,
The oak leviathans, whose huge ribs make
Their clay creator the vain title take
Of lord of thee, and arbiter of war ;
These are thy toys, and as the snowy flake,
They melt into thy yeast of waves, which mar
Alike the Armada's pride, or spoils of Trafalgar.

Thy shores are empires, changed in all save thee—
Assyria, Greece, Rome, Carthage, where are they ?
Thy waters wasted them while they were free,
And many a tyrant since ; their shores obey
The stranger, slave, or savage ; their decay
Has dried up realms to deserts :—not so thou.
Unchangeable save to thy wild waves' play
Time writes no wrinkle on thine azure brow—
Such as creation's dawn beheld, thou rollest now.

MODERN GREECE.

He who hath bent him o'er the dead
Ere the first day of death is fled,
The first dark day of nothingness,
The last of danger and distress,
(Before decay's effacing fingers
Have swept the line where beauty lingers,)
And marked the mild angelic air,
The rapture of repose that's there,
The fixed yet tender traits that streak
The languor of the placid cheek,
And—but for that sad shrouded eye,
That fires not, wins not, weeps not, now,
And but for that chill changeless brow,
Where cold Obstruction's apathy
Appals the gazing mourner's heart,
As if to him it would impart
The doom he dreads, yet dwells upon;
Yes, but for these and these alone,
Some moments, ay, one treacherous hour,
He still might doubt the tyrant's power;
So fair, so calm, so softly sealed,
The first, last look by death revealed!
Such is the aspect of this shore;
'Tis Greece, but living Greece no more!
So coldly sweet, so deadly fair,
We start, for soul is wanting there.
Her's is the loveliness in death,
That parts not quite with parting breath;

But beauty with that fearful bloom,
That line which haunts it to the tomb.
Expression's last receding ray,
A gilded halo hovering round decay,
The farewell beam of Feeling past away !
Spark of that flame, perchance of heavenly birth,
Which gleams, but warms no more its cherished earth

SOLITUDE.

To sit on rocks, to muse o'er flood and fell,
To slowly trace the forest's shady scene,
Where things that own not man's dominion dwell,
And mortal foot hath ne'er, or rarely been ;
To climb the trackless mountain all unseen,
With the wild flock that never needs a fold ;
Alone o'er steeps and foaming falls to lean ;
This is not solitude ; 'tis but to hold
Converse with Nature's charms, and view her stores
    unrolled.

But midst the crowd, the hum, the shock of men,
To hear, to see, to feel, and to possess,
And roam along, the world's tired denizen,
With none who bless us, none whom we can bless,
Minions of splendour shrinking from distress !
None that, with kindred consciousness endued,
If we were not, would seem to smile the less
Of all that flattered, followed, sought, and sued ;
'Tis to be alone ; this, this is solitude !
29*

TO INEZ.

Nay, smile not at my sullen brow,
  Alas! I cannot smile again;
Yet heaven avert that ever thou
  Shouldst weep, and haply weep in vain.

And dost thou ask, what secret wo
  I bear, corroding joy and youth?
And wilt thou vainly seek to know
  A pang, ev'n thou must fail to soothe?

It is not love, it is not hate,
  Nor low Ambition's honours lost,
That bids me loathe my present state,
  And fly from all I prized the most:

It is that weariness which springs
  From all I meet, or hear, or see;
To me no pleasure Beauty brings;
  Thine eyes have scarce a charm for me.

It is that settled, ceaseless gloom
  The fabled Hebrew wanderer bore;
That will not look beyond the tomb,
  But cannot hope for rest before.

What Exile from himself can flee ?
   To Zones, though more and more remote,
Still, still pursues, where'er I be,
The blight of life—the demon thought.

Yet others rapt in pleasure seem,
   And taste of all that I forsake ;
Oh ! may they still of transport dream,
   And ne'er, at least like me, awake !

Through many a clime 'tis mine to go,
   With many a retrospection curst ;
And all my solace is to know,
   Whate'er betides, I've known the worst.

What is that worst ? Nay do not ask—
   In pity from the search forbear:
Smile on—nor venture to unmask
   Man's heart, and view the hell that's there.

REMORSE.

The spirits I have raised abandon me—
The spells which I have studied baffle me—
The remedy I recked of tortured me ;
I lean no more on super-human aid,
It hath no power upon the past, and for
The future, till the past be gulfed in darkness,
It is not of my search.—My mother earth !
And thou, fresh breaking day, and you, ye mountains,
Why are ye beautiful ? I cannot love ye.
And thou, the bright eye of the universe,
Thou openest over all, and unto all
Art a delight—thou shin'st not on my heart.
And you, ye crags, upon whose extreme edge
I stand, and on the torrent's brink beneath
Behold the tall pines dwindled as to shrubs
In dizziness of distance ; when a leap,
A stir, a motion, even a breath, would bring
My breast upon its rocky bosom's bed
To rest forever—wherefore do I pause ?
I feel the impulse—yet I do not plunge ;
I see the peril—yet do not recede ;
And my brain reels—and yet my foot is firm :
There is a power upon me, which withholds,
And makes it my fatality to live ;
If it be life to wear within myself
This barrenness of spirit, and to be
My own soul's sepulchre, for I have ceased
To justify my deeds unto myself—
The last infirmity of evil.   Aye,

Thou winged and cloud-cleaving minister,
Whose happy flight is highest into heaven,
Well may'st thou swoop so near me—I should be
Thy prey, and gorge thine eaglets; thou art gone
Where the eye cannot follow thee; but thine
Yet pierces downward, onward, or above
With a pervading vision.—Beautiful!
How beautiful is all this visible world!
How glorious in its action and itself!
But we, who name ourselves its sovereigns, we,
Half dust, half deity, alike unfit
To sink or soar, with our mixed essence make
A conflict of its elements, and breathe
The breath of degradation and of pride,
Contending with low wants and lofty will
Till our mortality predominates,
And men are—what they name not to themselves
And trust not to each other.   Hark! the note,
The natural music of the mountain reed—
For here the patriarchal days are not
A pastoral fable—pipes in the liberal air,
Mixed with the sweet bells of the sauntering herd;
My soul would drink those echoes.—Oh, that I were
The viewless spirit of a lovely sound,
A living voice, a breathing harmony,
A bodiless enjoyment—born and dying
With the blest tone that made me!

DARKNESS.

I had a dream, which was not all a dream.
The bright sun was extinguished, and the stars
Did wander darkling in the eternal space,
Rayless, and pathless, and the icy earth
Swung blind and blackening in the moonless air ;
Morn came, and went—and came, and brought no day,
And men forgot their passions in the dread
Of this their desolation ; and all hearts
Were chilled into a selfish prayer for light :
And they did live by watchfires—and the thrones,
The palaces of crowned kings—the huts,
The habitations of all things which dwell,
Were burnt for beacons ; cities were consumed,
And men were gathered round their blazing homes
To look once more into each other's face ;
Happy were those who dwelt within the eye
Of the volcanoes, and their mountain torch :
A fearful hope was all the world contained ;
Forests were set on fire—but hour by hour
They fell and faded—and the crackling trunks
Extinguished with a crash—and all was black.
The brows of men by the despairing light
Wore an unearthly aspect, as by fits
The flashes fell upon them ; some lay down
And hid their eyes and wept ; and some did rest
Their chins upon their clenched hands, and smiled ;
And others hurried to and fro, and fed
Their funeral piles with fuel, and looked up

With mad disquietude on the dull sky,
The pall of a past world ; and then again
With curses cast them down upon the dust,   [shrieked,
And gnashed their teeth and howled : the wild birds
And, terrified, did flutter on the ground,
And flap their useless wings ; the wildest brutes
Came tame and tremulous ; and vipers crawled
And twined themselves among the multitude,
Hissing, but stingless—they were slain for food :
And war, which for a moment was no more,
Did glut himself again ;—a meal was bought
With blood, and each sate sullenly apart
Gorging himself in gloom : no love was left ;
All earth was but one thought—and that was death,
Immediate and inglorious ; and the pang
Of famine fed upon all entrails—men
Died, and their bones were tombless as their flesh ;
The meagre by the meagre were devoured,
Even dogs assailed their masters, all save one,
And he was faithful to a corse, and kept
The birds and beasts and famished men at bay,
Till hunger clung them, or the dropping dead
Lured their lank jaws ; himself sought out no food,
But with a piteous and perpetual moan,
And a quick desolate cry, licking the hand
Which answered not with a caress—he died.
The crowd was famished by degrees ; but two
Of an enormous city did survive,
And they were enemies ; they met beside
The dying embers of an altar-place,
Where had been heaped a mass of holy things

For an unholy usage ; they raked up,
And shivering, scraped with their cold skeleton hands
The feeble ashes, and their feeble breath
Blew for a little life, and made a flame
Which was a mockery ; then they lifted up
Their eyes as it grew lighter, and beheld
Each other's aspects—saw, and shrieked, and died—
Even of their mutual hideousness they died,
Unknowing who he was upon whose brow
Famine had written Fiend.   The world was void,
The populous and the powerful was a lump,
Seasonless, herbless, treeless, manless, lifeless—
A lump of death—a chaos of hard clay.
The rivers, lakes, and ocean, all stood still,
And nothing stirred within their silent depths ;
Ships sailorless, lay rotting on the sea,
And their masts fell down piecemeal ; as they dropped
They slept on the abyss without a surge—
The waves were dead ; the tides were in their grave,
The moon their mistress had expired before ;
The winds were withered in the stagnant air,
And the clouds perished ; Darkness had no need
Of aid from them—She was the universe.

THE DESTRUCTION OF SENNACHERIB.

The Assyrian came down like the wolf on the fold,
And his cohorts were gleaming in purple and gold ;
And the sheen of their spears was like stars on the sea,
When the blue wave rolls nightly on deep Galilee.

Like the leaves of the forest when summer is green,
That host with their banners at sunset were seen:
Like the leaves of the forest when Autumn hath blown,
That host on the morrow lay withered and strewn.

For the angel of Death spread his wings on the blast,
And breathed on the face of the foe as he passed ;
And the eyes of the sleepers waxed deadly and chill,
And their hearts but once heaved, and for ever grew still!

And there lay the steed with his nostril all wide,
But through it there rolled not the breath of his pride :
And the foam of his gasping lay white on the turf,
And cold as the spray of the rock-beating surf.

And there lay the rider distorted and pale,
With the dew on his brow, and the rust on his mail ;
And the tents were all silent, the banners alone,
The lances unlifted, the trumpet unblown.

And the widows of Ashur are laid in their wail,
And the idols are broke in the temple of Baal ;
And the might of the Gentile, unsmote by the sword,
Hath melted like snow in the glance of the Lord !
30

THE EAST.

Know ye the land where the cypress and myrtle
   Are emblems of deeds that are done in their clime,
Where the rage of the vulture, the love of the turtle,
   Now melt into sorrow, now madden to crime ?
Know ye the land of the cedar and vine,
Where the flowers ever blossom, the beams ever shine ;
Where the light wings of Zephyr, oppressed with perfume,
Wax faint o'er the gardens of Gúl in her bloom ;
Where the citron and olive are fairest of fruit,
And the voice of the nightingale never is mute ;
Where the tints of the earth, and the hues of the sky,
In colour though varied, in beauty may vie,
And the purple of ocean is deepest in die ;
Where the virgins are soft as the roses they twine,
And all, save the spirit of man, is divine ?
'Tis the clime of the East ; 'tis the land of the Sun—
Can he smile on such deeds as his children have done ?
Oh ! wild as the accents of lovers' farewell,
Are the hearts which they bear, and the tales which
       they tell.

BYRON.

LYRIC VERSES

The Isles of Greece, the Isles of Greece!
  Where burning Sappho loved and sung,
Where grew the arts of war and peace—
  Where Delos rose, and Phœbus sprung!
Eternal summer gilds them yet,
But all, except their sun, is set.

The Scian and the Teian muse,
  The hero's harp, the lover's lute,
Have found the fame your shores refuse;
  Their place of birth alone is mute
To sounds which echo further west
Than your sires' 'Islands of the Blest.'

The mountains look on Marathon—
  And Marathon looks on the sea;
And musing there an hour alone,
  I dreamt that Greece might still be free;
For, standing on the Persians' grave,
I could not deem myself a slave.

A king sate on the rocky brow,
  Which looks o'er sea-born Salamis;
And ships by thousands lay below,
  And men in nations; all were his!
He counted them at break of day—
And when the sun set, where were they?

And where are they ? and where art thou,
    My country ? On thy voiceless shore
The heroic lay is tuneless now—
    The heroic bosom beats no more !
And must thy lyre, so long divine,
Degenerate into hands like mine ?

'Tis something, in the dearth of fame,
    Though linked among a fettered race,
To feel at least a patriot's shame,
    Even as I sing suffuse my face ;
For what is left the poet here ?
For Greeks a blush—for Greece a tear.

Must *we* but weep o'er days more blest ?
    Must *we* but blush ?—Our fathers bled.
Earth ! render back from out thy breast
    A remnant of our Spartan dead !
Of the three hundred grant but three,
To make a new Thermopylæ !

What, silent still ? and silent all ?
    Ah ! no ;—the voices of the dead
Sound like a distant torrent's fall,
    And answer, " Let one living head,—
But one arise—we come, we come !"
'Tis but the living who are dumb.

In vain—in vain : strike other chords ;
    Fill high the cup with Samian wine !
Leave battles to the Turkish hordes,
    And shed the blood of Scio's vine !
Hark ! rising to the ignoble call—
How answers each bold bacchanal !

You have the Pyrrhic dance as yet,
    Where is the Pyrrhic phalanx gone ?
Of two such lessons, why forget
    The nobler and the manlier one !
You have the letters Cadmus gave—
Think you he meant them for a slave ?

Fill high the bowl with Samian wine !
    We will not think of themes like these
It made Anacreon's song divine :
    He served—but served Polycrates—
A tyrant : but our masters then
Were still, at least, our countrymen.

The tyrant of the Chersonese
    Was freedom's best and bravest friend
That tyrant was Miltiades !
    Oh ! that the present hour would lend
Another despot of the kind !
Such chains as his were sure to bind.
                30*

Fill high the bowl with Samian wine!
  On Suli's rock and Parga's shore,
Exists the remnant of a line
  Such as the Doric mothers bore;
And there, perhaps, some seed is sown,
The Heracleidan blood might own.

Trust not for freedom to the Franks—
  They have a king who buys and sells:
In native swords, and native ranks,
  The only hope of courage dwells:
But Turkish force, and Latin fraud,
Would break your shield, however broad.

Fill high the bowl with Samian wine!
  Our virgins dance beneath the shade
I see their glorious black eyes shine;
  But gazing on each glowing maid,
My own the burning tear-drop laves,
To think such breasts must suckle slaves.

Place me on Sunium's marbled steep—
  Where nothing save the waves and I,
May hear our mutual murmurs sweep;
  There, swan-like, let me sing and die:
A land of slaves shall ne'er be mine—
Dash down yon cup of Samian wine!

KEATS

FROM " ISABEL "

Fair Isabel, poor simple Isabel !
  Lorenzo, a young palmer in love's eye !
They could not in the self-same mansion dwell
  Without some stir of heart, some malady ;
They could not sit at meals but feel how well
  It soothed each to be the other by ;
They could not, sure, beneath the same roof sleep
But to each other dream, and nightly weep.

With every morn their love grew tenderer,
  With every eve deeper and tenderer still ;
He might not in house, field, or garden stir,
  But her full shape would all his seeing fill ;
And his continual voice was pleasanter
  'To her, than noise of trees or hidden rill ;
Her lute-string gave an echo of his name,
She spoilt her half-done broidery with the same.

He knew whose gentle hand was at the latch,
    Before the door had given her to his eyes;
And from her chamber-window he would catch
    Her beauty farther than the falcon spies;
And constant as her vespers would he watch,
    Because her face was turned to the same skies;
And with sick longing all the night outwear,
To hear her morning step upon the stair.

*   *   *   *   *   *

With her two brothers this fair lady dwelt,
    Enriched from ancestral merchandize,
And for them many a weary hand did swelt
    In torched mines and noisy factories,
And many once proud-quivered loins did melt
    In blood from stinging-whip—with hollow eyes;
Many all day in dazzling river stood,
To take the rich-ored driftings of the flood.

For them the Ceylon diver held his breath,
    And went all naked to the hungry shark;
For them his ears gushed blood; for them in death
    The seal on the cold ice with piteous bark
Lay full of darts: for them alone did seethe
    A thousand men in troubles wide and dark:
Half-ignorant, they turned an easy wheel,
That set sharp racks at work, to pinch and peel

*   *   *   *   *   *   *

In the mid-days of Autumn, on their eves
    The breath of Winter comes from far away,
And the sick west continually bereaves
    Of some gold tinge, and plays a roundelay
Of death among the bushes and the leaves,
    To make all bare before he dares to stray
From his north cavern.   So sweet Isabel
    By gradual decay from beauty fell,

Because Lorenzo came not.   Oftentimes
    She asked her brothers, with an eye all pale,
Striving to be itself, what dungeon climes
    Could keep him off so long?   They spake a tale
Time after time, to quiet her.   Their crimes
    Came on them, like a smoke from Hinnom's vale;
And every night in dreams they groaned aloud,
    'To see their sister in her snowy shroud.

TO AUTUMN.

Season of mist and mellow fruitfulness,
    Close bosom-friend of the maturing sun;
Conspiring with him how to load and bless
    With fruit the vines that round the thatch-eaves run;
To bend with apples the mossed cottage-trees,
    And fill all fruit with ripeness to the core;
        To swell the gourd, and plump the hazel shells
With a sweet kernel; to set budding more,
    And still more, later flowers for the bees,
Until they think warm days will never cease,
For Summer has o'er-brimmed their clammy cells.

Who hath not seen thee oft amid thy store?
　　Sometimes whoever seeks abroad may find
Thee sitting careless on a granary floor,
　　Thy hair soft-lifted by the winnowing wind;
Or in a half-reaped furrow sound asleep,
　　Drowsed with the fume of poppies, while thy hook
Spares the next swath and all its twined flowers:
And sometimes like a gleaner thou dost keep
　　Steady thy laden head across a brook;
　　Or by a cider press, with patient look,
Thou watchest the last oozings hours by hours.

Where are the songs of Spring? Aye, where are they?
　　Think not of them, thou hast thy music too,——
While barred clouds bloom the soft-dying day,
　　And touch the stubble-plains with rosy hue;
Then in a wailful choir the small gnats mourn
　　Among the river sallows, borne aloft
　　　Or sinking as the light wind lives or dies;
And full-grown lambs loud bleat from hilly boorn;
　　Hedge-crickets sing; and now with treble soft
The red-breast whistles from a garden-croft;
　　And gathering swallows twitter in the skies

TO THE NIGHTINGALE.

My heart aches, and a drowsy numbness pains
My sense, as though of hemlock I had drunk,
Or emptied some dull opiate to the drains
One minute past, and Lethe-wards had sunk :
'Tis not through envy of thy happy lot,
But being too happy in thine happiness,—
That thou, light-winged Dryad of the trees,
    In some melodious plot
Of beechen green, and shadows numberless,
Singest of summer in full-throated ease.

O, for a draught of vintage ! that hath been
Cooled a long age in the deep-delved earth,
Tasting of Flora and the country green,
    Dance, and Provençal song, and sunburnt mirth !
O for a beaker full of the warm South,
    Full of the true, the blushful Hippocrene,
        With beaded bubbles winking at the brim,
            And purple-stained mouth ;
    That I might drink, and leave the world unseen,
        And with thee fade away into the forest dim :

Fade far away, dissolve, and quite forget
    What thou among the leaves hast never known,
The weariness, the fever, and the fret
    Here, where men sit and hear each other groan,
Where palsy shakes a few, sad, last gray hairs,
Where youth grows pale, and spectre thin, and dies ;
        Where but to think is to be full of sorrow
            And leaden-eyed despairs,
        Where beauty cannot keep her lustrous eyes,
        Or new love pine at them beyond to-morrow

Away ! away ! for I will fly to thee,
    Not charioted by Bacchus and his pards,
But on the viewless wings of Poesy,
    Though the dull brain perplexes and retards:
Already with thee ! tender is the night,
    And haply the Queen-moon is on her throne,
    Clustered around by all her starry fays ;
        But here there is no light,
Save what from heaven is with the breezes blown
Through verdurous glooms and winding mossy ways.

I cannot see what flowers are at my feet,
    Nor what soft incense hangs upon the boughs,
But, in embalmed darkness, guess each sweet
    Wherewith the seasonable month endows
        The grass, the thicket, and the fruit-tree wild ;
    White hawthorn, and the pastoral eglantine ;
        Fast fading violets covered up in leaves ;
            And mid-May's eldest child,
The coming musk-rose, full of dewy wine,
    The murmurous haunt of flies on summer eves.

Darkling I listen ; and, for many a time
  I have been half in love with easeful Death,
Call'd him soft names in many a mused rhyme,
  To take into the air my quiet breath ;
    Now more than ever seems it rich to die,
To cease upon the midnight with no pain,
  While thou art pouring forth thy soul abroad
    In such an ecstasy !
Still would'st thou sing, and I have ears in vain—
  To thy high requiem become a sod.

Thou wast not born for death, immortal Bird !
  No hungry generations tread thee down ;
The voice I hear this passing night was heard
  In ancient days by emperor and clown :
    Perhaps the self-same song that found a path
Through the sad heart of Ruth, when, sick for home,
  She stood in tears amid the alien corn ;
    The same that oft-times hath
Charmed magic casements, opening on the foam
  Of perilous seas, in faery lands forlorn,

Forlorn ! the very word is like a bell
  To toll me back from thee to my sole self !
Adieu ! the fancy cannot cheat so well
  As she is famed to do, deceiving elf.
    Adieu ! adieu ! thy plaintive anthem fades
Past the near meadows, over the still stream,
  Up the hill side ; and now 'tis buried deep
    In the next valley-glades :
Was it a vision, or a waking dream ?
  Fled is that music :—Do I wake or sleep !
      31

ROBIN HOOD.

No! those days are gone away,
And their hours are old and gray,
And their minutes buried all
Under the down-trodden pall
Of the leaves for many years;
Many times have winter's shears,
Frozen North and chilling East,
Sounded tempests, to the feast
Of the forest's whispering fleeces,
Since men knew nor rent nor leases.

No, the bugle sounds no more,
And the twanging bow no more;
Silent is the ivory shrill
Past the heath and up the hill,
There is no mid-forest laugh,
Where lone echo gives the half
To some wight, amazed to hear
Jesting, deep in forest drear.

On the fairest time of June
You may go, with sun or moon,
Or the seven stars to light you,
Or the polar ray to right you,
But you never may behold
Little John, or Robin bold;
Never one; of all the clan,
Thrumming on an empty can
Some old hunting ditty, while
He doth his green way beguile
To fair hostess Merriment,

Down beside the pasture Trent;
For he left the merry tale
Messenger for spicy ale.

Gone, the merry morris din;
Gone, the song of Gamelyn;
Gone, the tough-belted outlaw
Idling in the " grenè shaw;"
All are gone away and past!
And if Robin should be cast
Sudden from his turfed grave,
And if Marian should have
Once again her forest days,
She would weep, and he would craze:
He would swear, for all his oaks,
Fallen beneath his dockyard strokes,
Have rotted on the briny seas;
She would weep that her wild bees
Sang not to her—Strange! that honey
Can't be got without hard money!

So it is: yet let us sing,
Honour to the old bow string!
Honour to the bugle horn!
Honour to the woods unshorn!
Honour to the Lincoln green '
Honour to the archer keen!
Honour to bold Robin Hood,
Sleeping in the underwood!
Honour to maid Marian,
And to all the Sherwood-clan!
Though their days have hurried by
Let us two a burden try.

FROM "HYPERION."

Deep in the shady sadness of a vale
Far sunken from the healthy breath of morn,
Far from the fiery noon, and eve's one star,
Sat gray-haired Saturn, quiet as a stone,
Still as the silence round about his lair;
Forest on forest hung about his head
Like cloud on cloud.   No stir of air was there,
Not so much of life as on a summer's day
Robs not one light seed from the feathered grass,
But where the dead leaf fell, there did it rest.
A stream went voiceless by, still deadened more
By reason of his fallen divinity
Spreading a shade: the Naiad 'mid her reeds
Pressed her cold finger closer to her lips.

Along the margin-sand large foot-marks went,
No further than to where his feet had strayed,
And slept there since.   Upon the sodden ground
His old right hand lay nerveless, listless, dead,
Unsceptered; and his realmless eyes were closed;
While his bowed head seemed listening to the earth,
His ancient mother, for some comfort yet.

It seemed no force could wake him from his place,
But there came one. who with a kindred hand

Touched his wide shoulders, after bending low
With reverence, though to one who knew it not.
She was a Goddess of the infant world ;
By her in stature the tall Amazon
Had stood a pigmy's height : she would have ta'en
Achilles by the hair and bent his neck ;
Or with a finger stayed Ixion's wheel.
Her face was large as that of Memphian sphinx.
Pedestaled haply in a palace court,
When sages looked to Egypt for their lore
But oh ! how unlike marble was that face :
How beautiful, if sorrow had not made
Sorrow more beautiful than beauty's self.
There was a listening fear in her regard,
As if calamity had but begun ;
As if the vanward clouds of evil days
Had spent their malice, and the sullen rear,
Was with its stored thunder labouring up.
One hand she pressed upon that aching spot
Where beats the human heart, as if just there,
Though an immortal, she felt cruel pain :
The other upon Saturn's bended neck
She laid, and to the level of his ear
Leaning with parted lips, some words she spake
In solemn tenor and deep organ tone :
Some mourning words, which in our feeble tongue
Would come in these like accents ; O how frail
To that large utterance of the early Gods !
" Saturn, look up !—though wherefore, poor old **King?**
I have no comfort for thee, no not one:
" I cannot say, ' O wherefore sleepest thou ?'
31*

" For heaven is parted from thee, and the earth
" Knows thee not, thus afflicted, for a God ;
" And ocean too, with all its solemn noise,
" Has from thy sceptre passed ; and all the air
" Is emptied of thine hoary majesty.
" Thy thunder, conscious of the new command,
" Rumbles reluctant o'er our fallen house ;
" And thy sharp lightning in unpractised hands
" Scorches and burns our once serene domain.
' O aching time ! O moments big as years !
" All as ye pass swell out the monstrous truth,
" And press it so upon our weary griefs
" That unbelief has not a space to breathe.
" Saturn, sleep on :—O thoughtless, why did I
" Thus violate thy slumbrous solitude ?
" Why should I ope thy melancholy eyes ?
" Saturn, sleep on ! while at thy feet I weep."

As when, upon a tranced summer-night,
Those green-robed senators of mighty woods,
Tall oaks, branch-charmed by the earnest stars,
Dream, and so dream all night without a stir,
Save from one gradual solitary gust
Which comes upon the silence, and dies off,
As if the ebbing air had but one wave ;
So came these words and went ; the while in tears
She touched her fair large forehead to the ground.

   *   *   *   *   *   *   *   *

KEATS. 367

It was Hyperion :—a granite peak
His bright feet touched, and there he staid to view
The misery his brilliance had betrayed
To the most hateful seeing of itself.
Golden his hair of short Numidian curl,
Regal his shape majestic, a vast shade
In midst of his own brightness, like the bulk
Of Memnon's image at the set of sun
To one who travels from the dusking East :
Sighs, too, as mournful as that Memnon's harp
He uttered, while his hands contemplative
He pressed together, and in silence stood.

MILLMAN.

FROM "THE FALL OF JERUSALEM."

Oh Thou ! thou who canst melt the heart ot stone,
And make the desert of the cruel breast
A paradise of soft and gentle thoughts !
Ah ! will it ever he, that thou wilt visit
The darkness of my father's soul ?   Thou knowest
In what strong bondage zeal and ancient faith,
Passion and stubborn Custom, and fierce Pride,
Hold the heart of man.   Thou knowest, Merciful '
That knowest all things, and dost ever turn
Thine eye of pity on our guilty nature :

For thou wert born of woman ! thou didst come
Oh Holiest ! to this world of sin and gloom,
Not in thy dread omnipotent array ;
  And not by thunders strewed
  Was thy tempestuous road ;
Nor indignation burnt before thee on thy way.
  But thee, a soft and naked child,
   Thy mother undefiled.
  In the rude manger laid to rest
   From off her virgin breast.

The heavens were not commanded to prepare
A gorgeous canopy of golden air ;
Nor stooped their lamps th' enthroned fires on high :
  A single silent star
  Came wandering from afar,
Gliding unchecked and calm along the liquid sky ;
  The Eastern sages leading on
   As at a kingly throne,
  To lay their gold and odours sweet
   Before thy infant feet.

The earth and ocean were not hushed to hear
Bright harmony from every starry sphere ;
Nor at thy presence brake the voice of song
  From all the cherub choirs,
  And seraph's burning lyres.   [along.
Poured through the host of heaven the charmed clouds
  One angel troop the strain began,
   Of all the race of man
  By simple shepherds heard alone,
   That soft Hosanna's tone.

And when thou didst depart, no car of flame
To bear thee hence in lambent radiance came ;
Nor visible Angels mourned with drooping plumes :
    Nor didst thou mount on high
    From fatal Calvary   [tombs
With all thine own redeemed outbursting from their
    For thou didst bear away from earth
    But one of human birth,
    The dying felon by thy side, to be
    In paradise with thee.

Nor o'er thy cross the clouds of vengeance brake ;
A little while the conscious earth did shake
At that foul deed by her fierce children done ;
    A few dim hours of day
    The world in darkness lay ;
Then basked in bright repose beneath the cloudless sun.
    While thou didst sleep beneath the tomb,
    Consenting to thy doom ;
    Ere yet the white robed Angel shone
    Upon the sealed stone.

And when thou didst arise, thou didst not stand
With devastation in thy red right hand,
Plaguing the guilty city's murtherous crew ;
    But thou didst haste to meet
    Thy mother's coming feet,
And bear the words of peace unto the faithful few.
    Then calmly, slowly didst thou rise
    Into thy native skies ;
    Thy human form dissolved on high
    In its own radiancy.

FROM "THE MARTYR OF ANTIOCH."

FABIUS.

Cease, Calanthias, cease ;
And thou, Charinus. Oh, my brethren, God
Will summon those whom he hath chosen, to sit
In garments dyed with their own blood around
The Lamb in Heaven ; but it becomes not man
To affect with haughty and aspiring violence
The loftiest thrones, ambitious for his own,
And not his Master's glory. Every star
Is not a sun, nor every Christian soul
Wrapt to a seraph. But for thee, Calanthias,
Thou know'st not whether even this night sha'.
The impatient vengeance of the Lord, or rest
Myriads of human years. For what are they,
What are our ages, but a few brief waves
From the vast ocean of eternity,
That break upon the shore of this our world,
And so ebb back into the immense profound,
Which He on high, even at one instant, sweeps
With his omniscient sight.
                         Beloved brethren,
And ye, our sisters, hold we all prepared,
Like him beside whose hallowed grave we stand,
To give the last and awful testimony
To Christ our Lord. Yet tempt not to our murder
The yet unbloody hands of men.
                         They come
Pale lights are gleaming through the dusky night,

And hurrying feet are trampling to and fro.
Disperse—disperse, my brethren, to your homes !—
Sweet Margarita, in the Hermitage
By clear Orontes, where so oft we've met,
'Thou'lt find me still.   God's blessing wait on all !
Farewell ! we meet, if not on earth, in heaven.

     *   *   *   *   *   *   *

CALLIAS.

And yet she stands unblasted !   In thy mercy
Thou dost remember all my faithful vows,
Hyperion ! and suspend the fiery shaft
That quivers on thy string.   Ah, not on her,
This innocent, wreck thy fury !   I will search,
And thou wilt lend me light, although they shroud
In deepest Orcus.   I will pluck them forth,
And set them up a mark for all thy wrath ;
Those that beguiled to this unholy madness
My pure and blameless child.   Shine forth, shine forth
Apollo, and we'll have our full revenge.

MARGARITA.

'Tis over now—and oh, I bless thee, Lord,
For making me thus desolate below ;
For severing one by one the ties that bind me
To this cold world, for whither can earth's outcasts
Fly but to heaven ?
                   Yet is no way but this,
None but to steep my father's lingering days

In bitterness? Thou knowest, gracious Lord
Of mercy, how he loves me, how he loved me
From the first moment that my eyes were opened
Upon the light of day and him. At least,
If thou must smite him, smite him in thy mercy,
He loves me as the life-blood of his heart,
His love surpasses every love but thine :

For thou didst die for me, oh Son of God !
   By thee the throbbing flesh of man was worn ;
Thy naked feet the thorn of sorrow trod ;
   And tempests beat thy houseless head forlorn
      Thou, that wert wont to stand
      Alone, on God's right hand,
Before the ages were, the Eternal, eldest born.

Thy birthright in the world was pain and grief,
   Thy love's return ingratitude and hate ;
The limbs thou healed'st brought thee no relief,
   The eyes thou opened'st calmly viewed thy fate :
      Thou, that wert wont to dwell
      In peace, tongue cannot tell,
Nor heart conceive the bliss of thy celestial state.

They dragged thee to the Roman's solemn Hall,
   Where the proud Judge in purple splendour sate ;
Thou stood'st a meek and patient criminal,
   Thy doom of death from human lips to wait ;
      Whose throne shall be the world
      In final ruin hurled,
With all mankind to hear their everlasting fate.
32

Thou wert alone in that fierce multitude,
   When " Crucify him !" yelled the general shout ;
No hand to guard thee mid those insults rude,
   Nor lip to bless in all that frantic rout ;
      Whose lightest whispered word
      The Seraphim had heard,
And adamantine arms from all the heavens broke out.

They bound thy temples with the twisted thorn,
   Thy bruised feet went languid on with pain ;
The blood, from all thy flesh with scourges torn,
   Deepened thy robe of mockery's crimson grain ;
      Whose native vesture bright
      Was the unapproached light,
The sandal of whose foot the rapid hurricane.

They smote thy cheek with many a ruthless palm,
   With the cold spear thy shuddering side they pierced ;
The draught of bitterest gall was all the balm
   They gave, t'enhance thy unslaked, burning thirst :
      Thou, at whose words of peace
      Did pain and anguish cease,
And the long buried dead their bonds of slumber burst.

Low bowed thy head convulsed, and, drooped in death,
   Thy voice sent forth a sad and wailing cry ;
Slow struggled from thy breast the parting breath,
   And every limb was wrung with agony.
      That head, whose veilless blaze
      Filled angels with amaze,
When at that voice sprang forth the rolling suns or high.

And thou wert laid within the narrow tomb,
  Thy clay-cold limbs with shrouding grave-clothes
                        [bound
The sealed stone confirmed thy mortal doom,
  Lone watchmen walked thy desert burial ground,
    Whom heaven could not contain,
    Nor th' immeasurable plain
Of vast Infinity inclose or circle round.

For us, for us, thou didst endure the pain,
  And thy meek spirit bowed itself to shame,
To wash our souls from sin's infecting stain,
  T' avert the Father's wrathful vengeance flame:
    Thou, that could'st nothing win
    By saving worlds from sin,
Nor aught of glory add to thy all-glorious name.

FROM "BELSHAZZAR."

HYMN.

Oh, thou that wilt not break the bruised reed,
  Nor heap fresh ashes on the mourner's brow,
Nor rend anew the wounds that inly bleed,
  The only balm of our afflictions thou,
Teach us to bear thy chastening wrath, oh God!
To kiss with quivering lips—still humbly kiss thy rod!

We bless thee, Lord, though far from Judah's land;
  Though our worn limbs are black with stripes and
                                              [chains;
Though for stern foes we till the burning sand;
  And reap, for others' joy, the summer plains;
We bless thee, Lord, for thou art gracious still,
Even though this last black drop o'erflow our cup of ill!

We bless thee for our lost, our beauteous child;
  The tears, less bitter, she hath made us weep;
The weary hours her graceful sports have guiled,
  And the dull cares her voice hath sung to sleep!
She was the dove of hope to our lorn ark;
The only star that made the stranger's sky less dark!

Our dove is fallen into the spoiler's net;
   Rude hands divide her plumes so chastely white ;
To the bereaved their one soft star is set,
   And all above is sullen, cheerless night !
But still we thank thee for our transient bliss :
Yes, Lord, to scourge our sins remained no way but this?

As when our Father to mount Moriah led
   The blessing's heir, his age's hope and joy,
Pleased, as he roamed along with dancing tread,
   Chid his slow sire, the fond, officious boy,
And laughed in sport to see the yellow fire
Climb up the turf-built shrine, his destined funeral pyre.

Even thus our joyous child went lightly on ;
   Bashfully sportive, timourously gay,
Her white foot bounded from the pavement stone
   Like some light bird from off the quivering spray ;
And back she glanced, and smiled, in blameless glee ;
The cars, and helms, and spears, and mystic dance to see

By thee, O Lord, the gracious voice was sent
   That bade the Sire his murtherous task forego :
When to his home the child of Abraham went
   His mother's tears had scarce begun to flow.
Alas ! and lurks there in the thicket's shade,
The victim to replace our lost devoted maid ?
        32*

Lord, even through thee to hope were now too bold ;
    Yet 'twere to doubt thy mercy to despair.
'Tis anguish yet, 'tis comfort, faint and cold,
    To think how sad we are, how blest we were !
To speak of her is wretchedness, and yet
It were a grief more deep and bitterer to forget !

Oh Lord our God ! why was she e'er our own ?
    Why is she not our own—our treasure still ?
We could have passed our heavy years alone.
    Alas ! is this to bow us to thy will ?
Ah, even our humblest prayers we make repine,
Nor, prostrate thus on earth, our hearts to thee resign.

Forgive, forgive—even should our full hearts break,
    The broken heart thou wilt not, Lord, despise :
Ah ! thou art still too gracious to forsake,
    Though thy strong hand heavily chastise.
Hear all our prayers, hear not our murmurs, Lord ;
And, though our lips rebel, still make thyself adored.

MILLMAN.

FROM "BELSHAZZAR"

HYMN.

God of the Thunder! from whose cloudy seat
   The fiery winds of Desolation flow ;
Father of vengeance! that with purple feet,
   Like a full wine-press, tread'st the world below
The embattled armies wait thy sign to slay,
Nor springs the beast of havoc on his prey,
Nor withering Famine walks his blasted way,
   Till thou the guilty land hast sealed for wo.

God of the Rainbow! at whose gracious sign
   The billows of the proud their rage suppress :
Father of Mercies! at one word of thine
   An Eden blooms in the waste wilderness !
And fountains sparkle in the arid sands,
And timbrels ring in maidens' glancing hands,
And marble cities crown the laughing lands,
   And pillared temples rise thy name to bless.

O'er Judah's land thy thunders broke, O Lord,
   The chariots rattled o'er her sunken gate,
Her sons were wasted by the Assyrian sword,
   Even her foes wept to see her fallen state ;
And heaps her ivory palaces became.
Her princes wore the captive garb of shame,
Her temple sank amid the smouldering flame,
   For thou didst ride the tempest cloud of fate.

O'er Judah's land thy rainbow, Lord, shall beam,
  And the sad City lift her crownless head ;
And songs shall wake, and dancing footsteps gleam,
  Where broods o'er fallen streets the silence of the dead
The sun shall shine on Salem's gilded towers,
On Carmel's side our maidens cull the flowers,
To deck, at blushing eve, their bridal bowers,
  And angel feet the glittering Sion tread.

Thy vengeance gave us to the stranger's hand,
  And Abraham's children were led forth for slaves ;
With fettered steps we left our pleasant land,
  Envying our fathers in their peaceful graves.
The stranger's bread with bitter tears we steep,
And when our weary eyes should sink to sleep,
'Neath the mute midnight we steal forth to weep,
  Where the pale willows shade Euphrates' waves.

The born in sorrow shall bring forth in joy ;
  Thy mercy, Lord, shall lead thy children home ;
He that went forth a tender yearling boy,
  Yet, ere he die, to Salem's streets shall come.
And Canaan's vines for us their fruit shall bear,
And Hermon's bees their honied stores prepare,
And we shall kneel again in thankful prayer,
  Where, o'er the cherub-seated God, full blazed
      th' irradiate dome.

WOLFE.

THE BURIAL OF SIR JOHN MOORE.

Not a drum was heard, not a funeral note,
 As his corse to the rampart we hurried;
Not a soldier discharged his farewell shot
 O'er the grave where our hero we buried.

We buried him darkly at dead of night,
 The sods with our bayonets turning;
By the struggling moonbeam's misty light,
 And the lantern dimly burning.

No useless coffin enclosed his breast,
 Nor in sheet nor in shroud we wound him;
But he lay like a warrior taking his rest,
 With his martial cloak around him.

Few and short were the prayers we said,
  And we spoke not a word of sorrow :
But we stedfastly gazed on the face of the dead,
  And we bitterly thought of the morrow.

We thought as we hollowed his narrow bed,
  And smoothed down his lonely pillow,
That the foe and the stranger would tread o'er his
  And we far away on the billow !

Lightly they'll talk of the spirit that's gone,
  And o'er his cold ashes upbraid him,—
But little he'll reck, if they let him sleep on
  In the grave where a Briton has laid him.

But half of our heavy task was done,
  When the clock struck the hour for retiring;
And we heard the distant and random gun
  That the foe was sullenly firing.

Slowly and sadly we laid him down,
  From the field of his fame fresh and gory;
We carved not a line, and we raised not a stone,
  But we left him alone with his glory !

STANZAS.

If I had thought thou couldst have died,
   I might not weep for thee ;
But I forgot when by thy side,
   That thou couldst mortal be :
It never through my mind had past,
   That time would e'er be o'er,
And I on thee should look my last,
   And thou shouldst smile no more.

And still upon that face I look,
   And think 'twill smile again ;
And still the thought I will not brook,
   That I must look in vain !
But when I speak, thou dost not say,
   What thou ne'er left'st unsaid ;
And now I feel, as well I may,
   Sweet Mary ! thou art dead !

If thou wouldst stay, e'en as thou art,
   All cold and all serene—
I still might press thy silent heart,
   And where thy smiles have been !
While e'en thy chill, bleak corse I have,
   Thou seemest still mine own ;
And there I lay thee in thy grave—
   And I am now alone !

WOLFE

I do not think, where'er thou art,
    Thou hast forgotten me ;
And I, perhaps, may sooth this heart,
    In thinking too of thee :
Yet there was round thee such a dawn
    Of light ne'er seen before,
As fancy never could have drawn,
    And never can restore !

MRS. HEMANS.

THE HOUR OF DEATH

LEAVES have their time to fall,
And flowers to wither at the North-wind's breath,
    And stars to set—but all,
Thou hast all seasons for thine own, O Death!

    Day is for mortal care,
Eve for glad meetings round the joyous hearth,
    Night for the dreams of sleep, the voice of prayer;
But all for thee, thou mightiest of the earth!

    The banquet hath its hour,
Its feverish hour of mirth, and song, and wine;
    There comes a day for grief's o'erwhelming power,
A time for softer tears—but all are thine!

    Youth and the opening rose
May look like things too glorious for decay,
    And smile at thee!—but thou art not of those
That wait the ripened bloom to seize their prey!

Leaves have their time to fall,
And flowers to wither at the North-wind's breath,
    And stars to set——but all,
Thou hast all seasons for thine own, O Death!

    We know when moons shall wane,
When summer-birds from far shall cross the sea,
    When Autumn's hue shall tinge the golden grain
But who shall teach us when to look for thee?

    Is it when spring's first gale
Comes forth to whisper where the violets lie?
    Is it when roses in our paths grow pale?
They have one season——all are ours to die!

    Thou art where billows foam,
Thou art where music melts upon the air;
    Thou art around us in our peaceful home,
And the world calls us forth——and thou art there;

    Thou art where friend meets friend,
Beneath the shadow of the elm to rest,
    Thou art where foe meets foe, and trumpets rend
The skies, and swords beat down the princely crest.

    Leaves have their time to fall,
And flowers to wither at the North-wind's breath,
    And stars to set——but all,
Thou hast all seasons for thine own, O Death!

MOZART'S REQUIEM

A Requiem!—and for whom?
For beauty in its bloom?
For valour fallen—a broken rose or sword?
A dirge for king or chief,
With pomp of stately grief,
Banner, and torch, and waving plume deplored?

Not so, it is not so!
The warning voice I know,
From other worlds a strange mysterious tone;
A solemn funeral air,
It called me to prepare,
And my heart answered secretly—my own!

One more then, one more strain,
In links of joy and pain
Mighty the troubled spirit to enthral!
And let me breathe my dower
Of passion and of power
Full into that deep lay—the last of all!

The last!—and I must go
From this bright world belo   ,
This realm of sunshine, ringing   ith sweet sound !
Must leave its festal skies,
With all their melodies,
That ever in my breast glad ecl oes found.

Yet have I known it long:
Too restless and too strong
Within this clay hath been th' o'ermastering f me
Swift thoughts, that came and went,
Like torrents o'er me sent,
Have shaken, as a reed, my thrilling frame.

Like perfumes on the wind,
Which none may stay or bind,
The beautiful come floating through my soul;
I strive with yearnings vain,
The spirit to detain
Of the deep harmonies that past me roll !

Therefore disturbing dreams
Trouble the secret streams
And founts of music that o'erflow my breast;
Something far more divine
Than may on earth be mine,
Haunts my worn heart, and will not let me rest.

Shall I then fear the tone
That breathes from worlds unknown ?—
Surely these feverish aspirations *there*
Shall grasp their full desire,
And this unsettled fire,
Burn calmly, brightly, in immortal air

One more then, one more strain,
To earthly joy and pain
A rich, and deep, and passionate farewell !
I pour each fervent thought
With fear, hope, trembling, fraught,
Into the notes that o'er my dust shall swell.

THE PALM TREE.

It waved not through an Eastern sky,
Beside a fount of Araby ;
It was not fanned by southern breeze
In some green isle of Indian seas,
Nor did its graceful shadow sleep
O'er stream of Afric, lone and deep

But fair the exiled Palm-tree grew
Midst foliage of no kindred hue ;
Thro' the laburnum's dropping gold
Rose the light shaft of orient mould,
And Europe's violets, faintly sweet,
Purpled the moss-beds at its feet.

Strange looked it there !—the willow streamed
Where silvery waters near it gleamed ;
The lime-bough lured the honey bee
To murmur by the desert's tree,
And showers of snowy roses made
A lustre in its fan-like shade.

There came an eve of festal hours—
Rich music filled that garden's bowers :
Lamps, that from flowering branches hung,
On sparks of dew soft colours flung,
And bright forms glanced—a fairy show—
Under the blossoms to and fro.

But one, a lone one, midst the throng,
Seemed reckless all of dance or song :
He was a youth of dusky mein,
Whereon the Indian sun had been,
Of crested brow, and long black hair—
A stranger, like the Palm-tree there.

And slowly, sadly, moved his plumes,
Glittering athwart the leafy glooms :
He passed the pale green olives by,
Nor won the chesnut flowers his eye ;
But when to that sole Palm he came,
Then shot a rapture through his frame !

To him, to him, its rustling spoke,
The silence of his soul it broke !
It whispered of its own bright isle,
That lit the ocean with a smile ;
Aye, to his ear that native tone
Had something of the sea-waves moan

His mother's cabin home, that lay
Where feathery cocoas fringed the bay;
The dashing of his brethren's oar,
The conch-note heard along the shore;
All thro' his wakening bosom swept:
He clasped his country's Tree and wept!

Oh! scorn him not!—the strength, whereby
The patriot girds himself to die,
Th' unconquerable power, which fills
The freeman battling on his hills,
These have one fountain deep and clear—
The same whence gushed that child-like tear!

MRS. HEMANS.

THE MEETING OF THE BROTHERS.

The voices of two forest boys,
  In years when hearts entwine,
Had filled with childhood's merry noise
  A valley of the Rhine.
To rock and stream that sound was known
Gladsome as hunter's bugle tone

The sunny laughter of their eyes
  There had each vineyard seen ;
Up every cliff whence eagles rise,
  Their bounding step had been ;
Ay! their bright youth a glory threw
O'er the wild place wherein they grew

But this, as day-spring's flush, was brief
  As early bloom or dew ;——
Alas! 'tis but the withered leaf
  That wears the enduring hue !
Those rocks along the Rhine's fair shore,
Might girdle in their world no more.

For now on manhood's verge they stood,
  And heard life's thrilling call,
As if a silver clarion woo'd
  To some high festival ;
And parted as young brothers part,
With love in each unsullied heart.

They parted—soon the paths divide
   Wherein our steps were one,
Like river-branches, far and wide
   Dissevering as they run,
And making strangers in their course
Of waves that had the same bright source.

Met they no more?—once more they met,
   Those kindred hearts and true !
'Twas on a field of death, where yet
   The battle-thunders flew,
Though the fierce day was well-nigh past,
And the red sunset smiled its last.

But as the combat closed, they found
   For tender thoughts a space,
And ev'n upon that bloody ground
   Room for one brief embrace,
And pour'd forth on each other's neck
Such tears as warriors need not check.

The mists o'er boyhood's memory spread
   All melted with those tears
The faces of the holy dead
   Rose as in vanish'd years :
The Rhine, the Rhine, the ever blessed
Lifted its voice in each full breast !

Oh ! was it *then* a time to die ?
   It was !—that not in vain

The soul of childhood's purity
   And peace might turn again.
A ball swept forth—'twas guided well—
Heart unto heart those brothers fell.

Happy, yes, happy thus they go !
   Bearing from earth away
Affections, gifted ne'er to know
   A shadow—a decay,
A passing touch of change or chill,
A breath of aught whose breath can kill.

And they, between whose sever'd souls,
   Once in close union tied,
A gulf is set, a current rolls
   For ever to divide,—
Well may *they* envy such a lot,
Whose hearts yearn on—but mingle not.

FINIS.

POETRY AND THE DRAMA.

THE COMPLETE WORKS OF SHAKSPEARE. In eight volumes 8vo., printed upon extra calendered paper, with forty steel engravings. Price, in muslin, $16; in library style, $20; with calf or morocco backs and corners, $25; in morocco, full gilt, $40; in calf or turkey antique, $50.

This is widely known as the "Boston Illustrated Edition," and it has received the most unqualified commendations for clearness of type, beauty of paper, elegance of illustrations, and excellence of binding, as being by far the finest edition published in America.

Another edition, in eight volumes. Price, in muslin, $10.

SHAKSPEARE. In one volume, 8vo., with portrait, etc., printed upon fine paper. Price, in muslin, $3; half calf, $5; full calf or turkey, antique or gilt, $6.

THE COMPLETE POETICAL AND DRAMATIC WORKS OF BEAUMONT AND FLETCHER. In two volumes, octavo. Edited by Rev. Alexander Dyce. With Memoirs, copious Notes, Glossary, and Index, and two splendid steel portraits.

The only American edition of these great dramatists. Price, in muslin, $5; library style, $6. Bound in costlier styles to order.

The price of the English edition from which this work is reprinted is $30.

THE POETICAL WORKS OF JOHN MILTON. Edited by Sir Egerton Brydges, Bart. With a portrait, and engravings, from designs by John Martin and J. M. W. Turner, R. A. In one volume 8vo.

This edition of Milton is believed to be the best before the public, as regards the care and taste of the editor, the genius of the artists, and the elegance with which the book is printed and bound.

THE COMPLETE POETICAL WORKS OF SIR WALTER SCOTT. With the Author's Introductions and Notes. In one volume, 8vo.; with illustrations, and portraits.

THE COMPLETE WORKS OF LORD BYRON. With a Memoir, portrait and other illustrations. In one volume, 8vo. Same edition, bound in a splendid quarto, turkey, antique, $15.

THE POETICAL WORKS OF THOMAS MOORE. Complete in one volume, royal octavo. A new edition, from the last London edition. With a portrait, and other fine illustrations.

THE COMPLETE WORKS OF ROBERT BURNS: Containing his Poems, Songs, and Correspondence. With a Life of the Poet, and Notices Critical and Biographical. By Allan Cunningham. With elegant steel illustrations. In one volume 8vo.

THE WORKS OF BEN JOHNSON. With a Memoir. By William Gifford. In one volume, 8vo., with portrait.

THE WORKS OF WILLIAM COWPER; his Life, Letters, and Poems. (Now completed by the introduction of his private correspondence.) Edited by Rev. T. S. Grimshawe, A. M., F. S. A. In one volume, 8vo., illustrated.

THE POETICAL WORKS OF JAMES MONTGOMERY. With a Memoir, by Rev. Rufus W. Griswold. In one volume, 8vo., with portrait and illustrations.

THE POETICAL WORKS OF FELICIA HEMANS. Complete in one volume, 8vo. With a Memoir, by Mrs. L. H. Sigourney. A new edition, from the last London edition, elegantly illustrated from original designs.

THE COMPLETE WORKS OF LETITIA E. LANDON. In one volume, royal 8vo. with portrait.

*** The price of the edition of the Poets above, per volume is, bound in muslin, $2.50; in library style, $3; in muslin, gilt, extra, $4; in morocco, gilt, $4.50.

Same edition, printed upon fine calendered paper. Price, in black muslin, $3; in half turkey or half calf, gilt or antique, $5; in full turkey, antique or gilt, $6.

☞ For a complete list of the British Poets, published by P. S. & Co., see their Catalogue, copies of which are furnished, post-paid, upon application.

PUBLISHED BY

PHILLIPS, SAMPSON & CO., Boston,

And for sale by all Booksellers in the United States.

THE STANDARD
Eras Sargent, Esq., author of " The Standard Speaker," etc. rrivate Schools. By
The most successful, and the best reading books before the public.
. For the particulars respecting their size, character, price, postage, etc., etc., see the general advertise-
nent on the last printed page of the first volume of this work.

THE PRINCIPLES OF CHEMISTRY; Illustrated by Simple Experiments. By
Dr. JULIUS ADOLPH STOCKHARDT. Translated by C. H. Peirce, M. D. With an Introduction
bj
Sup
AT
A
2$
A n
epart
NTI
U
Thi
RO

Th
be
: G
UB
T
P.
IB
a
p
A

o
1
L

l
d

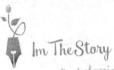

Im TheStory

personalised classic books

JANE
IN
WONDERLAND

LEWIS
CARROLL

"Beautiful gift.. lovely finish,
My Niece loves it, so precious!"

Helen R Brumfieldon

⭐⭐⭐⭐⭐

UNIQUE
GIFT

FOR KIDS, PARTNERS
AND FRIENDS

Timeless books such as:

Kids

Alice in Wonderland · The Jungle Book · The Wonderful Wizard of Oz
Peter and Wendy · Robin Hood · The Prince and The Pauper
The Railway Children · Treasure Island · A Christmas Carol

Adults

Romeo and Juliet · Dracula

Highly Customizable · **Change** Books Title · **Replace** Characters Names with yours · **Upload** Photo/let inside pages · **Add** Inscriptions

Visit
Im TheStory .com
and order yours today!

CPSIA information can be obtained
at www.ICGtesting.com
Printed in the USA
BVHW042351150819
555860BV00045B/2190/P